This Fine Piece of Water

This Fine

AN ENVIRONMENTAL HISTORY OF

Piece of

LONG ISLAND SOUND

Water

TOM ANDERSEN

Foreword by Robert F. Kennedy Jr.

Yale University Press *New Haven & London*

Designed by Sonia L. Shannon.
Set in Galliard type by Integrated Publishing
Solutions, Grand Rapids, Michigan.
Printed in the United States of America
by R. R. Donnelley and Sons,
Harrisonburg, Virginia.

Library of Congress
Cataloging-in-Publication Data
Andersen, Tom, 1954–
This fine piece of water : an environmental
history of Long Island Sound / Tom Andersen ;
foreword by Robert F. Kennedy Jr.
p.   cm.
Includes bibliographical references and index.
ISBN 0-300-08250-9 (hardcover : alk. paper)
1. Marine pollution—Long Island Sound
(N.Y. and Conn.)—History. 2. Long Island
Sound (N.Y. and Conn.)—Environmental
conditions—History.   I. Title.
GC1212.N7 A53 2002
363.739'4'0916346—dc21   2001006401

A catalogue record for this book is available
from the British Library.

The paper in this book meets the guidelines for
permanence and durability of the Committee on
Production Guidelines for Book Longevity of
the Council on Library Resources.

10 9 8 7 6 5 4 3 2 1

For Gina,
and for Elie and Kaare

CONTENTS

FOREWORD
Robert F. Kennedy Jr.

Pete Seeger says that if you put a frog in a pot of cold water and slowly bring it to a boil the frog will sit calmly and simmer. In contrast, a frog tossed into boiling water will energetically try to escape. Before 1987, the changes in Long Island Sound's ecology were dramatic but so gradual that people just accepted them. Like the frog placed in cold water, no one noticed the slow-but-lethal environmental changes. In the summer of 1987, Long Island Sound finally succumbed. Its western half died. Scientists found zero dissolved oxygen in the water, the lowest levels ever recorded. As a result, the fin fish left the area or perished. The barnacles, crustaceans, clams, quahogs, and lobsters died. For the first time, people who lived around the Sound experienced more or less a universal consciousness that something important was being lost. In truth, those losses began long ago.

The first explorers to see Long Island Sound described a region of mythical productivity. They smelled aromas from Long Island's flowers before sighting land and found four hundred bird species, many of which are gone today. Henry Hudson's lieutenant Robert Juett described rivers choked with salmon (probably striped bass) and mullet. Giant dolphin pods schooled in the East River and New York Harbor. F. Scott Fitzgerald, one of Long Island's most faithful chroniclers in recalling its legendary abundance, suggested that the Sound appeared to the first Dutch sailor as the "fresh green breast of the new world," compelling him to hold his breath in "an aesthetic contemplation he neither understood nor desired, face to face for the last time in history with something commensurate with his capacity for wonder."

Two hundred years after contact, the European invasion had little impact on the estuary's extraordinary productivity. During the eighteenth century, enough lobsters still washed ashore each night from natural die-offs to fertilize the coastal farms of Connecticut, New York, and Massachusetts. Inmates protesting endless servings of Long Island Sound lobster rioted in New England prisons, and New Yorkers ate more oyster than any other kind of meat, the product of a bivalve — now extinct — called the East River oyster, whose eleven-inch shell housed seven pounds of succulent flesh. The Industrial Revolution's impacts were noticeable but still lacked the drama needed to cause an outcry. The dolphins disappeared during the Civil War, but entire communities continued to thrive on the Sound's terrapin, ducks, striped bass, bluefish, clams, and other estuarine bounties. Waterfront market hunters and fishermen prospered.

By the 1920s, the terrapin, duck, and lobster populations were in decline, and periodic algal blooms clouded the waters, once gin-clear. Somewhat less exuberant, Fitzgerald christened his contemporary Long Island Sound "that great wet barnyard," acknowledging its modern function as the primary waste receptacle for the enormous human population now crowding its shores. But even in Fitzgerald's time, life filled the Sound, supporting its thriving commercial and recreational facilities.

In the three decades before 1987, the pace of change accelerated, becoming noteworthy even in the memory of a single generation. I grew up on Cape Cod, which is part of the hydrology of Long Island Sound. For a brief time, my family had a home in Glen Cove, on Long Island. There are fishes that I knew as a boy that are gone today; among them the smelt, once so numerous they could be scooped with a bucket. Long Island Sound's flounder catch dropped from forty million pounds in 1982 to one million pounds in 1987. The oyster catch sank from three million bushels annually to fifteen thousand. The blue crabs and razor clams, abundant in every bay and mud flat when I was a boy, disappeared altogether.

The year 1988 began the first economic downturn in United States history during which New York City's unemployed could not go to the shores of Long Island Sound and reliably catch a fish for the family dinner table. The fish were mostly gone. Shellfish beds were closed, as organic chemicals and bacteria poisoned the clams and oysters. After three hundred and fifty years of putting food on our tables and enriching our culture, commercial fishermen left their profession in droves, turning their backs on the Sound to seek other occupations, such as hanging Sheetrock or tiling roofs.

Clearly there are serious economic impacts when we lose an estuary like Long Island Sound. As Tom Andersen points out in this wonderful book, diminished fisheries are only a part of the annual $6 billion water-based income losses to the Long Island Sound region caused by pollution. The cultural and historical losses are equally disturbing. Long Island Sound has a special role. It gives New Yorkers, prisoners of asphalt and steel, their best opportunity to retouch the land and water. When we destroy this resource, we lose our sense of the seasons and the tides and the life cycles of the fishes and our sense of the earth and our place on it.

Andersen shows that Long Island Sound is also part of our history. Our cultural and political institutions are rooted on its shores. When we destroy the Sound, we destroy a tangible component of our history and culture — our link with our own past and to other generations of Americans. If we succeed in divorcing ourselves completely from nature, we will become a rootless people, strangers in our own country, separated from our sources of values and identity. At that point, we may begin to question our humanity.

Reminiscent of Rachel Carson's opening chapter of *Silent Spring*, *This Fine Piece of Water* begins with a description of the Sound during the summer of 1987. Carson sounded the clarion call against pesticides and toxins in our environment. Now Tom Andersen has called us back to the barricades to save our dying estuaries.

Mount Kisco, New York

ACKNOWLEDGMENTS

This book took so long to come together that it requires a prodigious feat to remember everyone who helped me. My apologies ahead of time to anyone I've forgotten. My specific thanks to the following:

Two friends and former colleagues, Joey Asher and Cameron McWhirter, read and critiqued the manuscript, and then for years prodded me to keep working to get it published. Their encouragement helped me to keep believing it was a worthwhile project when I otherwise would have given up.

At the U.S. Environmental Protection Agency, Rosemary Monahan and Sue Beede answered every question and sent me every report and document I asked for during the early years of the Long Island Sound Study. In more recent years, Mark Tedesco at EPA's Long Island Sound office has been, if possible, even more helpful. Paul Stacey at the Connecticut Department of Environmental Protection and Karen Chytalo at the New York State Department of Environmental Conservation were available to help whenever I called. Penelope Howell of the Connecticut DEP was patient with me while seining for fish, spent as much time on the phone with me as I needed, and sent me research reports that her department produced; she also read a draft of the chapters on fish and hypoxia. Philip T. Briggs, who, until he retired, was the New York State DEC's lobster expert, provided me with numerous reports and spent uncounted hours on the phone with me. John Volk of the Connecticut Aquaculture Department helped me understand the contemporary oyster industry in the Sound. Ralph Lewis of the Connecticut DEP's Geological Survey helped me fine-tune the chapter on the Sound's geology by sending me the latest research and by reading and commenting on the chapter.

Barbara Welsh took my phone calls and was patient with me when I tracked her down in person in unlikely places even on the hottest days during the busy research seasons in 1987, '88, and '89, and later sat down for a long taped interview and gave me the scientific reports that her research resulted in.

Jeannette Semon, who runs Stamford's sewage plant, Joseph Lauria and Fred Treffeisen at Malcolm Pirnie Inc., and Adam Zabinski of the Westchester County Department of Environmental Facilities tried to teach me about sewage treatment.

Three Westchester County environmentalists — Robert Funicello, Nancy Seligson, and Kathryn Clarke — were always available to talk to me about Sound issues and were uncompromising in holding government officials and developers accountable for the Sound's problems.

Phil Reisman, Ron Patafio, and Larry Beaupre were my editors at *The Journal News* and its predecessor, and were encouraging and enthusiastic about the newspaper reports that led to this book.

Lyn Chu and Glen Hartley made helpful editing suggestions. I am grateful to Robert F. Kennedy Jr. for the kind words in his foreword.

Finding and assembling the photographs that appear in the book were major tasks made easier by numerous people. Helen Federico helped select photographs at the Connecticut State Library, where the librarians and photo archivists were helpful and efficient in person and on the phone. Thanks especially to archivist Nancy Shader and Joy Floyd at the library. Mary Cohn and Henry Gloetzner at the Rowayton Historical Society made their photo collection available to me and trusted me to borrow what I needed. Bob Ritter let me use photographs from *The Journal News,* and Larry Nylund arranged to have copies made for me. Thanks to Howard Golub and Peter Sattler at the Interstate Environmental Commission for the use of the 1947 aerial photo of the East River. Robert T. Augustyn of Martayan Lan, a rare book and map dealer in Manhattan, generously let me use the 1635 Blaeu map and also explained the map's history to me. John Atkin of Save the Sound graciously let me go through his organization's large photo collection and choose what I wanted. Thomas G. Siccama of the Yale University School of Forestry and Environmental Studies let me choose photos from his collection of lantern slides and glass plate negatives. Elie Andersen helped organize the photos for publication.

Jean Thomson Black at Yale University Press was extremely patient and skillful in shaping my manuscript and guiding it through the publication process. And thanks to Rebecca Gibb at Yale University Press for bringing the manuscript to the editors' attention, and to Manushag Powell for helping me make sure the manuscript was in proper shape, and to manuscript editor Jeffrey Schier for suggesting dozens of ways to fine-tune the writing.

Thanks especially to my wife, Gina Federico, who made sure I had the time at home to finish this project and who made the connection with Yale University Press that led to its getting published.

The Sound

I ts beauty rivaled that of any waterway in the world.

To Daniel Webster, Long Island Sound justified a metaphor that conjured classical landscapes and seascapes: he called it the Mediterranean of the Western Hemisphere.

The Sound's "beautiful, varied and picturesque . . . inlets, 'necks' and sea-like expansions" charmed Walt Whitman, who as a boy growing up in Huntington, Long Island, found it a serene contrast to the wildness of the Atlantic shore.

Long after he had retired as the nation's first chief justice of the Supreme Court, John Jay, living on his own manor elsewhere in New York, considered his true home to be the family seat in Rye, where he had roamed the salt marshes along the shore of the Sound in colonial Westchester County.

Old sea cards and books called it the Devil's Belt, but Timothy Dwight, the president of Yale College two hundred years ago, thought that no sea or ocean or bay could be more pleasant than the Sound, nothing could compare to the seascapes and landfalls that make up what he called "this fine piece of water."

A century or so after Dwight, F. Scott Fitzgerald described the Sound as "the most domesticated body of salt water in the Western Hemisphere," and Nick Carraway was gazing at it under the stars when it called to mind the awesome spectacle that confronted the first European visitors: "For a transitory enchanted moment man must have held his breath in the presence of this continent, compelled into an aesthetic contemplation he neither understood nor desired, face to face for the last time in history with something commensurate to his capacity for wonder."[1]

Yet Long Island Sound had more than beauty. Commerce thrived as well. Sea creatures from whales to mossbunkers to oysters were caught in the Sound. Market sloops transported virtually every commodity local residents needed and every product they could grow on the bucolic hillsides that rose beyond the harbor villages. Throughout the nineteenth century Connecticut industrialists found the Sound and its tributaries to be convenient receptacles for their factories' byproducts, and by the 1880s oil terminals were starting to squat along the shore at its far western end.[2]

For a time it seemed like Long Island Sound was ideally proportioned to accommodate everybody. It was big: thirteen hundred and ten square miles of water compressed into a belt one hundred and ten miles long, constricting to barely fifteen hundred yards wide at Throgs Neck but bulging to 21 miles between New Haven and Shoreham. It was robust and dynamic: Twice a day the tides rushed in and out of the Sound, rising and falling three feet near the Connecticut–Rhode Island border and seven feet west of where Connecticut meets New York, draining marshes, broadening beaches, and exposing acre after acre of mudflat. Salinity ranged from an oceanlike thirty-two parts per thousand in its eastern end to about twenty-two parts per thousand in the west. Water temperatures fell as low as 32 degrees in winter and rose to 76 in August, a range greater than that of any other body of water in the world.[3] It was deep: an average of seventy-nine feet, with a lopsided underwater profile, slipping down gradually away from the Connecticut shore, bottoming out in a trough about three-quarters of the way south, and then ascending steeply to meet Long Island. Shoals and sills in several places rose to within ten or twelve feet of the surface. At the Race, the eastern entrance to the Sound, the roiling tides and currents scoured out trenches and holes more than three hundred feet deep. It was continually revitalized: six-knot currents filled the Sound with seawater at the Race and freshened it with brackish water at Hell Gate, the western terminus; and water poured down the Connecticut River at a rate of eighty-four thousand gallons a second, a flow greater than that of the Hudson. It was vibrant: The Sound was home to fish and bivalves and crustaceans by the millions, microscopic plants and animals by the billions. Birds that are now rare depended on the Sound — roseate terns and least terns and piping plovers nested on its beaches — and others, like bald eagles and peregrine falcons, visited regularly. And one truly rare animal, a sea turtle called the Kemp's ridley, rode the Gulf Stream north from the Gulf of Mexico each year, slipping into the Sound in August, and exiting again in October.

But Long Island Sound became among the most heavily used waterways in the world. Use evolved into abuse as the population rose, the industries grew, the cities expanded, and the suburbs sprawled. More than eight million people live on the lands that drain into the

Sound, a territory that spreads over 16,246 square miles. Those lands are crossed by more than seventy-five streams in a watershed that ranges far to the north. When a man hoses off his driveway in the eastern part of Hillsdale, New York, in Columbia County, twenty miles southeast of Albany, the water and the particles it transports seep into the Green River, which empties into the Housatonic River in Berkshire County, Massachusetts, which flows to the Sound at Stratford, Connecticut. Part of Rhode Island drains into the Sound via the Pawcatuck River. The watershed of the Connecticut River alone is 11,263 square miles.[4] Rain that filters through the spruce trees in the boggy forests of southern Quebec trickles into the Connecticut and flows 407 miles to the Sound. Brooks that run through Vermont's dairy land, cascades that tumble off New Hampshire's mountains, and storm sewers that rush under the streets of Springfield, Massachusetts, empty into the Connecticut and the Sound.

Ninety-three harbors and bays indent its shores.[5] New Haven's wide harbor cuts far inland and is the Sound's busiest. The deep New London–Groton harbor at the mouth of the Thames (pronounced Thaymes) River is home to General Dynamics' Electric Boat plant, manufacturers of nuclear submarines. Norwalk supports an oyster industry; Stonington the Sound's only commercial fishing fleet. The harbors of the western Sound—Little Neck and Eastchester bays in Queens and the Bronx; Manhasset Bay and Hempstead Harbor in Nassau County; Larchmont, Mamaroneck, New Rochelle's Echo Bay, and Rye's Milton Harbor in Westchester County; Greenwich and Stamford harbors in Connecticut—are some of the best and busiest recreational ports in the country. Boat registrations approach 200,000, and on a given Saturday or Sunday in summer 90,000 vessels may slip out of the cozy harbors to sail or motor along the Sound. Each summer season, 60 million people swim at its beaches.[6]

Despite the size, resiliency, and depth of Long Island Sound, the surprise is that it has survived for as long as it has. The people and the industry, the very routines of everyday life, have brought the Sound to the brink of disaster. Its fish and lobsters are tainted with cancer-causing PCBs. Copper and lead coat its sediments. Litter by the ton defaces its beaches. Its marshes and mudflats are poisoned by oil spills. And most significantly, the Sound has become the Northeast's sewer.

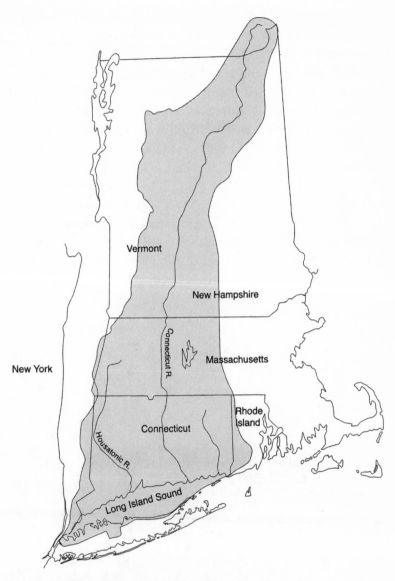

Long Island Sound and Its Watershed
Parts of New York, Connecticut, Rhode Island, Massachusetts, New Hampshire,
Vermont, and Quebec drain into Long Island Sound's 1,310 square miles. The
watershed covers 16,246 square miles and is home to 8.4 million people.

Each day 1.047 billion gallons of treated sewage pour into the Sound, supplemented by another 18 million gallons of raw sewage—almost one-fifth the flow of the Connecticut River.

The result is that Long Island Sound is undergoing an ecological crisis that threatens to turn it into a dead sea. The stakes are high. The Sound supports well over a hundred species of fish. From the 1960s through the 1980s, commercial fishermen working the Sound caught an average combined total of about 1.5 million pounds a year of black-fish, bluefish, butterfish, mackerel, scup, striped bass, fluke, weakfish, and winter flounder. But the commercial take is only a fraction of all the fish caught in the Sound, and inadequately conveys the Sound's true abundance. Recreational fishermen reel in far more fish than are caught commercially. Sport fishermen make 3–4 million fishing trips a year and catch an annual average of 23 million pounds. They land almost 3.5 million pounds of winter flounder, 2 million pounds each of

A Party Boat Searching for Bluefish
Party boats like the *Klondike,* based in New Rochelle, carry thousands of fishermen each year. Sport fishermen make 3 million to 4 million fishing trips a year and catch an annual average of 23 million pounds. The most popular sport fish is bluefish. Courtesy of Save the Sound.

Herring Dipping on the Mianus
Blueback herring and alewives still make a spring spawning run up some of the
Sound's tributaries. In this picture, taken on the Mianus River in Greenwich
in the 1980s, fishermen are scooping up herring during the spring run.
Courtesy of Art Glowka/Save the Sound.

fluke and of porgy, 1 million pounds of blackfish, and 240,000 pounds
of striped bass. The most popular catch is the bluefish. Sport fishermen catch about 15 million pounds a year,[7] and party boats like the
Klondike, out of New Rochelle, have been known to land 3,500 bluefish in a day, 30 per person — more than a hundred people reeling in
fish after fish, up to 70 at once, when the boat settles over a school.

But the problems besetting the Sound also present an incipient
economic crisis: the towns along the Sound reap at least $6 billion a
year in economic gain from the industries whose well-being depend
on a clean Sound.[8]

What follows is an attempt to tell the story of how Long Island
Sound has been pushed to the brink of destruction. It is also an instruc-
tive story, because in its beauty, bounty, and pollution, in its history as
a stage for a destructive conflict between commerce and nature, and in
its ultimate solution, the Sound is typical of coastal waters worldwide.

The misuse of the Sound culminated in a series of sobering events during the last years of the 1980s, events that shook the foundation of scientists' and the public's confidence in the Sound. But that crisis also led to a massive effort by the government and an amazingly diverse public constituency to pull the Sound back from the brink of disaster and restore it as a healthy estuary.

As long ago as 1938, Aldo Leopold posed what he called "the standard paradox of the twentieth century: our tools are better than we are, and grow better faster than we do. They suffice to crack the atom, to command the tides. But they do not suffice for the oldest task in human history: to live on a piece of land without spoiling it."[9] That remains the paradox of Long Island Sound. But it is a paradox that within the last two decades of the twentieth century went from being almost overwhelming to almost being solved. With the right knowledge applied with intelligence and sensitivity—qualities rarely used during Long Island Sound's last four hundred years of history—we might still succeed.

The Sound Is Dying

The first loud groan of a dying ecosystem was heard on Long Island Sound during the third week of July 1987. Barbara Welsh recognized it immediately. Welsh was the lead scientist on a research boat cruising outside Hempstead Harbor, above a submerged knoll called Hempstead Sill, where the Sound is only about forty feet deep. Welsh was testing and measuring, checking the water's saltiness, its clarity, its temperature, its oxygen concentrations. As she worked, her mind fixed on the mechanics of the instruments, the blue-gray water all around her turned brown.

The epicenter of this strange discoloration seemed to be the water over Hempstead Sill. It spread east across the state line into Connecticut and west over Execution Rocks and Gangway Rock, off Manhasset, toward Throgs Neck. It hung suspended in the water like a fog so thick that visibility extended only an inch or two below the surface.

It was not sewage, as swimmers and sailors who encountered this brown pall assumed. It was algae, a big-bang universe of tiny one-celled plants, reproducing, growing, spreading across the western third of the Sound like some out-of-control science fiction creature. Millions of microscopic plants can be crammed into a square meter of water. The bloom Barbara Welsh was witnessing covered dozens of square miles—a mass of vegetation ominous in its unnaturalness.

"I think something's going to happen—I *really* think something's going to happen," Welsh recalled saying. "This is very unusual. I think this is going to really knock us."

Welsh went home to Waterford that night and slept uneasily. She had first noticed isolated splotches of discolored water a week earlier, but, immersed in her research, had given it little attention. Her mind instead had been on oxygen levels. They had been falling all summer. By mid-June the waters west of Hempstead Sill, between City Island and Manhasset Bay, which under ideal conditions hold eight milligrams of oxygen per liter, were down to just three milligrams per liter. Three milligrams is the threshold of a condition called hypoxia—a dissolved oxygen deficit severe enough to make it impossible for many kinds of fish and crustaceans to survive. Welsh and her crew had been expecting oxygen levels to fall, and they were occupied with assembling a complete record of the drop. The early splotches of algae had not alarmed her. But the massive discoloration she saw that day was something different.

The next morning she called scientists from the environmental departments of New York and Connecticut. Whatever was about to befall the Sound, she wanted others to see it as well. New York assigned biologists to work the harbors of Long Island's north shore. Connecticut sent a research vessel to trawl for fish alongside Welsh's boat, which steamed between the gravelly necks of Nassau County two miles south and the rocks and islands of Westchester and Fairfield counties two miles north. Welsh herself continued to document strange events. Symptoms of ecological catastrophe were everywhere.

First, the curtain of algae died, almost as one being, and the microscopic plants sank. The water became unusually clear. As the algae drifted down, they began to decompose. Oxygen levels collapsed. From July 28 to August 4, as far east as Bridgeport, Welsh found less than three milligrams of oxygen per liter. Off Stamford, oxygen concentrations fell below two. In an arc of water spreading from New Rochelle and Manhasset Bay east to Greenwich and Matinecock Point, Welsh measured less than one milligram, perhaps one-tenth of what the water would hold in the best of times. And at the core of the arc—between Hempstead Harbor and Rye–Mamaroneck—there was no oxygen at all.

Welsh thought her instruments were broken. She had her technicians check them, and when the equipment proved to be working properly she had her crew take another set of measurements. She is a cautious scientist, with almost two decades of teaching and research experience at the University of Connecticut and Yale, a sturdily built woman and an accomplished mariner, whose face wears the alert and weathered look that only uncounted hours on a boat can give. But her experience had not prepared her for this. When the instruments duplicated the earlier data—no oxygen—she was astonished.

"I've seen some things here I've never seen before," Welsh said. "Never in an estuary like this have I seen zero oxygen."

It was not to be the only unprecedented phenomenon observed in the glare and heat and humidity of that summer on the Sound.

Hypoxia in the Sound's center trough spread up and out toward the shoals, linking up with hypoxia in the harbors. Pockets of healthy water that could have provided refuge for fish and lobsters vanished. Blackfish breached the surface, gasping pitifully for air.

In the newsroom of the New Rochelle newspaper I worked for, I took a call from a man who said he had been fishing at New Rochelle's Hudson Park the evening before. He heard a curious noise in the dusk and, looking down to the rocks below the sea wall, saw lobsters crawling out of the water. At the park's beach, listless bluefish swam in the shallows — an unusual spectacle, to say the least: bluefish are energetic swimmers with sharp teeth and a reputation for being quick to use them on the fingers of careless anglers. People at the park grabbed these now-docile fish and carted them home to eat.

Several miles east, in Mamaroneck, the harbor was awash with dead fish. Flounder. Mossbunker. Striped bass. Bluefish. Bergall. I phoned Jim Mancusi, Mamaroneck's harbor master. We're loading dead fish into garbage bags by the shovelful, he told me.

And in Rye, a lobster fisherman named John Fernandes eased his boat into the rocky waters off Playland Amusement Park and hauled his holding pen thirty feet to the surface. It contained every lobster he had caught from July 15 through July 19 — three-hundred pounds' worth. Every one was dead. Other lobstermen in other ports began reporting the same distressing tale — there were few lobsters around to be caught; those few that did wander into a trap were half-dead, as Fernandes put it, or all-dead if they had been left in the traps for more than a day. Holding pens with several days' labor became lobster morgues.

Welsh continued her daily research. What she found astonished her. Oxygen levels dropped below one milligram per liter and continued to fall toward zero, igniting a chemical reaction that let loose hydrogen sulfide from the Sound's bottom sediments. The rotten-egg stench of the toxic gas pierced the surface.

"You could smell it," Welsh said. "You could smell it and you knew what had happened. It was awful. Once the hydrogen sulfide gets there — whop! The system really gets toxic. It just kills everything right off."

The trawler manned by the marine fisheries bureau of the Connecticut Department of Environmental Protection confirmed what Welsh already knew was taking place. On a late-July day, the boat made four twenty-minute trawls over Hempstead Sill. It is an area that might normally yield fifteen hundred fish of ten or twelve species in one trawl. Now, each time the researchers hauled in their net, it held no fish of any kind, and 80 percent of the invertebrates it snagged — starfish, spider crabs, mantis shrimp, lobsters — were dead.

Welsh instructed two divers on her research team to descend for a look and to take photographs. Within ten minutes they resurfaced. To their dismay, they found that in the warm summer water the curtain of algae had been replaced by a curtain of decomposing fish, a veil of flesh so thick it clogged the divers' breathing apparatus. Moving several miles to the east, off Greenwich, and descending again, they found thousands of tiny crabs clinging to the daisy frame that held Welsh's scientific instruments, desperately trying to climb toward where the water might hold more oxygen.

Throughout the western Sound, fish kills became routine, spreading like a fire from west to east. On July 27, in Hempstead Harbor and Manhasset Bay, lobsters, fluke, summer flounder, windowpane flounder, blackfish, pipefish, rock crabs, horseshoe crabs, lady crabs, mossbunkers, eels, and killifish died. Two days later, again in Manhasset Bay, winter flounder, windowpane flounder, and rock crabs were found floating on the surface; off Sands Point, at the tip of Manhasset Neck, more than five hundred pounds of lobster died in traps, while across the Sound in New Rochelle, all but two of sixty-five lobsters hauled to the surface were dead. In the waters near City Island, on July 31, mossbunkers, rock crabs, and winter flounder suffocated, and traps pulled from seventy feet of water off Northport yielded dead crabs and lobsters. On August 3, hogchokers, winter flounder, fluke, eels, and crabs died in Hempstead Harbor; just east of the harbor's mouth, off Matinecock Point, the toll included lobsters, crabs, and blackfish. Lobsters died off Lloyd Point on August 7, and crabs suffocated in Smithtown Bay on August 11.

Through it all, scientists somehow were trying to prevent panic. "This is not a life-threatening, environment-threatening situation. We don't want to turn it into a Long Island Sound-is-dying kind of thing, because it's not," Donald Squires, the head of UConn's marine sciences department, told me at the time. Welsh agreed. "The Sound has a great deal of robustness," she said.

What remained unsaid was the darker knowledge that the Sound's robustness was far from unlimited. The scientists knew — there was no denying it — that something dramatic and disturbing had descended with an intensity beyond anyone's expectations: A large pocket of Long Island Sound — once a great and beautiful estuary crowded with magnificent schools of fish and uncounted millions of lobsters and crabs — had somehow been transformed into a dead zone.

ONE

The Birth of the Sound

L ong Island Sound was born fifteen thousand years ago, the progeny of ice and rivers and the surging sea. Geologically, it's a current event, but its birth was the culmination of a force that began about three million years ago, when, century after century, the earth's cooling climate prevented snow from melting in the far north and allowed it to build into a mass of Arctic ice that exerted so much pressure on itself it began to flow south. The Pleistocene Ice Age had begun. In the ensuing years at least four and perhaps as many as sixteen glaciers descended and retreated over much of North America, each ice sheet cataclysmically grinding and scouring the landscape. At least two — the Illinoisan and then the Wisconsinan — crept as far south as Long Island Sound.[1]

Twenty-six thousand years ago, the Wisconsinan ice sheet began plowing slowly across Connecticut. Its leading edge was an irregular wall of ice, perhaps two miles high, that eventually would span the breadth of North America, from Nova Scotia to Washington. It inched forward with awesome power. On its descent the glacier scraped soil off the bedrock and dragged boulders across it, ripping off chunks of the bedrock itself. It sheared forests, softened the sharp contours of the river valleys, and gouged out depressions near the rivers. It crossed what is now the coast of Connecticut and New York's Westchester County, and swept over a lowland that had been sculpted by rivers and the earlier Illinoisan ice sheet.[2]

Then, just like that (in geological time), weather conditions at the face of the ice changed, and, by twenty-one thousand years ago, the glacier had advanced as far as it would go. Ice kept flowing from the glacier's northern source, but only enough to keep pace with the melting at its southern terminus. The wall of ice held its ground. Water poured from its face. The air was milky with mist. Rivers of sand, rock, and soil that had been locked in the ice flowed in torrents of meltwater. The debris piled up, forming a long, lumpy terminal moraine that, on the east coast of the United States, now emerges from the ocean at Block Island, Martha's Vineyard, and Nantucket Island, and lies across much of central Long Island and its South Fork, where it is called the Ronkonkoma moraine.[3]

In another two thousand years, the ice sheet retreated slightly and paused again, dumping out sand and gravel continuously. When it stopped, it spread another moraine — this one a recessional moraine — north of the terminal moraine. It forms the north shore and the North Fork of Long Island and is called the Harbor Hill–Roanoke Point moraine. Sail past the steep bluffs of eastern Long Island's north shore and you're looking at a rough mirror image, its focus softened by centuries of erosion, of the glacier's face. East of Port Jefferson the bluffs stretch virtually without indentation for forty miles, dropping into the water at Orient Point. The moraine slithers east through Plum Island and Great Gull and Little Gull islands. It drops under water at the Race, the eastern entrance of the Sound, and forms a submerged sill that forces the tidal current to ride up and over it, causing the roiling water that is so notable in that section of the Sound and gouging out depressions that are almost three hundred feet deep on either side of the sill. The moraine rises again at Fishers Island and forms the barrier beaches of Rhode Island and, eventually, Cape Cod. West of Port Jefferson, beaches and bluffs form the mouths of a series of harbors that cut deep into Long Island — Oyster Bay, Hempstead Harbor, Manhasset Bay, Little Neck Bay.[4]

Over the next fifteen hundred years the glacier retreated north from the Harbor Hill–Roanoke Point moraine, leaving smaller recessional moraines in the Sound itself and along the Connecticut coast as well, near Norwalk, for example, and in Milford at the mouth of the Housatonic River, and between Madison and Old Saybrook at the mouth of the Connecticut River.[5]

As the glacier receded, its melt water settled into the lowland that the ice had helped to create south of New England. The moraine acted as a dam between Orient Point and Fishers Island, and a cold lake — glacial Lake Connecticut, almost three hundred feet deep — covered what is now Long Island Sound. For a thousand years, the land just north of the lake was little more than exposed rock and glacial debris, whipped by cold winds off the glacier's face. The glacier's melt water swept a vast amount of sediment into the lake. It drifted down and accumulated on the bottom, nearly filling the lake with two hundred feet of clay deposits.

During these centuries sea level was two hundred and fifty or three hundred feet lower than it is today because of the amount of water locked in the glacial ice. The coast of North America was one hundred

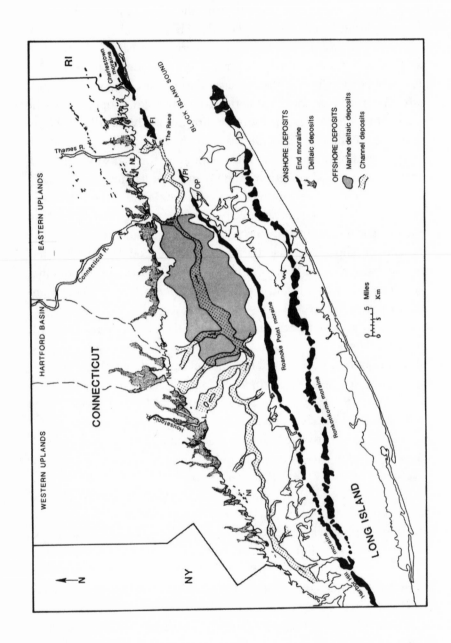

WESTERN UPLANDS

HARTFORD BASIN

EASTERN UPLANDS

CONNECTICUT

Connecticut R.

Thames R.

Housatonic R.

NH

NL

FI

The Race

BLOCK ISLAND SOUND

PI

OP

NY

NI

Harbor Hill moraine

Ronkonkoma moraine

Roanoke Point moraine

LONG ISLAND

RI

Charlestown moraine

N

ONSHORE DEPOSITS

End moraine

Deltaic deposits

OFFSHORE DEPOSITS

Marine deltaic deposits

Channel deposits

0   5   Miles
0   5   Km

The Glacier That Shaped the Sound

The biggest force in shaping Long Island Sound was the Wisconsinan ice sheet, which descended on the region about 20,000 years ago. The black lines that run across Long Island and over to Rhode Island on this map mark the farthest southern extent of the glacier, where the ice dumped a mass of sand, soil, and rock to form a terminal moraine. As the glacier retreated, rivers, streams, and deltas formed in what would become the Sound's basin and the Connecticut shoreline. Courtesy of the *Journal of Coastal Research*.

miles south of present-day Long Island, at the edge of the Continental Shelf. As the ice sheet melted, sea level rose and the water approached the moraines.[6]

Wind and water eroded the dam, enlarging a spillway at the Race, and Lake Connecticut drained steadily. By 15,500 years ago it was empty, leaving a network of rivers and streams to crisscross the lake bed. Five hundred years later the sea had risen sufficiently to flow in through the same breach that had drained the lake, sending salty water across the old lake bed and mixing it with the freshwater of the region's rivers. The Long Island Sound estuary was born.

The ice continued to melt north, and south winds began to dominate. As the climate moderated, the tiny, boggy plants of the tundra took root. The first trees to return were the spruces, followed a thousand years later by the first deciduous trees, the alders.[7] The sea continued to encroach and was well-established in the old lake basin by 13,500 years ago.[8] Eventually it filled beyond the basin, creeping up into north–south valleys, creating the drowned coastline that characterizes the Sound's north and south shores. The rising water delineated the Sound's harbors and bays. It flooded river valleys, creating smaller tidal estuaries in the lower reaches of freshwater streams. "Native Americans recognized the important difference in the character of these rivers," wrote Michael Bell, author of *The Face of Connecticut;* "the syllable 'tuck' and its corruption 'tic' contained in [their] names mean 'tidal river'" — examples being the Pawcatuck, the Mystic, the Niantic, and the Saugatuck. The Indians settled the area and eventually thrived for the same reason that Europeans would: because it was a benign environment, protected from the vicissitudes of the ocean by Long Island and containing ample fresh water in its rivers, whose valleys were fertile and whose waters became the easiest roads to the interior.[9]

The rising sea also surrounded higher points of land, creating many of the islands along the Sound's north shore. The Fish Islands, off Darien, are but bedrock hills that were too tall to be covered by the sea. Some islands are glacial moraines — the Norwalk Islands, for example, and the Captain Islands, off Greenwich. Falkner's Island, off Branford, is a drumlin, a hill of debris dumped by the glacier, which, in its uneroded form, is shaped like an upside-down spoon. The debris that forms Falkner's, though, was left by the Illinoisan ice sheet, not the Wisconsinan, one hundred and fifty thousand years ago. The Thimble Islands, just west of Falkner's Island, are bedrock knobs topped with glacial leftovers.[10]

Some of the scoured bedrock was not high enough to form significant islands but not low enough to be completely underwater. Lighthouses were built on at least two of these exposed rocks in the nineteenth century. One, Stepping Stone Light, sits among a string of mostly intertidal knobs running between City Island and Little Neck Bay—knobs that can be disastrous for unwary speed boaters. Another, Execution Light, marks the perilous Execution Rocks off New Rochelle. Local legend has it that, during the Revolutionary War, Tories chained traitors to the rocks to await drowning when the tide rose. In truth, though, Execution Rocks was named because it is a dangerous shipping area. The lowest tides still expose the remains of wrecked vessels.[11]

The south shore of the Sound, by contrast, has no islands. The glacier smothered the bedrock with the sand and gravel that make up Long Island. It also dumped thousands of offshore boulders, glacial erratics like the rocks in the fields and woods of New England and New York.

Ten to twelve thousand years ago sea level was still significantly lower than it is today. (It did not rise enough to form the Sound's present-day coastline until about four thousand years ago.) Islands and peninsulas were mainland hills; shoals and sills were islands.[12] The moderating temperature around this infant estuary invited settlement by creatures from the warmer lands to the south. Among them, probably, were human beings, elk hunters who also may have grown a few crops. Assertions about those people are necessarily conditional. They left behind scant evidence. There is no doubt, however, that as the centuries passed, the population of those people grew and prospered. They developed closely related languages. They established well-defined territorial boundaries. They lived a life governed by the rhythms of the natural year, synchronized with the migrations of wildlife, attuned to the vicissitudes and benevolences of climate and weather.

They were a people who were keenly aware of their place in the natural world. It was a wild creature, they believed, who gave rise to their forefathers. An old Indian called Jasper, who lived on Long Island in the seventeenth century, explained their origins to European visitors by drawing an oval on the ground and adding four paws, a head, and a tail. "This is a tortoise lying in the water around it," he told them. "This was or is all water, and so at first was the world or the earth, when the tortoise gradually raised its round back up high, and the water ran off of it, and thus the earth became dry."

Jasper stuck a straw into the middle of the tortoise's back. "The earth was now dry, and there grew a tree in the middle of the earth, and the root of this tree sent forth a sprout beside it and there grew upon it a man, who was the first male. This man was then alone, and would have remained alone; but the tree bent over until its top touched the earth, and there shot therein another root, from which came forth another sprout, and there grew upon it the woman, and from these two are all men produced."[13]

Descended from trees and supported by animals, the people prospered on this island that was the back of a turtle. For centuries they lived in relative peace, isolated from and utterly ignorant of the fantastic technological changes burgeoning half a world away as Europe emerged from the Middle Ages — changes that would first lead to the extinction of the native population and later put the Sound itself on the brink of disaster.

TWO

Early Residents

Canoo, five Naviculæ
e corticibus arborum.

I t might have been that they saw the first ship in 1525. A Portuguese navigator named Esteban Gómez, sailing for Spain in that year, had explored north along the coast of North America, ignoring the mouths of Chesapeake Bay and Delaware Bay before turning east with the shore at New York Harbor. Beyond Montauk Point he aimed his vessel northwest, in all likelihood pushed through the Race, and poked into the eastern end of Long Island Sound. Among the rivers and bays that Gómez noted between Cape Charles and Cape Cod is one that contemporary charts called "Rio de buena madre" — probably the Thames or the Connecticut. If there were people watching the ship's progress, they would have been Shinnecocks, Montauks, or Corchaugs on Long Island or, to the north, Pequots, Niantics, or perhaps Quinnipiacs. Gómez, who as a pilot five years earlier had led a mutiny on one of Magellan's ships off Patagonia, was the first European known to have entered Long Island Sound.[1]

The Indian nations that watched him would wait almost ninety years before seeing another ship that differed markedly from the dugout canoes in which they skimmed over the waters, or the bark canoes favored by the natives to the north. This vessel, captained by a Dutch merchant-explorer named Adriaen Block, sailed from Marblehead Bay in Massachusetts to the Hudson River via Long Island Sound. The captain explored for more than twenty leagues up the Connecticut River, to present-day Enfield, before he was halted by rapids. He noted the red hills beyond New Haven Harbor. He sailed through the roiling water of Hell Gate. He estimated the distance of the "Great Bay," as he called the Sound, at thirty-seven leagues, or one hundred and eleven miles, which is almost precisely its length. And he produced a chart of the region that located the "Archipelagus" off Norwalk and showed for the first time the landforms we now call Long Island and Manhattan Island. The voyage also marked the first time that a white man viewed the Sound from end to end.[2]

What those sailors encountered ninety years apart was not the virgin land of American myth. It was neither an unspoiled Eden nor a howling wilderness with danger lurking in the dark forest. Long-settled cultures were scattered through the woods and encamped on the river banks and tidal inlets. Coastal New York and southern New England

Canoe, sive Navicula
e corticibus arborum.

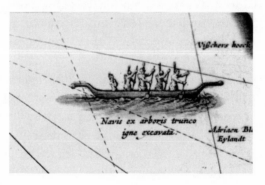

Vijschers hoeck

Navis ex arboris trunco
igne excavata.

Adriaen Bl.
Eylandt

Indian Canoes
The native Americans who lived near the Sound
traveled in dugout canoes — of oak, pine, or
chestnut — that held from fifteen to forty
men. Indians farther north used bark
canoes. This detail is from a Dutch
map produced in 1635. Courtesy
of Martayan Lan Fine Antique
Maps, New York, N.Y.

was the territory of about ninety thousand people. Connecticut may have had two hundred and eighty-seven people per hundred square miles, or a total population of fourteen thousand. As many as twenty-five hundred lived in coastal New York. Those nations husbanded the land, the rivers, and the sea. They hunted, fished, planted, maintained a subsistence economy, warred with their enemies, migrated from the woods in winter to the shore of the Sound in summer, and celebrated the passing of the seasons.[3]

Each year they longed for winter's end. They looked for the signs that presage the warm weather: a hint of vernal mildness in the afternoon air, the tempering of the harsh calls of winter birds into the urgent songs of spring. The winds that blew off the Sound were cold, and would stay cold for many weeks, but the days grew noticeably longer and the angle of the sunlight eased from its winter sharpness. The people waited for the new moon after the last full moon of February. When it arrived, the new year arrived with it.

"They watch it with great devotion," a Dutch observer wrote in 1624, "and when it comes, they compliment it with a festival; then they collect together from all quarters, and revel in their way, with wild game or fish, and drink clear river water to their fill."[4] He was describing the natives of "New Netherland," which to the Dutch encompassed the lands from Cape Cod west to Manhattan Island, and south at least to Delaware Bay, an area inhabited by the tribes or nations known collectively as the Algonquians. The waning of winter was their signal that the cycle of the seasons was about to return to the renewal of life on land and in the sea.

As the mild days became more frequent and the soil grew soft and warm, the women set to work, tilling their gardens with spades of hardwood. They watched for the signs that would tell them when to plant — the opening of the leaves of certain trees or the rush upstream of spawning fish. Then, molding the earth with the shells of horseshoe crabs, they formed small hills, into which they planted corn and beans, whose vines would climb and be supported by the cornstalks; nearby they planted squash, sunflowers, and tobacco.[5]

The men had their own tasks. As the crops sprouted, fish moved inshore. Every coastal stream and river supported a spring run of fish drawn upriver, from saltwater to fresh, by the urge to spawn. The bounty was staggering, almost incredible by today's standards. From March until June, day after day, species after species jammed from bank to bank—shad, alewives, striped bass, salmon, sturgeon, blue-back herring: fresh food and, smoked over fires or dried in the sun on scaffolds, provender for the return of the cold weather.[6]

They caught fish in weirs and nets, the Siwanoys at streams like the Premium River, which slides past a spit of sand at the border of what is now Larchmont and New Rochelle; the Pequots, probably, at Bride's Brook, a stream snaking through the marshes and oak forests of East Lyme, Connecticut; and the Matinecocks at the Nissequogue River, which cuts through the bluffs at Smithtown Bay, on Long Island. They caught individual fish by fashioning a gorge and line from the shank bone of a fawn and strands of spun Indian hemp. Sturgeon, a favorite among the Indians, were gulled at night with an early form of jacklighting: waving a blazing torch alongside their dugout canoes, the Indians waited, poised with lances, for the intrigued fish to approach their vessels. When a sturgeon, whose armored back was impenetrable, turned its white belly toward them, they speared it and hauled it to shore.[7]

The Indians caught and trapped more than two dozen kinds of fish and shellfish. At archaeological sites along New York's portion of the Sound, researchers have unearthed the remains of bluefish, black-fish, winter flounder, weakfish, goosefish, eel, porgy, herring, sturgeon, lobster, and crab, along with many species that don't find their way onto modern tables—sea robin, bergall, smooth dogfish, spiny dogfish, oyster toadfish, angler, black drum, sting ray, whale, grubby, skate, shark, and puffer.[8] The men pursued these fish in dugout canoes, described by some witnesses as steady, by others as prone to tipping if the mariners were not skillful; by some as big enough for fifteen men, by others as big enough for forty.

The canoes often were the product of one man's labor. With a supply of parched corn to sustain him, he would leave his coastal camp for the woods, select a tree, and fell it. The tree could be oak, or pine, or chestnut, the last of which resisted decay particularly well. He hewed the wood with stone tools, fashioning the vessel from sunrise to sunset, and then slept next to his work. The labor progressed for ten or twelve days. The finished canoes, especially those of chestnut, were heavy boats, and several men were needed to launch one.[9] When not used for fishing or for crossing the Sound on other errands, the dugouts were an efficient vessel for hunting waterfowl. Ducks, geese, and other migratory birds, as well as fish, were the Indians' staples from late winter until crops were ready in midsummer.

The rafts of geese and ducks that still winter on the Sound and its tributaries, or stop to rest and feed during their migrations north and south, pale in number before the wildfowl of several centuries ago. Scoters, scaup, and canvasbacks in winter, widgeons, mergansers, mallards, shovelers, Canada geese, and brant in fall and spring—all were netted or shot with arrows. Under cover of darkness, Indians plucked cormorants from their rocky offshore roosts.[10] Other birds—some for eating, some not—were abundant as well. Herons, egrets, and bitterns stalked the marshes. Gulls and terns crowded into coastal colonies, which the Indians raided for fresh eggs—no doubt under harrowing conditions given breeding birds' panic at intruders. Grackles, in return, raided cornfields, and some Indians kept tamed hawks on hand to control the blackbirds. Passenger pigeons, now extinct, filled the woods with their calls and darkened the sky for days on end during migration.[11]

Who were these people who lived off the land, who indeed were as much a part of the land as the animals and fish they hunted, the plants they gathered? They were Algonquians, linked by their closely related languages. On eastern Long Island they were called Shinnecocks and Montauks and Corchaugs, three tightly allied nations. Across the Sound, the Pequots claimed the lower Mystic River valley as their land, and their kin, the Mohegans, lived about twelve miles north of the Pequots; culturally and linguistically, both were almost identical to the eastern Long Island nations. Flanking the Pequots were the two Niantic tribes, who shared a name but had conflicting political ties. The eastern Niantics—linked to the Narragansetts of Rhode Island—lived east of the Pequots, along the Pawcatuck River. The western Niantics, allies of the Pequots, lived on the eastern shore of the Connecticut River. West of the river, the broad harbor and red hills of New Haven were the lands of the Quinnipiacs. The Quiripi, the Naugatucks, and the Schaghticokes lived in the valley of the Housatonic. And further west, the Norwalks' territory reached to the Five Mile River, in Darien.

Indian Villages
These villages were depicted in an early Dutch map
of New Netherland. Courtesy of Martayan Lan
Fine Antique Maps, New York, N.Y.

The Five Mile River marked the border separating the Algonquians of New England with another nation, also Algonquian, which spoke Munsee and Unami, and which, after being forced onto reservations in places such as Ontario and Oklahoma, became known as the Delaware. Their territory stretched west through New Jersey and into Pennsylvania. Among them, the Tankitekes lived along the coves and creeks and in the chestnut- and oak-covered hills west of Five Mile River, reaching about to the Byram River. And beyond, along the Westchester County shore to the Bronx River, lived the Siwanoys. Opposite them on Long Island, on the necks and along the bays, in Hempstead, Huntington, Oyster Bay, and Flushing, were the Matinecocks and Massapequas, who probably were Delaware but may have traced their lineage to the New England Algonquians.[12]

"To make sense of it," wrote James Wilson in *The Earth Shall Weep: A History of Native America,* "you have to realize that what you are seeing is a snapshot of one moment in a constantly changing situation: these are not nation states, but groups of culturally — and often physically — related peoples who move within frontiers shaped by custom and mutual understanding rather than legal definition. But the impression of chaos — one of the key European perceptions of the eastern Indian — is illusory: although they managed their relationship with the land and with each other in a profoundly different way, their world was at least as orderly as contemporary Europe's."[13]

Exactly how many Indians lived along the Sound before Europeans arrived is impossible to say. Believable estimates have been made for populations in a wider area that includes the region of the Sound. The late anthropologist Lynn Ceci estimated that in all of coastal New York—including the south shore of Long Island, Manhattan, and Staten Island—the maximum population of "sedentary Indians" ranged from seventeen hundred to about twenty-five hundred. The historian William Jennings argues that southern New England sustained a much greater population than earlier historians believed. Using estimates from a European traveler during the early colonial period—one Daniel Gookin, who reported hearing from tribal elders that eighteen thousand warriors populated lower New England before 1600—Jennings infers a population in Massachusetts, Rhode Island, and Connecticut of from seventy-two thousand to ninety thousand, based on an estimate of three or four dependents for each warrior. Another historian, William Cronon, says that in southern New England, where tribes grew crops (unlike the northern regions, where the climate did not allow much planting), the land supported two hundred eighty-seven people per hundred square miles. By that estimate, about fourteen thousand Indians lived in Connecticut before Europeans began settling in the area.[14]

Rivers, hills, and bays bounded the Indians' territories. Within their regions they were migratory, with few possessions to tie them to any one location. In warm weather they dispersed to the shore; in cold, they retreated into the protected interior of the forest. If too many years of planting corn in one field depleted the soil, they abandoned it for another. Their most substantial houses were long and narrow—one hundred feet by ten feet—or circular, fourteen or fifteen paces in circumference, and made of poles and mats of straw, which could be dismantled and carried to a new site. Several families lived in each dwelling. The houses were clustered into villages. When the men went hunting or fishing they often took along smaller, more portable shelters.[15]

With crops ripening and needing little attention, and with no domestic animals to tend, the Indians were most mobile in summer.

"Some of them lead a wandering life in the open air with no settled habitations," wrote Johan deLaet, a director of the Dutch West India Company, in 1625. "Lying stretched upon the ground or on mats made of bulrushes, they take both their sleep and food, especially in summer, when they go nearer to the sea for the sake of fishing."[16]

Summer was the season of living off the fat of the land, and on the Sound a good portion of the "fat" was shellfish. Lobsters were large and numerous. Mussels seemed infinite. One observer in New England claimed to have seen clams "as big as a penny white loaf" of English bread. Oyster beds stretched for a mile in length, and individual oysters were a foot long. To get at the oysters, Indians invented a precursor of the modern oyster rake, a long-tined forked branch that worked the bivalves up from the shallows.[17]

Shellfish had another use, too, besides nourishment. Along the shores of Long Island Sound, and east to the Narragansett region, Indians laboriously fashioned the shells of three species of mollusks into wampum, the tiny beads that had enormous importance culturally and economically both before and after Europeans arrived. Only the Indians who lived near the shore and who had a guaranteed supply of shells could make wampum. They ground down the choice parts of the shells on stone slabs, carefully forming beads a quarter of an inch long and an eighth of an inch in diameter. Then, using stone drills, they bore a hole through each tiny bead. For white beads the Indians chose the central column of two kinds of whelks, the channeled whelk (*Busycon canaliculatum*) and the knobbed whelk (*Busycon carica*). "Black" beads were crafted from the small purple part of the inner shell of the quahog.

It is unclear if Indians used wampum as money before Europeans arrived—the fact that it seems not to have been manufactured in abundance is perhaps an indication that they did not. Wampum, however, had many other uses. Its possession, especially inland, where its value was greater than along the waterfront areas near where it originated, was a sign of individual power or wealth: sachems wore small amounts of it, and if accumulated by someone whose status was unrecognized by society, it was taken as a challenge to the powerful. Weaker nations paid it in tribute to more powerful ones; the Pequots, for one, were renowned for demanding, and receiving, tribute from their neighbors.

Wampum was used as reparations for murder. It was exchanged during marriage proposals. It was given as gifts to friends and allies. Wampum belts of impressive size were painstakingly crafted: one belt that survived contained ten thousand five hundred beads in rows two hundred and ten beads wide by fifty beads long. Wampum was powerfully symbolic and important, probably the most important non-utilitarian item produced by the people of the Long Island Sound area.[18]

Often it was the women who waded into the shallows and dug along the mudflats for oysters and lobsters and clams for food, as well as whelks for wampum. The women also were responsible for gathering berries. "In the wilds are found all sorts of fruits: plums, wild cherries, peaches; yea, fruits in great profusion." The ripening marked the progression of the season: wild strawberries in June, wineberries, raspberries, and blueberries in July, raspberries and blackberries in August.[19]

The shore of the Sound also was ideal for waiting out the humid days of hazed-in horizons and afternoon thunderstorms. But the increased activity necessitated by autumn came early. The first new moon of August signaled a harvest feast. Preparation for winter intensified. Corn ripened and was made into cornmeal cakes, which the women baked in the ashes of a fire.[20] Corn and kidney beans, with chunks of fish or game sometimes thrown in, made a succotash-like porridge. They had no table salt, so the meat and liquor of clams were added for savor. Later in the season the porridge was fortified with pumpkin and ground nuts. Autumn provided nuts in abundance — black walnuts, hickory nuts, butternuts, chestnuts. Acorns were boiled or dried, and added to stews, or eaten instead of corn if the harvest had been poor. At least five kinds of oaks produced edible acorns — white oak, swamp white oak, chestnut oak, bur oak, and post oak.[21]

The bounty of nuts was available in the autumn woods, where the Indians retreated for the cold months. Because they also needed animals in abundance and easy passage through the woods, they set fire to the forest's undergrowth twice a year, in fall and spring — a simple and effective form of game- and land-management. The blazes burned quickly and lightly, clearing brush before it got too thick but allowing room for the succulent plants that game animals thrived on. The technique worked well: in spring, herds of up to a hundred deer were common. For the most part, the Indians let these springtime animals be because fish and birds were so common in that season. The game animals, especially deer, would be there when the fish and birds were not. And, adding weight for winter, they would be much more desirable as food. Some archaeological evidence indicates that deer accounted for ninety percent of the Indians' meat.[22]

The Indians hunted deer with bows and arrows tipped with points of bone, stone, iron, or copper.[23] They held communal drives, two hundred to three hundred men forcing herds into pounds, or to the shore, where they could be easily dispatched. A Dutchman named David de Vries described an early seventeenth-century communal hunt that involved about one hundred men:

> They stand a hundred paces more or less from each other, and holding flat thigh-bones in the hand, beat them with a stick, and so drive the creatures before them to the river. As they approach the river, they close nearer to each other, and whatever is between any two of them, is at the mercy of their bows and arrows, or must take to the river. When the animals swim into the river, the savages lie in their canoes with lassos, which they throw around their necks, and tighten, whereupon the deer lie down and float with the rump upwards, as they cannot draw breath. At the north, they drive them into a *fuyk,* which they make of palisades split out of trees, and eight or nine feet high, and set close to each other, for a distance of fourteen or fifteen hundred paces on both sides; the opening is one or two thousand paces wide. When the animal is within the palisades, the savages begin to come nearer to each other, and pursue it with great ardor, as they regard deer-hunting the noblest hunting. At the end of the *fuyk* it is so narrow that it is only five feet wide, like a large door, and it is there covered with the boughs of trees, into which the deer or animal runs, closely pursued by the savages, who make a noise as if they were wolves, by which many deer are devoured, and of which they are in great fear. This causes them to run into the mouth of the

fuyk with great force, whither the Indians pursue them furiously with bows and arrows, and from whence they cannot escape; they are then easily caught.[24]

There were other game animals too, especially in the cold weather and after the first snow fell, when tracking was easy: elk, beaver, wild turkey, and black bear, the bear being easy targets once they had denned for the winter. The Indians loved bear for its fat, using it for food and anointing their bodies with it as insulation against the cold. And although they were less important, many other animals became prey for Indian hunters — otter, skunk, squirrel, woodchuck, wolf, marten, mink, muskrat, raccoon, gray fox, red fox, porcupine, lynx, bobcat, and cottontail rabbit.[25] This is not to suggest that the region of Long Island Sound, or indeed any part of North America, was an Acadian utopia of native peoples. The Indians went to war. There were murders and assaults. Goods were stolen, pacts made and broken. They were said to be kind and generous, but if victimized they sought revenge, and they held long grudges if vengeance was delayed, an encounter with the wrongdoer often ending with a slaying. Thievery was rarely punished unless it went too far; then the accused was stripped of his goods and left to start anew. If a husband deserted his wife, or vice versa, without just cause, he was forced to abandon all his possessions to her. They cherished their children and estranged couples would often remain together for their sake. And, observers noted, the Indians appeared remarkably healthy, with few infirmities or crippling deformities.[26]

In short, they were a people characterized by all the faults and qualities of any other nation. Yet they were a people who lived with nature, not against it, who were dwellers in the land, not consumers of it. They were also a people who were in no way prepared for the changes the seventeenth century would bring — changes heralded by the coming of a Dutch merchant named Adriaen Block.

THREE

Adriaen Block and the First Explorers

By the seventeenth century, European sailors had been visiting the New World for more than a hundred years. Following Columbus, there was John Cabot, who ventured along the North American coast in 1497 and 1498; his son Sebastian made a similar journey in 1508–9. Amerigo Vespucci explored the coast of South America in 1499 and more extensively in 1501–2. Balboa crossed Central America to view the Pacific in 1513, and Magellan set sail for South America in 1519 and almost three years later his fleet—or what remained of it—succeeded in circumnavigating the globe. And fishermen from Portugal, the Basque territory, Breton, and Bristol had been seeking cod off the coasts of Canada and New England since well before Columbus.

The first time a European even approached the waters connected with Long Island Sound was probably in 1524, when Giovanni da Verrazzano explored the east coast of North America for France. He sailed from the Carolinas to Rhode Island, passing by Chesapeake Bay and Delaware Bay but poking into the Hudson River estuary, where boatloads of natives in headdresses greeted his ship. His survey of New York Bay was as close as he got to the Sound, however. After a brief stay, Verrazzano retreated to the ocean and coasted along the south shore of Long Island, apparently ignoring the waters north and west of Montauk Point in favor of a route that took him further east and into Narragansett Bay. A map that his brother, Girolamo, produced in 1529 shows a wide bay at the eastern entrance to the Sound; the headland curves to the west to form the south shore of Long Island, although it is part of the mainland—Europeans did not yet know that Long Island was in fact an island. Near the bay, the map shows a triangular island that might represent Nantucket, Martha's Vineyard, or Block Island. A year after Verrazzano's visit, Esteban Gómez nudged his way into the eastern Sound.[1] It was not until 1609 that another European navigator, Henry Hudson, again explored the New York area. In 1609, aboard his ship the *Half Moon,* he found a great tidal river, along the shores of which lived a population willing to barter furs. He returned to Europe with the news and a rough map, but they stirred little interest among his employers, the East India Company.

The merchants thought it so unpromising, in fact, that they took no trouble to keep Hudson's discovery a secret, and soon others were mounting expeditions to the New World, not only to find Hudson's trading territory but in hopes that diligent searching might still yield a Northwest Passage to China. Among the first to follow Hudson was Adriaen Block.[2]

Block's achievement has gotten little attention in the stories of the early exploration and settlement of the Northeast, but he was foremost among the group of mariners who opened European trade with the Indians of northeast North America, which led to the establishment of permanent trading posts and then towns in New York. He made at least three, and perhaps four, journeys to New Netherland and the Hudson River: on the *St. Pieter* in 1611, as captain of the *Fortuyn* in 1612 and again in 1612–13, and as captain of the *Tijger* in 1613–14. He was the first European to sail Long Island Sound from one end to the other, and he did it at least twice, probably, before anyone else did it once. Like many European navigators who sailed to lands little known by the Renaissance world, Captain Adriaen Block was not primarily an explorer. He was a businessman, a merchant who journeyed across the Atlantic to waters that were only rudimentarily charted, to barter and deal with people whose good will and honesty were hardly guaranteed, a venture that doubtless required courage and surely required success if a mariner such as Block was to mount the financial backing for return voyages. Almost single-handedly he opened the Sound and its tributaries to European trade. And although it is true that if he had not done it, someone else would have in very short order, it nevertheless was an achievement — one that would have cataclysmic, even devastating, effects on nature and native life in the region.

Adriaen Block was born in Amsterdam in about 1567. On October 26, 1603, he married Neeltgen Heyndricx van Gelder, with whom he had five children. Three years after their wedding they settled on Amsterdam's Oude Waal, in the house — called the "Twee Bontecraijen" — in which he would live for the rest of his life.

By the time he married, he was already busy in the shipping trade, hauling wood from northern Europe to Spain, where deforestation had forced the importation of timber as early as 1500. Block sailed to

Norway for wood in April 1596, delivering his cargo to Bilbao, in the Basque region of Spain. From there he headed for Rivadeo, where he loaded more timber, this time to be sold in Cádiz.

On April 23, 1601, Block left Amsterdam for the East Indies, part of a convoy of fourteen ships that returned to Holland two years later. In the spring of 1604 he delivered goods to the Italian province of Liguria, and received as payment eleven thousand pieces of eight. He then sailed to Cyprus, passing among a group of islands, which he knew as Archipelagus, between Greece, Crete, and Turkey. In Cyprus he bought one thousand eight hundred and twenty-eight bales of rice and one hundred bags of gall-nuts, as well as cotton, currants, and malmsey. He hoped to sell them in Venice, but he had no luck there and so returned to Amsterdam. Before reaching home, however, Block seized an opportunity off Lisbon, when he encountered a ship from the Baltic port of Lübeck, in Germany. Block had with him a letter of marque—permission from Dutch authorities to capture enemy merchant ships—and he put it to use, taking the ship and its cargo of sugar and Brazil wood. He sailed into Amsterdam in August 1605, and although Dutch authorities returned the seized ship and some of its goods to its owners, Block saw a substantial profit, which he probably used to buy his house on the Oude Waal.[3]

Block and the merchants who financed Holland's trade then looked west, across the Atlantic and specifically to the region that Hudson had visited. Block's first voyage to North America might have been in 1611—two years after Hudson—when he sailed with Captain Cornelis Rijser on the *St. Pieter*, a 120-ton ship owned by a small group of Lutheran merchants in Amsterdam. The *St. Pieter* had a crew of thirteen. If Block was on board, he was one of three supercargoes—a merchant ship officer who is in charge of a voyage's goods and commercial concerns. The *St. Pieter* carried 2,950 guilders' worth of goods to trade for pelts, and enough food for seven months. In 1611 no one knew how profitable a voyage to the New World would be, so the owners made sure there was a contingency plan: if the trading was bad, the crew was to help out with fishing.[4] The journey from Holland to New Amsterdam took ten weeks or longer, and Block's ships probably sailed along the Labrador Current, past Newfoundland, and then down the coast of New England to New York Bay.[5]

Block must have done his job well on the *St. Pieter* — and the beaver trading must have been successful — because on January 17, 1612, acting again on behalf of the Lutheran merchants, he bought a square-sterned ship of 110 tons, called the *Fortuyn*. With Block as its captain, the *Fortuyn* sailed for New Netherland in February 1612, a departure date that probably had the ship approaching the mainland in mid to late April.

In December of 1612, Block left Amsterdam for his third voyage, again on the *Fortuyn,* arriving no sooner than mid February to mid March.[6] It was on one of these two journeys that Block became the first European to sail the length of Long Island Sound. Whether it was the journey of 1612 or of 1612–13 is unknown, but that it was one of the two is clear from the events of Block's fourth visit to New Netherland, in 1614.

Block no doubt entered the Sound to scout out areas for expanding his trade. Such a purpose is suggested by his description of his journey, which is filled with notations of depths, distances, safe anchorages, harbors, rivers, islands, and inlets — remarks on phenomena and features that might later prove useful to him. (The descriptions were published in 1625, in a book called *New World,* by Johan deLaet, who used Block's log as his source.[7])

Block's survey of the coast began off Massachusetts, probably at Marblehead Bay, and proceeded around Cape Cod. He noted Nantucket Island, Martha's Vineyard, and the Elizabeth Islands, and sailed into Buzzard's Bay and Narragansett Bay. Then, cruising along the line of barrier beaches that form Rhode Island's Atlantic shore, he veered south and visited Block Island, the only land in North America that now bears his name. He probably entered Long Island Sound by slipping between the eastern extreme of Fishers Island and Rhode Island's Napatree Point, "a curved promontory," as deLaet described it, "behind which there is a small stream or inlet" — the Pawcatuck River, which the Dutch called East River.

The *Fortuyn* then poked into the Mystic River, referred to in deLaet as "the river of Siccanamos," named after the sagamore of the "Pequatoos," or Pequots, whose territory flanked the river. DeLaet's account seems to confuse the Mystic with the next river along the coast, the Thames. He reports that the Mystic supported salmon (which it

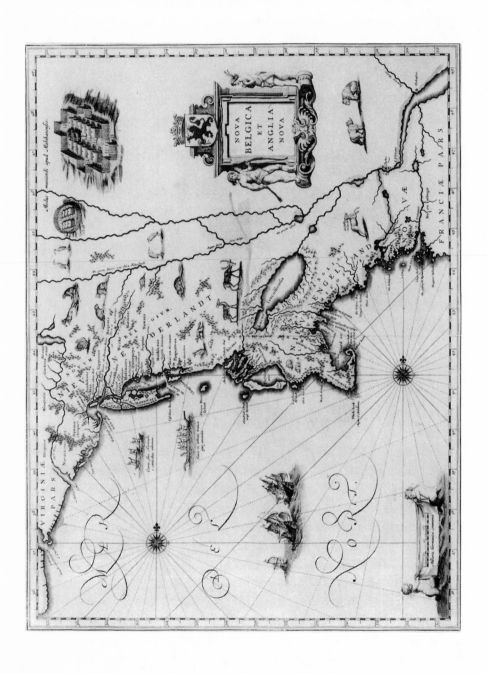

The Region in the Early Seventeenth Century

The so-called Blaue map of 1635 was produced in the Netherlands as part of an atlas and is based on a chart that Captain Adriaen Block made during his early explorations of the region. Block's original map was the first chart to show that Long Island was indeed an island. In this reproduction, north is at the top of the page, but the map originally was published with west at the top; the Sound region is near the illustrations of the Indian canoes, and Long Island, with its many bays and inlets, is shown as several islands separated by small waterways. Among the map's features are Long Island Sound (labeled as De Groote Baye, or the Great Bay), Fishers Island (called Lange Eylandt, or Long Island), Adriaen Block Eylandt (Block Island), Archipelagus (the Norwalk Islands), Hellegat (Hell Gate), and Versche Riviere (the Connecticut River). Courtesy of Martayan Lan Fine Antique Maps, New York, N.Y.

could have), and that it had a point of sand that protected an anchorage fifteen feet deep, about a mile and a half from the western shore. The depth of the river itself varied widely, deLaet wrote; some shallows had as little as six feet of water while elsewhere there were "holes with full five fathoms," or thirty feet. According to deLaet, ships could sail upstream perhaps as much as eighteen miles from the river's mouth.[8]

Block noted Fishers Island, then poked up the Thames, apparently trading with the Mohegans, who lived inland along the river.[9] Sailing again along the mainland, he continued to scout up streams and inlets in search of a route to the interior. He soon found what he was look-ing for: not Hudson's river but the Connecticut or, as Block called it in Dutch, *de Versche Riviere* — the Fresh River. This river, deLaet wrote, "is shallow at its mouth, and lies between two courses, north by east and west by north; but, according to conjecture, its general direction is from the north-northwest. In some places it is very shallow, so that at about fifteen leagues up the river [forty-five miles] there is not much more than five feet of water. There are few inhabitants near the mouth of the river, but at a distance of fifteen leagues above [Middletown, Connecticut] they become numerous; their nation is called Sequins. From this place the river stretches ten leagues, mostly in a northerly di-rection, but is very crooked; the reaches extend from northeast to southwest by south, and it is impossible to sail through them all with a head wind. The depth of water varies from eight to twelve feet, is sometimes four and five fathoms [twenty-four to thirty feet], but mostly eight and nine feet."

Other potential trading partners, the Nawaas, lived on the Fresh River north of the Sequins. They and their sagamore, Morahieck, lived in present-day Hartford. They planted maize and baked it into a bread they called "leganick." Further north lived "another nation of savages, who are called Horikans," who navigated the river in bark canoes. It is doubtful, however, that Block came face-to-face with them — at least on this first exploration — for north of Hartford he and his vessel were turned back by the rapids.

From the Connecticut, Block continued west, sailing eight leagues — or about twenty-four miles — to New Haven Harbor, the Sound's next wide bay. At the head of the harbor, he found that the river, the Quinnipiac, was "about a bow-shot wide." He also noted the river valley's most prominent feature — West Rock, the rust-colored, four-hundred-foot basalt escarpment north of present-day New Haven. To mark it, Block called the tributary the "river of Royenberch," or red hills. As for the Indians, he noted that they were called Quiripeys and, judging from deLaet's remarks, were in the practice of hunting just as many beavers as they needed for their own use, and no more — a practice Block held in contempt: "They take many beavers, but it is necessary for them to get into the habit of trade, otherwise they are too indolent to hunt the beaver."

Still sailing west, Block stopped at "a small island, where good water is to be found" — perhaps Charles Island, off Milford, although either he or deLaet mistook its distance, locating it twelve miles from New Haven when it lies just six miles away. The measurement of the distance from New Haven to the Norwalk Islands, though, was on the mark: eight leagues, or twenty-four miles. Block called the islands "Archipelagus," a name that hearkened back to his days as a young merchant captain among the archipelago of islands between Greece, Crete, and Turkey.

At Rowayton, Block noted that the Five Mile River became a mere stream — or less: he said it was "perfectly dry" — half a mile inland. He also must have sailed south, because he reported that at Norwalk the Great Bay was four leagues, or twelve miles, wide — a generous estimate: Norwalk is only about eight miles north of Long Island. The natives at Norwalk were Siwanoys, Block reported, and they lived along the coast for at least as far as Hellegat — Hell Gut or Strait, by which Block meant not only the swirls and whirlpools of Hell Gate at Wards Island but the entire East River.[10]

If his exploration of the Sound took place during his third journey to North America, then Block would have reached the Hudson in the spring. He remained there for about two months, trading peacefully until, to Block's surprise, another Dutch ship arrived, the *Jonge Tobias*. There could be no doubt about the purpose of the ship's skipper, Thijs Mossel, or its supercargo, Hans Hontom — they were there to compete with Block for beaver. They began with a tactic guaranteed to win over any producer of raw materials: they offered the Indians double what Block was paying. The maneuver forced Block to negotiate, and the two captains eventually agreed that Block would receive two-thirds of all the pelts traded on the river, with Mossel getting one-third. For verification, both captains assigned trade representatives to the other's ship.

Given Block's advantage, it was not surprising that Mossel's voyage was not profitable, if the later complaints of the merchants who backed him are evidence. Block, however, did better. On July 30, 1613, one of the Lutheran merchants, Francoys Pelgroms Geerartsen, wrote to his wife that Block and his supercargo, Jan Kindt, had returned to Amsterdam "in good health and made a good voyage, yes, a better voyage even than last year."

Block, in fact, did so well that he tried to hide his success from potential competitors. In August on the Amsterdam Exchange, he met an old acquaintance and former partner, the merchant Simon Williamsen Nooms, who, like Block, had owned a one-sixteenth share in the ship Block had sailed to Cyprus in 1604. Block indicated to Nooms that the journey to New Netherlands had been a poor one, the trading inconsequential. Nooms was no fool. If the trading had been so unprofitable, he remarked, why was Block outfitting two ships to sail to North America again? Nooms also told Block that the trading in New Netherland had attracted interest among other merchants. But that was no matter, Block responded, because his company had acquired a patent, giving it sole rights to trade on Hudson's river. But as Nooms knew — and as Block should have known — the patent merely meant that Block's voyage was lawful, not that the company owned by the Lutheran merchants should be free from competition.

The two ships that Block and his merchants were preparing were the *Fortuyn,* this time to be commanded by Block's colleague, Hendrick Christiaensen, and the *Tijger,* which Block himself was to sail. Thijs Mossel, in the meantime, had gotten rid of the *Jonge Tobias* and was preparing for a return voyage on another ship, the *Nachtegael.* Christiaensen and Mossel set sail first, embarking at the end of September 1613. Block followed about a month later, carrying not only the patent as "proof" that he and Christiaensen were to be allowed to trade unencumbered by competition, but more substantial evidence, perhaps, that Block expected the patent to carry little weight in the waters of North America: he had asked the Admiralty of Amsterdam for six to eight guns, and the Admiralty consented, lending him six that weighed as much as 1,600 pounds each.

Dutch Ships
These ships are a detail from the 1635 Blaue map.
Adriaen Block sailed to the region probably four
times—on the *St. Pieter* (1611), the *Fortuyn* (1612 and
1612–13), and the *Tijger* (1613–14). Although most
accounts of Block's journeys say he made his first
exploration of the Sound in 1614 on a yacht called the
Onrust, which he had built after the *Tijger* burned,
there is strong circumstantial evidence that his first
trip through the Sound was actually on one of his
two journeys on the *Fortuyn.* Courtesy of Martayan
Lan Fine Antique Maps, New York, N.Y.

Christiaensen reached the river first and then, when Mossel finally
arrived, considered him an interloper who had no business trading on
the Hudson and who should, in fact, be forced from the area. The ten-
sion eased with the appearance of Block, who was Christiaensen's su-
perior. Negotiating for his company, Block proposed that he and his
merchants receive three-fifths of all the skins bartered on the river,
while Mossel and Hontom take rights to two-fifths. As part of the bar-
gain, Block was to depart the river and trade elsewhere, leaving Christiaensen and Mossel to continue bartering with the Indians on the
Hudson and its tributaries.

The deal was struck in January 1614, and suggests that Block had
already explored the Sound, for if he was so willing to quit the Hudson's proven trading grounds it is likely that he knew he could journey
elsewhere and find comparable numbers of beaver—up the Connecticut River, for example, where the Indians planted corn and ate corn-

bread, or to the Quinnipiac, where the river was a bow-shot wide and the "indolent" natives would need to be prodded to hunt enough beaver to satisfy him. This knowledge would have been his only if he had already made his exploratory voyage along the Sound.

But wherever he planned to go, Block was forced to remain on the Hudson until the river became free of ice. While he was waiting to sail, in January or February of 1614, the *Tijger* caught fire and was destroyed.[11] Mossel and Hontom quickly sought to exploit Block's troubles. They offered to take on half the *Tijger*'s crew — and pay their wages — in return for a modification in the trade agreement: instead of a 60:40 split, they wanted half the furs. Block and the rest of his crew would then, presumably, remain with Christiaensen on the *Fortuyn*. Or, if Block needed more help than that, Mossel and Hontom would take all of the *Tijger*'s men onto the *Nachtegael* and, not surprisingly, most of the furs. Block and Christiaensen rejected both offers, which did little to ease the bad blood between the competitors. Rather than capitulate, Block ordered that a new vessel be constructed. His shipbuilder, Herman Hillebrantsen, set to work designing and building a smaller boat, called the *Onrust*.[12]

As February passed into March, the ice on the river began to break up. On March 3 Christiaensen and the *Fortuyn* — accompanied by a crew member from the *Nachtegael* to verify that the trade agreement was being kept — sailed north in search of furs. The next day Block and his supercargo, Jan Kindt, learned that Mossel and Hontom planned to sail the *Nachtegael* through Hell Gate, in search of pelts. Block and Kindt immediately visited Mossel's ship to confront their rivals, reminding them that their deal forbade Mossel and Hontom from trading in the region beyond Hell Gate.

Mossel and Hontom disagreed. Their deal allowed them to trade on the Hudson and its tributaries, they pointed out. Yes, countered Block, but Hell Gate was not a tributary; the waters beyond Hell Gate were reserved for Block and were off-limits to Mossel and Hontom because Hell Gate led to a Great Bay, which in turn led to the sea, one hundred and eleven miles away — information that Block would have had no way of knowing had he not already explored the Sound. Mossel and Hontom, though, were not dissuaded. On March 6 Hontom took two sloops and seventeen men — the majority of the *Nachtegael*'s crew — and headed for the East River and the Sound beyond in search of furs. The next day, when Mossel and some of the *Nachtegael*'s remaining men went ashore to fetch firewood, a treacherous band of Block's men — apparently without Block's approval and knowledge — boarded the *Nachtegael* and took control of Mossel's vessel. Mossel appealed to Block for help, and together the two captains negotiated with the renegades. The talks failed and Block and Mossel returned to the *Onrust,* where preparations were made to recapture the *Nachtegael* by force. Armed with muskets and spears, Mossel and Jan Kindt first perched on a hill and shot down at the mutineers, who returned their fire. Then, with Block's permission, Mossel, Kindt, and three men sailed in Block's sloop to find Christiaensen for reinforcements. Block, meanwhile, attacked the *Nachtegael* with some of his crew and Mossel's crew. But the mutineers fought back and threatened to steal to the *Onrust* at night and set fire to it if Block did not stop shooting.

Christiaensen returned after hearing from Mossel and Kindt of the insurrection. He caught sight of the *Nachtegael* on the morning of March 8. Block and all but three of Block's crew — who stayed behind with the *Onrust* — boarded the *Fortuyn,* which chased the *Nachtegael* to the mouth of the Hudson. But when Christiaensen's ship caught the *Nachtegael,* the *Fortuyn*'s crew refused to fight the mutineers — men who had been, just days before, their comrades. When Hontom and his crew of seventeen finally returned from their trading along the Sound, they found that the *Nachtegael* had departed eight days earlier, bound for the West Indies, where the crew took up piracy, returning eventually to the Hudson, and then sailing to Ireland.

Only the *Fortuyn* and the much smaller *Onrust* remained on the Hudson. Two other Dutch ships soon sailed up the river — one also named the *Fortuyn* and the other the *Vos.* With Mossel's ship gone, and with the presence of two new competitors, Block and Mossel dissolved their trade agreement and forged a new deal among all four captains — namely, to divide equally all the skins acquired in New Netherland. They bartered with the Indians probably until May or June, when the *Onrust* set sail through Hell Gate for further trading along the Sound and the Connecticut River — a voyage mistakenly considered to be the first European exploration of the Sound. The three larger ships departed for Europe shortly after. Block took the *Onrust* as far as Cape Cod, where he met Christiaensen and the *Fortuyn*. He boarded the *Fortuyn* and left the yacht under the command of a mariner named Cornelis Hendrickson, who continued to trade on the Hudson and Delaware rivers. The *Fortuyn* returned to Amsterdam in July 1614, carrying about 2,500 skins.

For the Dutch, the return of the fur traders to the Netherlands led to an agreement to eliminate the kind of contention that caused the loss of the *Nachtegael*. On October 11, 1614, soon after the ships reached Holland, the government authorized four groups of merchants to form one company with exclusive Dutch rights to all trading in New Netherland — the New Netherland Company. Its birth led directly to the founding of New Amsterdam. The *Fortuyn* — the first ship to sail the length of Long Island Sound — remained in the employ of the New Netherland Company until it was sold in 1617.[13]

For Block, who was by then about forty-seven years old, the return to Amsterdam in July of 1614 meant the end of his adventuring in the New World. His next challenge was to be the head of whaling operations for the Northern Company in the Bellsund on Spitsbergen, in the Arctic Ocean off Norway. He held that job for a year, but even then, pushing fifty years of age, he remained on the sea for another decade, sailing until he died, on April 7, 1627. He was buried at Amsterdam's Old Church, in a grave next to his wife.[14]

Captain Adriaen Block had been a merchant on the Mediterranean, a privateer off Spain, an explorer on the Sound and the Connecticut River, and a fur trader throughout the Hudson River valley and southern New England. He had sailed across the Atlantic four times. He had visited lands and had piloted through waterways that no white man had seen. He had been the first European to see that Long Island was indeed an island, and the first to sail the Sound from one end to the other, a feat he accomplished at least twice, probably, before anyone else did it once. He had met and bartered with people who were probably as wondrous to him as he was to them.

It is certainly true that Indians in the region had traded with Europeans long before Adriaen Block arrived. Fishermen probably exchanged goods with New England natives before Columbus; in the Sound region, a blue bead found at an Indian village at Throgs Neck dates from 1570 to 1595 and may be the oldest European artifact from coastal New York.[15] But the fishermen and the owner of the blue bead were incidental traders. For Block, trading was business. He injected into the world of the Indians of New Netherland an economy that had no use for subsistence. The natural world upon which the Indians of the Sound region depended became a commodity. Forests became timber, animals became food and furs, waterways became roads for transporting goods, wampum became money. And the native culture became a thing of the past.

Wampum provides an excellent example. It took the Dutch until 1622, eight years after Block's departure, to recognize the value wampum could have. For five years they alone used it for trade. But the Dutch realized that it would not be long before colonists from other countries learned of its usefulness, which likely would inject, into a fur-trading region they had for themselves, an unwanted element — competition. Being unable to halt that tide, the Dutch at least tried to control its direction. The English at Plymouth did not know about wampum until a Dutch agent sold them some in 1627 and urged them to trade it with the natives along the coast of Maine, thus pointing the English away from the Connecticut valley, where the Dutch were doing a good business. Within two years wampum was the most important commodity Plymouth had to offer.

As the Europeans created a value for wampum that had not existed previously, the coastal Indians' painstaking method of crafting the shell with stone tools became too slow. Traders helpfully provided metal drills, which immeasurably speeded the process of boring the tiny holes through the eight-sided whelk and quahog beads. The tool revolutionized wampum-making, and for about thirty years, starting in 1635, wampum ruled the economy in the region surrounding Long Island Sound. Its value was roughly four to six beads to the penny; for five shillings, or sixty pence, one could obtain a "fathom" — an assemblage of two hundred and forty to two hundred and sixty beads.[16] Traders carried goods from Europe such as kettles and guns, exchanged them along the Sound and Rhode Island for wampum, and then transported the wampum inland, where they traded it for valuable furs. Wampum's use as currency was acknowledged by Linnaeus, the pioneering Swedish taxonomist, who gave the name *Mercenaria mercenaria* to quahogs, the edible bivalves which, when served by the dozen, are known as cherrystones or little necks.

For the European traders, New England and New Amsterdam were a vast market of furs and skins—deer, bear, otter, mink and marten, fox and raccoon, and the most valuable of all, beaver. Against a force as powerful as European musketry, *Castor canadensis* disappeared in a flash. It was vanishing from coastal Massachusetts by 1640, and by 1660 was no longer an important part of the economy of the Narragansett region.[17] In the Sound's drainage basin, beaver were hunted relentlessly, especially in the Connecticut River valley, yet managed to hang on somewhat longer.

The Dutch were the first to profit from the Connecticut valley's beaver. They monopolized trade along the river starting in 1614, when the founding of the New Netherland Company abolished their competition among themselves. From 1623 through 1632—the period immediately following their discovery that wampum could be used for trading—the Dutch shipped more than one hundred thousand beaver pelts to Europe, or ten thousand pelts a year. In 1632 English colonists began to trade along the Connecticut, establishing posts at what would become the settlements of Wethersfield, Hartford, and Windsor, Connecticut, and Springfield, Massachusetts. The Dutch monopoly was over, their two decades of prosperity-by-plunder yielding to the similarly insatiable English.[18]

For the next fifty years two men dominated trade in the valley— William Pynchon and his son, John. William Pynchon was one of the holders of an original patent of the Massachusetts Bay Colony. He arrived in Boston from England in 1630 and, while serving simultaneously as treasurer of the colony, established himself in the fur trade. By 1636, however, beaver were too scarce near Boston to be profitable, and so he recruited a dozen families and journeyed west.

The emigrants traveled a well-used path from Boston, stopping at the Connecticut River, where Pynchon established a trading post and founded the settlement that grew into Springfield. He built a warehouse to the south, just below the Enfield Rapids, in Connecticut (the same rapids that halted Block on his exploration of the river). That location assured him access by boat to the Sound and the Atlantic.

With his son sometimes serving as his European buyer, Pynchon imported mirrors, knives, hatchets, hoes, cloth, and other goods. He exchanged them along the Sound for wampum or had them carried upriver to the warehouse, where they were unloaded onto smaller boats or oxcarts and taken to Springfield. Furs that had been stockpiled in the warehouse were then loaded onto ships and sent down the river and on to Europe. By this method, William Pynchon shipped perhaps six–nine thousand pounds of beaver a year from 1636 until 1652 — a year in which he was considered one of New England's richest men.

But the monopoly that was responsible for Pynchon's prosperity was over by 1650, and the competition, combined with what by then must have been an obvious scarcity in raw material, prompted one observer of the time to judge the beaver trade in the Connecticut valley to be of "little worth." That may have been true for inexperienced men. Yet for those who had served a diligent apprenticeship — Pynchon's son John, for example — there remained wealth to be extracted for a number of years.

From 1652 until 1658 John Pynchon traded almost nine thousand beaver pelts, weighing about fourteen thousand pounds, plus smaller numbers of other fur bearers. In the sixteen years following 1658, Pynchon-the-younger shipped another nine thousand pounds of beaver pelts. He also sold during that time four hundred and fifteen moose skins, four hundred otter, seven hundred and eighteen muskrats, three hundred and fifteen fox and raccoon, and lesser numbers of mink, marten, and lynx. And as late as 1675, a fur trader and liquor maker named David Wilton shipped to Pynchon during the four months from April to July three hundred pounds of beaver, one hundred and seventy-three otter skins, sixty-four raccoon skins, fifty-two martens, as well as muskrat, mink, fox, and lynx. Such carnage was obviously unsustainable, in the Connecticut valley or anywhere else. In southern New England, the beaver was gone by the end of the century.[19]

The change caused by wampum and the fur trade was no less than an economic revolution, and it in turn changed not only Indian–European relations, but the way Indians got along with each other as well. When the function of wampum was still largely symbolic, strong peoples such as the Pequots received it in tribute from weaker neighbors, who took protection for their payment. Tribute signaled respect, an acknowledgment that one tribe was more powerful than another. Because it was a symbol, small quantities served the purpose. But when wampum became worth possessing for other reasons, tribes began to mount looting raids to acquire it by force. The Niantics, for example, crossed the Sound in 1638 to loot the Montauks on Long Island, who were reputed to make the highest quality wampum. Symbolism and ritual now meant nothing. Quantity was paramount.[20]

With a new economy driving them, the Indians of the Long Island Sound region dropped their custom of moving from the forest in winter to the coast in summer, a custom established over centuries to correspond with the ebb and flow of nature's bounty. Indians now settled on the waterfront year-round, in villages that sprung up at places such as Throgs Neck, Pelham Bay, Tallmans Island, Matinecock Point, Shoreham, and Stony Brook. There they made wampum, watched over traffic along the Sound, and traded with Europeans who approached the continent via young ports at Stamford, Norwalk, Fairfield, Milford, New Haven, and New London. Indians used the design expertise of the colonists to build several forts near the Sound—Shantok in eastern Connecticut, for example, and Corchaug on eastern Long Island—which probably became centers of wampum manufacture.[21]

Other changes tore at the traditions of the New Netherland and New England Indians as well. Wildlife besides beaver disappeared quickly, wiped out by market hunters—both Indians and whites—who supplied fresh meat to Europeans. Judging from archaeological records, the Indians along the Sound had a taste for wild turkey; virtually every Indian site excavated on New York's Sound shore yielded turkey bones.[22] Colonists liked it as well. Although wild turkeys of today are the wariest of birds, in the 1600s flocks had the foolhardy habit of hardly bothering to flee when one of their number was killed. Hunters would roll a buckboard under a tree in which turkeys were roosting, shoot as many as they could, and take only those that landed on the buckboard. By 1672 wild turkeys were rare. Black bears, loved by the Indians as meat and as a source of insulating grease, quickly followed suit. Deer, the Indians' most important source of protein, were hunted so relentlessly and effectively that colonists imposed hunting seasons as early as 1692, and a century later the only deer in New England lived in northern Vermont, New Hampshire, and Maine.[23]

Once the furs and meat had vanished, the Indians were coerced into bartering their land. Land was a matter of no small importance for the natives of North America. It was essential to the Indians' way of life. They had no notion of private property; ownership of land, as the author Kirkpatrick Sale has put it, would have been as incomprehensible as ownership of the wind or the clouds. "In a way that few Europeans could understand, the land *was* Indian culture: it provided Native Americans with their sense of a fixed place in the order of the world, with their religious observances, and with their lasting faith in the importance of the struggling but united community as opposed to the ambitious, acquisitive individual."

The Indians' land, as Sale explained, was the Indians' soul. It was not a commodity that could be sold, notwithstanding the historical record of deeds and transactions between Indians and Europeans. Indians who "sold" their land to Europeans were selling the rights to use the land; in no way could they have thought they were being forever dispossessed.[24] Yet that is precisely what happened, and not only in straightforward transactions like the sale of Manhattan Island for twenty-four dollars' worth of goods. John Pynchon, for example, was particularly successful at exploiting the Indians' vulnerability to an alien economy. According to Francis Moloney, the author of a 1931 history of New England's fur trade, "The Pynchons rarely employed Indians in their business, for they made poor workers, being lazy, shiftless, and unreliable." But those characteristics did not stop the Pynchons from selling the Indians more goods — including liquor — than the Indians could pay for, and then demanding a mortgage on Indian land. The Pynchons wanted furs as payment. But with the beaver and other fur bearers declining rapidly, making it impossible for the Indians to pay, another commodity would do just as well: the mortgage holders foreclosed and took over their debtors' land. "Thomas Cooper, an agent of the Pynchons, acquired land in this manner in 1664. John Pynchon foreclosed a mortgage on a large tract of Indian land at Westfield in 1666 upon the native's failure to pay his trading debt, and Joseph Parsons of Northampton did the same thing."[25]

Once the colonists had the land, they cut down the forests — Long Island was virtually without trees by 1700 — and established farms with cornfields and with pastures for grazing animals.[26] Their forests gone, their free range impeded by fences, their ability to browse hindered by farmers protecting their crops, the wildlife of southern New England and coastal New York disappeared. Yet the destruction was hardly limited to food, land, and a way of life. Within decades of the arrival of Adriaen Block, the Indians themselves had all but vanished too. Before Columbus, the natives of not only New England and New Netherland but of the entire Western Hemisphere had virtually no contact with deadly pathogenic diseases. They lived in "almost a paradise of well-being," as the anthropologist Henry Dobyns described the New World. But having had no contact with dangerous viruses and bacteria, neither did the Indians have any immunity when the viruses and bacteria arrived with the Europeans. The first epidemic was smallpox, which raged through the hemisphere starting in 1520. Maybe as many as a dozen other smallpox epidemics devastated New York and New England Indians until as late as 1783. In 1564, New England natives were hit hard by an epidemic that remains unidentified, and typhus struck the area as early as 1586. Bubonic plague was wiping out an untold number of people by the time Block was making his first voyage along the Sound. Measles tore through the region at least three times, from 1633 to 1728. Five epidemics of influenza hit before 1783, and diphtheria struck twice, in 1659 and 1735–36. "Viruses and germs constituted the true shock troops with which the Old World battered the New," as Dobyns put it.[27]

The diseases devastated the Indians, physically and psychologically. As early as 1674, the Pequots, the fiercest people of the Sound region, saw their force of warriors depleted to only three hundred men, down from four thousand before the epidemics. Nine out of every ten native Americans died of an imported disease.[28] "The effect of such a high mortality, and in such a short period of time, could have been only to shatter and distort a great part of the Indians' belief systems," Kirkpatrick Sale wrote, "disrupt their political and social institutions, discredit their medical practices and the healers among them, produce psychological disorientation and demoralization, kill off most of the elders who were the repositories of tribal history and traditional knowledge, demand the simplification of the cultural inventory and its technologies, force migration and regrouping of the remnant populations often in areas far from sacred lands, and increase the likelihood of warfare either in the clash of migrating groups or in the search for new populations."[29]

With the aid of the occasional massacre, like that of the Pequots near Mystic in 1637, the Europeans found themselves to be the inheritors of a land not virgin, as the American myth would have it, but widowed.[30] As the eighteenth century waned, the Indians' condition was nothing if not abject. On May 14, 1789, several surviving Mohegans — the people who lived along the Thames north of the Pequots — traveled to Hartford to petition the "Most Honorable Assembly of the State of Connecticut" with a pitiable plea:

We beg Leave to lay our Concerns and Burdens at Your Excelencies Feet. The Times are Exceedingly Alter'd, Yea the Times have turn'd everything upside down, or rather we have Chang'd the good Times, Chiefly by the help of the White People, for in Times Past, our Forefathers lived in Peace, Love and great harmony, and had everything in Great plenty. When they wanted meat they would just run into the Bush a little ways with their Weapons and would Soon bring home good venison, Raccoon, Bear, and Fowl. If they choose to have Fish, they wo'd only go to the River or along the Sea Shore and . . . presently fill their Cannoons With Variety of Fish, both Scaled and shell Fish, and they had abundance of Nuts, Wild Fruit, Ground Nuts and Ground Beans, and they planted but little corn and Beans and they kept no Cattle or Horses for they needed none — And they had no Contention about their lands, it lay in common to them all, and they had but one large dish and they Cou'd all eat together in Peace and Love — But alas, it is not so now, all our Fishing, Hunting and Fowling is entirely gone. . .

"And so we are now Come to our Good Brethren of the Assembly With Hearts full of Sorrow and Grief for Immediate help. . .

"Your Excellencies Compliance and Assistance at this Time will make our poor hearts very Glad and thankful.[31]

FOUR

The American Mediterranean

ithin decades colonial America had usurped the land of the Algonquians. Indian culture hung on only in remnants. Colonists, for example, scraped oysters from the Sound's shoals using a long-tined rake designed by the Indians. They had learned from the Indians where oysters grew in the estuaries that fanned out mostly from the Sound's north shore—the rich beds near Norwalk, the broad marshes near the mouth of the Housatonic River, the flats along the Quinnipiac in New Haven. Until well into the nineteenth century, New Haven's oystermen maintained a flotilla of dugout canoes of native design. And the early colonists opened oysters by propping them near hot rocks ringing an open fire, and eating them when the heat forced the shells apart—a trick also learned from the Indians.[1]

But the Algonquians themselves were gone. In their place was a prosperous, small-town American life whose chief geographic resources were the Sound and its tributaries. In fine weather it must have been a prospect of uninterrupted beneficence. Timothy Dwight, president of Yale, described it at the start of the nineteenth century:

> In the mild season there is perhaps no voyage in any part of the world pleasanter than that which is taken on the Sound, especially when the course is directed near the shore of the main. No expanse of water can be handsomer, or bounded by more beautiful shores. The various points, successively stretching into its bosom, with the intervening indents; the villages, which succeed each other at small distances, with their white spires seen over the tops of the trees or rising in open view; the rich fields which everywhere form the margin; the hills, elegantly ascending as the eye advances into the interior, covered with farms and crowned with groves; and the multitude of vessels skimming the surface in every direction, combine in their succession as many varieties of beauty, serenity and cheerfulness as can easily be united within the same limits.[2]

Although it might have seemed to be nearly perfect in the mild season, the Sound was not without its hazards, in fine weather or foul. Travelers were issuing warnings to mariners as long ago as the seven-

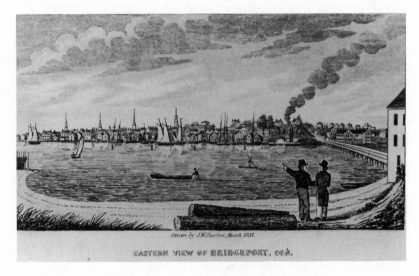

"Eastern View of Bridgeport, Con."
This woodcut from 1837 depicts the Bridgeport waterfront at a time when
Connecticut cities and towns were in the early years of becoming
manufacturing centers. Courtesy of the Connecticut
State Library, State Archives.

teenth century. In 1619, Captain Thomas Dermer from England sailed
west through the Sound: "I feared I had beene imbayed, but by the
helpe of an Indian I got to the Sea againe, through many crooked and
streight passages . . . wee found a most dangerous Catwract amongst
small rockie Ilands, occasioned by two unequall tydes, the one ebbing
and flowing two houres before the other: here we lost an Anchor by
the strength of the current, but found it deepe enough."[3]

In 1679, a Dutch visitor named Jasper Danckaerts gave more details of this "most dangerous Catwract"—perhaps more than any
mariner could need or make sense of:

> The river then runs up northerly to Hellgate, where there is
> an island, in front of which on the south side are two rocks,
> covered at high water, and close to the island, besides others
> which can be easily seen. Hellgate is nothing more than a
> bend of the river, which, coming up north, turns then straight

to the east. It is narrow here, and in the middle of the bend or elbow lie several large rocks. On either side it is wider, consequently the current is much stronger in the narrow part; and as it is a bend the water is checked, and made to eddy, and then, striking these rocks, it must make its way to one side or the other, or to both; but it cannot make its way to both, because it is a crooked bay, and therefore it pursues its course until it is stopped on the opposite side of the bay, to which it is driven, so much the more because it encounters these rocks on the way. Now between the rocks there is no current, and behind them it is still; and as the current for the most part is forced from one side, it finds liberty behind these rocks, where it makes a whirlpool. You must therefore be careful not to approach this whirlpool, especially with small vessels, as you will be in danger of being drawn under. It makes such a whirlpit and whistling that you can hear it for a quarter of an hour's distance, but this is when the tide is ebbing, and only, and mostly, when it is running the strongest. . . . When you have passed the large bay of Flushing, which is about eight miles from Hellgate, or rather, as soon as you get round the point, and begin to see an opening, you must keep well to the northeast, in order to sail clear of a long ledge of rocks, some of which stick out of the water like the Lizard in the channel near Falmouth.[4]

These rocks were the Stepping Stones, of which Dwight issued his own warning, some one hundred and twenty years after Danckaerts: "Several reefs run out some distance from the shore, and sometimes take up vessels ignorant of the navigation, as do also a few solitary shoals and rocks hidden beneath the surface. Of the latter, the Executioners over against Cow Neck on Long Island and Mamaroneck on the main, and the Stepping Stones against Great Neck and Pelham . . . are the most remarkable."

Hell Gate and the various rocks and reefs were not much of an impediment to shipping, however. In fact, shipping thrived, because overland roads were few and miserable. Sloops and packets traded along the coast; larger vessels worked international markets. With

New York to the west and Boston to the east attracting most of the commerce, the Sound failed to develop a truly large, important harbor. But small to medium-sized ports grew every several miles on the coast and up the Thames and Connecticut rivers, at Stonington, New London, Norwich, Middletown, Hartford, New Haven, Bridgeport, Norwalk, Stamford, Port Chester, Cold Spring, Port Jefferson, and elsewhere. "Every township on either shore has one or more harbors," Dwight wrote, "sufficiently capacious and convenient for the commerce which it will ever be able to carry on."[5] The river ports, in particular, shipped fresh produce from the fertile valleys and, in a region in which manufacturing had yet to develop, were an entry point for the European goods craved by farmers in the countryside.

Vessels carried passengers from port to port and from one side of the Sound to the other, not always with the greatest convenience or reliability. Dwight wrote of a journey he and two companions made by boat from Norwalk to Huntington, in early May of 1804. They and their horses boarded the ferry at five a.m. "After leaving Norwalk River, the mouth of which is a good harbor for vessels of less than one hundred tons, the wind became very feeble, shifted suddenly and frequently throughout the whole day; and, what was very tedious, shifted in almost every instance in such a manner as to retard our progress. We had breakfasted eagerly and on meager diet, and were miserably provided with food, both as to quantity and quality, for the day. . . . To add to our troubles, a thunderstorm overtook us in the mouth of Huntington harbor at nine o'clock in the evening. Our quarter deck was leaky and permitted the rain to descend upon us in streams. . . . Time, patience, and apathy, however, helped us through the train of our difficulties; and, at half after two, we landed at the usual place." The trip from Norwalk to Huntington, a journey of maybe sixteen miles by boat, took twenty-one and a half hours.

Dwight's description of their inconvenience that day was a relative rarity for him. He seems to have been inclined to look for the good and ignore the bad. Connecticut's coastal towns, in particular, enthralled him. His accounts of his journeys through them are laced with so many superlatives that a reader now is tempted to wonder whether his judgment of the Sound region as a whole was impaired. But then, as if to reassure us that he is no Pollyanna, he describes a trip like the one from Norwalk to Huntington, or a later one along the north shore of Long Island. Dwight was pleased to see that Long Islanders had taken pains to improve their agriculture:

[T]he inhabitants . . . have set themselves to collect manure wherever it could be obtained. Not content with what they could make and find on their own farms and shores, they have sent their vessels up the Hudson and loaded them with the residium of potash manufactories; gleaned the streets of New York; and have imported various kinds of manure from New Haven, New London, and even from Hartford. In addition to all this, they have swept the Sound, and covered their fields with the immense shoals of whitefish with which in the beginning of summer its waters are replenished. No manure is so cheap as this where the fish abound; none is so rich; and few are so lasting. Its effects on vegetation are prodigious. Lands which heretofore have scarcely yielded ten bushels of wheat by the acre are said, when dressed with whitefish, to have yielded forty. The number caught is almost incredible. It is here said . . . that one hundred and fifty thousand have been taken at a single draft.

But what was good for the fields was less than pleasant for the farmer, or the traveler. Dwight complained of the "fetor." "Wherever the fish were gathered in considerable quantities near the road, their effluvia filled the atmosphere, and made our journey sufficiently unpleasant. The farmers, however, by force of habit and the prospect of gain are reconciled to this odor. Indeed many of them must, I think, be insensible to it, for they feed their swine in the near neighborhood of their houses, and some of them directly before their doors, with the fish called horsefoots, the remains of which yield a smell still less supportable."[6]

The Sound was as important to everyday life two centuries ago as the Long Island Expressway or Interstate 95 or the commuter railroads are today. By 1784, when it incorporated as a city of three thousand people, New Haven had become the Sound's chief port. The maritime trade flourished around the warehouses and docks near Long Wharf. New Haven was home to thirty ships in 1784. Its vessels hopped from

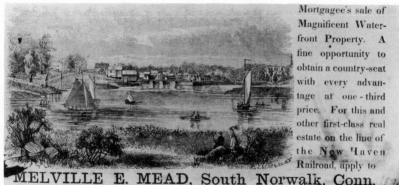

Mortgagee's sale of Magnificent Waterfront Property. A fine opportunity to obtain a country-seat with every advantage at one-third price. For this and other first-class real estate on the line of the New Haven Railroad, apply to

MELVILLE E. MEAD, South Norwalk, Conn.

Waterfront Property
The beauty of the Sound and its harbors was used as a selling point for land long before the modern era of land development. Courtesy of the Connecticut State Library, State Archives.

harbor to harbor along the coast and ventured to the West Indies and to Europe.[7] Virtually everything New Haven needed or wanted—wines, spices, tea, brandy, oils, opium, silks, textiles—was brought in by ship, from Marseilles, London, Bordeaux, Cádiz, the Spice Islands, and China.[8] Prosperity bred growth. Larger vessels needed a deeper harbor (they also needed to avoid new shoals created, probably, by silt washed downriver by poor farming practices inland), so laborers extended Long Wharf by 3,900 feet between 1765 and 1821.[9] In the first decades of the nineteenth century, one hundred ships embarked annually from New Haven for foreign ports.

For a handful of years after 1800, the dominant shipping venture in New Haven was sealing. The "New Haven South Sea Fleet" comprised twenty ships, with captains and crews recruited from along the Sound. They sailed south into the Pacific, hunted seals in the St. Felix Islands, in the Pacific west of Chile, dried the skins on a two-mile strip of Patagonian coast that came to be known as "New Haven Green," and traded the skins for silks and teas in Canton and for spices in the Spice Islands. But the sealing industry slammed to a halt around 1806, killed by mounting competition from other ports and by a crash in the seal population brought on by the years of slaughter.[10]

Another blow hit the shipping trade even harder: the Embargo Act of 1807, imposed by the young federal government of President Thomas Jefferson to force England and France to lift restrictions on trade with the United States. The act made it illegal for any American ship to embark for overseas ports. Foreign vessels could still ship goods to the United States but the law forbade them from leaving American ports with American cargo—a restriction that made imports impossible, for no foreign merchant could afford to send a ship abroad if it were to return without cargo to sell. As a guarantee that vessels in the domestic trade would land their merchandise in the United States, coastal vessels were forced to post bond worth twice the value of the boat and its cargo. Not until the spring of 1809, when Jefferson and his successor, James Madison, ended the embargo in stages, did overseas commerce resume. But the War of 1812 followed, and the hostilities made the high seas too dangerous for merchant vessels. The trade restrictions and the fighting crippled the shipping industry.[11] The ports on Long Island Sound never recovered the diverse commerce that was lost those decades. But two harbors above all others, New London in the east and Cold Spring in the west, established reputations in another branch of the maritime trade: whaling.

The first whaling voyages from Sound ports, in the late eighteenth century, were short, with ships venturing no further than the Newfoundland Banks.[12] There was no need for longer searches: whales were common all along the northeast coast, and they sometimes ventured into the Sound; even as late as 1799, two hundred whales were counted off Stonington.[13] When a whale was lugged home and towed to shore, virtually all the townspeople were needed to strip it of its blubber before it spoiled. They rendered the blubber into oil by boiling it down, around the clock, in huge kettles. A hundred barrels of oil could be extracted from a full-grown whale. Townsfolk peddled whale oil in nearby villages, or exported it to larger cities, or even used it as payment for local teachers and clergymen.[14]

Yet whales must have been getting noticeably scarcer as the end of the century drew near. As early as 1794, a ship from East Haddam became the first Connecticut vessel to hunt for whales in the Pacific. A whaler called the *Despatch,* from New London, ventured around Cape

Horn in 1802, but the voyage proved unprofitable. Three years later, whaling began in earnest in New London, only to be curtailed by the Embargo Act and the War of 1812. Not until 1819 did whaling truly establish itself in New London. A ship called the *Carrier* embarked first, disappearing down the Thames and through the Race, on a journey to the rich whaling grounds of the Pacific. When it next saw New London, a city of three thousand growing along the west side of the river valley, two and a half years had passed, and 2,074 barrels of sperm oil filled its cargo hold. Whaling's era of prosperity in New London had begun. By 1846 more than eight thousand people lived in the city, and its whaling industry counted seventy-eight barks, brigs, and schooners worth almost $2 million and manned by three thousand sailors — a fleet second in size only to that of New Bedford, Massachusetts. Whaling thrived as well in nearby Stonington, Mystic, and Norwich, in East Haddam and New Haven, and as far west as Bridgeport. But 1846 was to be New London's pinnacle as a whaling city. By the end of the decade, the California gold rush, a drop in demand for whale products, and a noticeable scarcity of whales themselves sent the industry into decline.[15]

Seventy-five miles to the west, and on the opposite shore of the Sound, whaling was developing into the backbone of another town's economy. Cold Spring Harbor never approached New London's stature; it never challenged New Bedford as the nation's dominant whaling port. But in the well-protected bay that pokes deep into Long Island, whaling survived on its own prosperous scale. Three brothers founded the whaling industry in Cold Spring Harbor — William H. Jones, Walter Restored Jones, and especially John H. Jones. In the 1820s and 1830s, John H. owned a general store, two textile mills, and a steamboat company and sold rugged clothing, knitted of merino wool spun from local sheep, to whalers. He also must have excelled as a salesman, because in 1836 he convinced thirty-three relatives, friends, and neighbors to invest in a bark called the *Monmouth*. Experience was not what Jones and partners were depending on — none of the thirty-four investors had any knowledge of whaling. But they were smart enough to recognize that limitation and to hire an experienced captain and crew from the well-established whaling port of Sag Harbor. The *Monmouth* sailed for the South Atlantic in July 1836, and returned to Cold Spring nine months later, hauling $20,000 worth of whale oil.

The Whaling Era
The *Sheffield* sailed out of Cold Spring Harbor during its heyday as a whaling
port. At 579 tons, the *Sheffield* was the largest whaling ship ever to sail
from Long Island and the third largest whaler in the United States.
Courtesy of Cold Spring Harbor Whaling Museum, New York.

The Jones brothers and their backers expanded, and soon Cold Spring
Harbor was home to nine whalers, ranging from the 280-ton *Mon-
mouth* to the 579-ton *Sheffield,* the largest whaling ship ever to sail from
Long Island and the third largest whaler in the United States.

The port thrived during the 1840s and into the 1850s. Blacksmiths
forged harpoons and lances by the score. John H. Jones himself built
a sail loft and a cooper shop, which at first made flour barrels but later
was modified to manufacture casks and barrels for whale oil. Sailors
from around the world gathered on Main Street, their foreign tongues
transforming the harbor side into a Babel. Shoes, woolen stockings,
and food were all produced locally to outfit and feed the whale men. A
sand spit kept the large ships away from shore, so provisions were
lined up on the wharf and lightered out to the vessels. When the ship
was loaded and the crew accounted for, a steamer towed it out of the
harbor and into the Sound.

But whaling was a doomed industry, no less in Cold Spring Harbor than in New London. Cold Spring's seasons of prosperity faded slowly. Its spirit and leadership began to slip away in 1855, when Walter Restored Jones died. When John H. Jones died four years later it vanished completely. Two of the fleet's nine ships were wrecked. When the Civil War started, the Confederate navy attacked northern whalers, and crewmen were needed to fight. And after the war, former whale men became merchant marines in the coast trade or began oystering along the shores of the Sound. Whaling was over, and with it went the period of the greatest shipping activity and prosperity the Sound's ports would ever see.[16]

The Industrial Age

When sealing and whaling were still at their peak, when packets, sloops, and steamships were still the best source of transportation for goods and people, two other industries that also depended on Long Island Sound and its tributaries were struggling to develop beyond infancy and adolescence. Metal manufacturing and oystering both were to have a profound effect on the Sound region. They came to clearly epitomize the conflict between unchecked economic expansion and a region's ecological health.

When Connecticut's delegates traveled to Philadelphia in 1787 to participate in the Constitutional Convention, they knew well the image they wanted their state to project. In representing Connecticut, they said, they were representing a manufacturing state. Reality had not quite caught up to concept, but before long it would. In 1790, Alexander Hamilton, the Secretary of the Treasury, argued that encouragement and protection were needed for American industries, "including Connecticut brass." A decade later, at the turn of the century, it was believed that farming had had its best days and that the state's economy would rise or fall with little effect from agriculture.

Small "manufactories" grew throughout Connecticut. Artisans made clocks, tin, paper, wool, and other goods, mostly for use in or near the home, but also to be peddled in nearby towns. As early as 1750, one John Allen was casting brass buttons and buckles at a factory in Waterbury, a Naugatuck River town acquired from the Indians in 1684 as part of a deal that gave the settlers one hundred and eighty square miles — land, it was reported to the colony's General Assembly, "capable of supporting 30 families." Another Yankee, Joseph Hopkins, also manufactured brass buttons and knee buckles, as well as silver pewter, in Waterbury, well before 1800.[1] In 1790, Henry Grilley, helped by his brothers, began casting pewter buttons in their home in Waterbury and two years later expanded into the manufacture of sheet brass — perhaps the first brass-rolling operation in the United States.

These early Yankee businessmen were hardly manufacturing specialists. Their skills included farming, spinning, blacksmithing, and peddling, and their shops were located in the barns and sheds of their homesteads. They produced goods as part of a diverse household economy in communities that were small and isolated; as late as 1819, in all of Connecticut only New Haven, Hartford, and Middletown had more than five thousand residents.

"To understand the conditions which preceded the rise of modern manufacturers," wrote Clive Day in a pamphlet published in 1935 for Connecticut's tercentenary celebration, "it is important to realize, not only that the large towns were rural but also that the little towns and villages were industrial to an extent unknown in a later period. . . . Self-sufficiency was the rule. . . . Each family made what it could for itself, and satisfied most of its remaining requirements by the labor of artisans living in the immediate vicinity." Every town had a sawmill, a grist mill, and a blacksmith. Most had a tannery, shoemakers, and wheelwrights. Early nineteenth-century residents would not have had to travel far to find people competent in making cabinets, harnesses, farm tools, hats, and tin kitchenware.[2] Each town also had a stream or a river that drained to Long Island Sound.

The diverse economy of the turn of the century was doomed by the Industrial Revolution, however. Stimulated by new technologies, new sources of power, new partnerships, and new laws, the brass industry was destined to break out of the farm shed and grow into the brick factories of Connecticut mill towns. The last two decades of the eighteenth century saw the invention, in England, of a brass manufacturing method that involved the direct fusion of zinc and copper. Two Englishmen, Abel and Levi Porter, brought the innovation to Waterbury in 1802, where it revolutionized the tiny domestic industry. The Porters became partners with the Grilleys—under the name Abel Porter and Company—which gave them manpower to couple with the new manufacturing method. Then in 1808 they added a third component crucial to the industry's growth: they bought an old grist mill, which supplied them with waterpower. Other men forged similar partnerships with their neighbors or relatives. Within decades these alliances would grow into the giant, Yankee-owned companies that dominated the brass industry.[3] The companies had much in common with each other, including their location—along the Naugatuck River, in which they could dump the copper residue of brass making, and this waste would then be swept downriver, by way of the Housatonic, into Long Island Sound.

These great manufacturing industries being born upriver of the Sound — clocks, tools, and firearms, as well as brass — needed something beyond manpower, waterpower, and a new manufacturing method. They needed the stimulant of economic demand. And it came, in 1807, in the same package that delivered to the Sound's shipping industry the blow that crippled it for good — the Embargo Act. By making it all but impossible for European products to be landed at American ports, the Embargo Act created an immediate demand for domestic goods. Connecticut responded by becoming a state of riverside mill towns.

Four brass foundries were established in Connecticut by 1810, eight years after the Porters and the Grilleys began their partnership. The new foundries' specialty was buttons — by 1819, four-fifths of all the metal buttons manufactured in the United States were from Connecticut. But Connecticut's dominance of domestic manufacturing was not tantamount to dominance of the industry. The best buttons, and the cheapest, were still made in England. The English brass industry, centered in Birmingham, had been refining its techniques since before 1700. The Connecticut companies did not begin to compete with England until about 1820. That's when American brass makers began luring skilled casters, rollers, toolmakers, die sinkers, platers, and burnishers across the ocean to Waterbury, and then wedded the English skills with the manufacturing innovations of Eli Whitney, the Yankee inventor whose cotton gin enabled cotton to become king of the South.[4]

Whitney revolutionized manufacturing. In 1798, while he was living in New Haven, he won a government contract to make ten thousand muskets. He built a factory and devised a system of manufacturing interchangeable parts. Rather than crafting the whole gun, each worker was assigned one small role in the production process, and each gun emerged from the factory practically identical, each trigger fitting with each butt, barrel, and flintlock. Other industries adapted the system to their own needs. Mills rose on seemingly every stream in Connecticut, making hardware, clocks, cotton, and wool, as well as brass.[5] Brass factories sprawled throughout the Naugatuck valley.

Ambitious Yankee captains of industry, with visages as severe as the nineteenth-century New England landscape, forged partnerships,

UNION MANUFACTORY, NORWALK, CONN.

The Age of Industry

This is a typical factory in Norwalk at a time when the cities along the Sound and its tributaries were becoming urban and industrial centers. Connecticut factories produced rubber, hats, silk, cotton, thread, wool, hardware, clocks, brass, and other goods, and typically dumped their waste and by-products into the nearest waterway. By the first quarter of the twentieth century, Norwalk had fifty-five factories. Courtesy of the Connecticut State Library, State Archives.

splintered into new firms, spawned offspring companies, expanded tiny rural outposts into manufacturing centers, and, when the needs of the business grew beyond what already existed, built brand new towns. The industrial activity was not limited to brass. Naugatuck produced rubber, Danbury hats, and Manchester silk. Norwich, Thompson, Putnam, Plainfield, Killingly, and Windham — all in the Thames River basin — were home to 70 percent of the state's cotton mills. Willimantic made thread; Rockville, Stafford Springs, and Broad Brook made wool. New Britain became the center of the hardware manufacturing industry.[6] "Sharon and Watertown made mousetraps by the hundred thousand. Brooklyn manufactured ten thousand pairs of spectacles a year. Woodbridge made five hundred dozen iron candlesticks. North Haven and Wallingford made razor strops by the thousand dozen. Chester manufactured thousands of dozens of inkstands; Manchester made ink to fill them."[7]

But, arguably, brass was king. In 1823, Aaron Benedict formed the A. Benedict Company in Waterbury, later to become Benedict & Burnham (spinning off still later into the American Brass Company and the Chase Company). In 1834, a New Yorker named Anson G. Phelps joined one of Benedict's former partners, Israel Coe, of the Coe Brass Company, to found the Wolcottville Brass Company, in what is now Torrington, eighteen miles upriver from Waterbury. Phelps soon left Coe and moved seventeen miles south of Waterbury, to Derby, where he opened the Smith & Phelps mill. In the early 1840s, Phelps moved on again, shifting two miles north of Derby to found not only another company — the Ansonia Brass & Copper Company — but a whole community, which he named after himself: Ansonia. Ansonia Brass & Copper later merged with American Brass. And so it went, along thirty-five miles of the Naugatuck. Brass mills were soon pounding out sheet brass and brass products in Thomaston, Winsted, Waterville, Naugatuck, Union City, Seymour, and Shelton, with industrial outposts in Bridgeport, Bristol, and New Haven. Brass manufacturing so dominated the corridor bounded by Torrington on the north and Shelton on the south, that the swath of land was soon known as Brass Valley.

Tariffs that barred competition from foreign goods protected the industry, allowing the Connecticut mills over the decades to control the American market. They made buttons, sheet brass, sheet metal and wire, tubing for gas pipes, kettles, and plates for daguerreotypes. Clocks manufactured in Bristol and Thomaston used Brass Valley brass. Whale-oil lamps, saddlery hardware, and carriage trimmings were made of brass. The factories turned out brass rifle shells, shrapnel shells (loaded and assembled), fuses for munitions, cartridge shells, and bullet cases. It manufactured thimbles and, later, vacuum cleaner motors. Pushed in one direction since the infancy of the Republic, Connecticut had become what its representatives to the Constitutional Convention had prematurely bragged of — a manufacturing state. In the first quarter of the twentieth century, Connecticut supported 3,968 manufacturers. New Haven and Bridgeport each had

Brass Valley
When this photo was taken in 1902, Seymour, Connecticut, was part of Brass
Valley, a string of factory towns along the Naugatuck River that were the center
of the nation's brass industry. The Naugatuck drains into the Housatonic River,
which empties into the Sound at Stratford. Copper wastes from brass factories
tainted the Sound's oysters, and to this day high levels of copper can be
found in the sediments of some of the Sound's harbors. Courtesy
of the Connecticut State Library, State Archives.

more than 500 factories. Waterbury had nearly 175, Stamford 100, South
Norwalk 90, and Norwalk 55.

Brass Valley alone in the early twentieth century had 381 factories.
In 1899, when the American Brass Company was formed in Waterbury,
there were 10,000 brass workers in the United States; half of them
worked for American Brass. During World War I the company employed 16,000 workers and produced 1 billion pounds of war material.
The largest brass plant in the world, however, was its rival Scovill. By
1925 Scovill's plant sprawled over 168 acres, encompassed 2.5 million
square feet of floor space, and did $35 million of business a year.

Industry on such a grand, American scale demanded labor, and the
demand brought dramatic population changes to the Sound region.
Connecticut factories employed 300,000 people in 1925. The population of Waterbury climbed from 10,000 in 1860 to 90,000 in 1920.
The combined population of other Brass Valley cities—Ansonia,

Connecticut Mill Towns
This is a river view of the Willimantic Company's mill number 2, which
manufactured thread. The idyllic New England village of elegant steeples and
white clapboard houses was more myth than reality in Connecticut. By the early
twentieth century, 3,968 factories had sprung up in the state. Virtually every one
dumped its wastes into rivers and maelstroms, all of which drained into the
Sound, or directly into the Sound's harbors. In Willimantic, the color of the
river told residents what color thread was being manufactured and dyed on
any given day. Courtesy of the Connecticut State Library, State Archives.

Derby, Naugatuck, Shelton, and Torrington — rose from 15,000 in 1890
to 75,000 in 1920. The pattern was no different along the Sound itself,
or throughout the state. The combined populations of Bridgeport,
New Haven, Stamford, and Norwalk jumped from 99,000 in 1880 to
almost 350,000 in 1920. The state's population in 1880 was 623,000;
by 1920 it rose to 1.4 million. In 1880, 42 percent of the population
lived in cities and 58 percent on farms; in 1920, 68 percent lived in
cities, 32 percent on farms.

There was no way that throngs of that magnitude could come together in concentrated locations among tremendous industry and not
have a severe effect on the environment. Not that nature was thought

of as an impediment to industrial or urban growth, however. Nature's function as America enjoyed the riches of the Gilded Age was to promote wealth. As the Chase Company, in Waterbury, prepared to expand for World War I, an official sent a memo to an underling: "Mr. O'Brien, Please change the location of the Naugatuck River as per enclosed blueprint."[8] Nothing would stand in the way of the region's growth, certainly not Long Island Sound and its tributaries.

Clearly, a region with such a heavy concentration of factories and people would produce a heavy concentration of wastes—not just industrial waste but sewage. Immense energy and thought and capital transformed Connecticut into an industrial power, but little of the same seems to have been expended on trying to keep the region's water clean. The Long Island Sound region was not unique, of course, or even unusual. Disposing of waste in inappropriate ways had been a hallmark of history—although sound advice was available to the ancients, from Yahweh himself, in Deuteronomy: "Thou shalt have a place also without the camp, whither thou shalt go forth abroad: and thou shalt have a paddle upon thy weapon; and it shall be, when thou wilt ease thyself abroad, thou shalt dig therewith, and shalt turn back and cover that which cometh from thee." But ever since then, heathens and believers, through laws divine and profane, had been trying to figure out what to do with their sewage.

As long as people were nomadic or lived in small groups—like the Israelites—disposal was easy, because the land and water were able to absorb human and animal wastes. But as people began to cluster in cities and towns, the buildup of wastes became too much for the land, the waterways, and the residents themselves to bear. As ancient as cities and urban civilization are, so too are sewage disposal problems. The earliest way to treat sewage was not to treat it at all but simply to send it away from the immediate vicinity as quickly as possible. Ancient Minoan sites on Crete had wastewater drainage systems, and covered drains coursed through Rome as early as the sixth century B.C., when the city was still dominated by the Etruscans. The Roman Empire itself built drains to discharge wastewater—Pompeii was served by such sewers in the first century A.D. But through the Middle Ages, the Renaissance, and into the Industrial Revolution, the Roman method was rarely copied and never improved upon. Sewage was trucked away from cities in carts, carried in buckets, or allowed to seep through ditches into waterways. If nothing else was available, people resorted to the custom of the ancient Israelites.

To the residents of those dark cities, the lack of communal sanitation was more than a problem of intolerable sights and smells. Unsanitary sewage disposal contributed to the epidemic diseases that wiped out enormous percentages of the population over the centuries. Yet nobody realized that poor sanitation was the source of the disease-causing bacteria—indeed, nobody knew about microscopic pathogens—and where sewage disposal was attempted, it was meant to solve aesthetic problems. Cesspools were invented, privy vaults were emptied periodically, and wealthy families used some of their riches to acquire land near waterways, into which they could dump their wastes. It was only when a cholera epidemic hit London for a second time, in 1854—after having reached England in 1849, following a centuries-long march from India and through Continental Europe—that a link was recognized between the epidemic disease and sewage: privy vaults in the city were contaminating a drinking well. London officials ordered residents to dump their household wastes into storm drains that washed into the Thames, a system of disposal that came to be known as the English, or water-carriage, method—sewage diluted with water and carried off to some convenient outlet.[9] In smaller towns, the preferred solution was to spread sewage across farmland. In the 1870s, Kendall, England, a town of fourteen thousand inhabitants, was disposing of its sewage on five and a half acres of land. In 1876, England's Local Government Board issued a "Report of Committee on Treating Local Sewage," which recommended the "land irrigation" method as the best and cheapest way to get rid of town sewage.[10]

For many London residents, the Thames had been the easiest and most efficient sewage outlet even before the epidemic. An unchecked influx of far more sewage than it could absorb had already transformed the Thames from a productive estuary to an oxygen-starved wasteland. The Thames was thriving in 1750, when London's population was three-quarters of a million. By 1840 the city had grown to two million people, and the river was in ruins. The cholera epidemic merely made inevitable what should have been done for the river's sake: in 1889, London built the first municipal sewage treatment facility on the banks of the first estuary destroyed by human waste. By 1900, when the city's population had reached six million, six hardy species of fish had returned to the Thames.[11]

In America, colonists built the first sewers in Manhattan in 1676 — open trenches to drain storm water. The Common Council of New York allowed a stone-reinforced storm sewer to be built under Broad Street in 1747. It was supposed to drain into the East River, but the sewer never worked properly, and pedestrians were left to trod through pools of rank water that collected in the streets. Underground sewers, though, were apparently the exception. In 1800, broad open trenches, constructed of stone, brick, cement, or wooden planks, through which foul water flowed sluggishly, commonly coursed down the center or along the sides of Manhattan's streets. These early sewers were meant for storm water — in fact, in 1819, the Common Council specifically prohibited human waste from being dumped into storm sewers. Human waste had to be removed in other ways. In the eighteenth century, Manhattan residents were allowed to dump their ordure tubs into the East and Hudson rivers. Not all of the contents made it directly into the water, though, and the wharves and docks became coated with excrement. In the late eighteenth and early nineteenth centuries, the city hired "necessary tubmen" to empty privies. They hauled the waste away at night or before dawn in closed carts, which were emptied into landfills, delivered to fertilizer makers, or dumped into the rivers. "The one thing tubmen were *not* allowed to do with human waste was put it in the sewers," wrote Edwin G. Burrows and Mike Wallace in *Gotham: A History of New York City to 1898.* The inadequacy of this disposal method became evident by about 1830, when researchers estimated that each day New Yorkers were dumping more than one hundred tons of excrement into areas from which it could seep down to the water table, contaminating drinking-water wells. In the cholera epidemic of 1832, 3,513 New Yorkers died.

By the middle of the century, Manhattan was crowded to the point beyond which the ground could absorb human waste; thousands of cesspools and privies were overflowing. In 1854 the city required that houses be hooked up to sewers, and two years later it passed a law requiring that all newly built houses be connected to sewers. "That New

York was drowning in garbage was in large measure a by-product of the explosive and unregulated growth that few were willing to impede. . . . [I]n 1857 . . . only 138 miles of the city's five hundred miles of paved streets had been sewered. That left two-thirds of all New Yorkers still reliant on backyard and basement privies, whose overflow continued to seep to the water table, infect public wells used by the poor, flood cellars, and leave missionaries and physicians routinely horrified to find children playing and mothers hanging the wash in yards coated with human excrement and swarming with flies."[12]

The general disregard for rudimentary pollution prevention was hardly limited to New York City. Ditches, both covered and uncovered, were still in use in some Connecticut cities in the 1880s, although by 1900 city and town health officials throughout the region were attempting to dispose of sewage to control outbreaks of typhoid fever and other diseases. Some smaller communities, like Meriden, adopted the English town method of spreading waste over agricultural areas.[13] For cities, the solution almost invariably was to send the sewage into the Sound or its tributaries.

In Bridgeport, almost twenty miles of sewers were discharging into Bridgeport Harbor or the tidal creeks along the Sound in 1878. But sewers had yet to reach the eastern section of the city, a district of small houses and tenements inhabited by poor factory workers in surroundings that were "not such as wealth and intelligence might procure. Indeed many glaring violations of hygiene laws are here noticed, such as privies heaped full, cess-pools emptied out on the ground, and both in close proximity to wells which supply several families with drinking water." In Norwich, two tributaries of the Thames — the Yantic and Shetucket rivers — were lined with outhouses that drained into the waterways; and in Derby, on the Naugatuck, "The house refuse and filth is removed by the river."[14]

Along the Connecticut River, Hartford used wooden logs to flush sewage along Ann Street, a public works project that was undertaken in 1844 for $840; from 1844 to 1855, the city built thirty-two sewer lines. By the 1870s, Hartford had invested $530,000 to build forty miles of sewers. But they did not keep waterways clean or the city free of water-borne diseases, and by the 1890s, forty-four of Hartford's forty-eight miles of sewers, which were made of old brick and stone pipes, failed to adequately convey the city's waste. Local waterways remained a convenient alternative. Park River, which flowed past the Capitol, carried the sewage and industrial waste of both Hartford and nearby New Britain, which also dumped waste directly into Piper's Brook and the Sabethe River. Although Hartford had stopped dumping sewage into the Connecticut River — one of its drinking water sources — by the 1870s, even that decision failed to protect its citizens. An 1879 typhoid outbreak in the city was traced to Connecticut River water, which had been contaminated not by Hartford but by Springfield, Massachusetts.[15] Closer to the Sound, crumbling brick and stone pipes made up half of New Haven's fifty-eight miles of sewers in the 1890s, and as late as 1911, more than a thousand New Haven households still relied on privies.[16]

Stamford had a public water supply that carried up to three hundred thousand gallons a day to city residents, but until 1880 city fathers did not recognize the need to get rid of all that water once it passed through the city's houses. The wastewater was discharged into the soil, "carrying with it the kitchen slops, grease, human excrement and other filth from nearly every habitation within our limits." Equally troubling was the city's industrial waste, particularly from a woolen mill that sat along the Mill River, about half a mile from where it discharged into Stamford's harbor. The mill washed its wool with water from the river, discharging it "in a condition hard to describe. It carries with it a vast amount of grease and animal matter removed from the dirty wool, together with the alkalies and other chemical agents employed in the separation of the greasy impurities. Added to this are the waste dye-stuffs, acids, and other refuse products of manufacturing, the stream as it leaves the mill being dark and turbid, and offensive in every way."[17] In 1880, Stamford decided to spend $100,000 for a sewer system.

In New York, sewage was recognized as a critical problem by the beginning of the twentieth century, and government response was characteristic of American bureaucracy: it formed commissions and ordered studies. In 1903, the state legislature appointed the New York Bay Pollution Commission, and then formed the Metropolitan Sewerage Commission in 1906. New York City set up a Sewer Plan Commission in 1913. In 1924, New York, Connecticut, and New Jersey formed a Joint Legislative Committee to study water pollution, and the next year the United States Engineers also studied the situation. In 1931 the Governor's Special Long Island Sanitary Commission was established, and in 1935 the Nassau County Sanitation Commission studied pollution in its local waters.[18]

The work of the commissions and committees and engineers resulted in a paper edifice of studies and reports, but little concrete was poured or mortar troweled to solve the problem through the first third of the century. An exception was in Westchester County, where sewage clogged the Bronx River, destroying the stream's ecological value and, most critically from the standpoint of motivating government, depressing real estate values. Unfortunately, the county's actions also set a precedent, followed assiduously through the decades, of providing as little treatment for sewage as it could get away with.

For years the suburban towns from North White Plains to the Bronx border—White Plains, Scarsdale, Mount Vernon, Yonkers, Bronxville—had been dumping their sewage into the Bronx River, which empties into the westernmost end of the Sound. By 1906 it was apparent to officials in Westchester that the pleasant rural and suburban brook that had been the Bronx River was now a turbid, stagnant sewer. The county Board of Supervisors established the Bronx Valley Sewer Commission, which built a large sewer line to intercept the sewage before it reached the Bronx River. The solution was hardly revolutionary—in keeping with the time-honored tradition of giving your headache to someone else, the new pipe diverted the sewage to the Hudson River—but its completion in 1912 was unusual in that it was a successful attempt to clean up a tributary to the Sound.[19]

SIX

Oystering

Connecticut's evolution into an urban manufacturing state during the nineteenth century was almost matched by the growth of the oystering industry on Long Island Sound. Oysters seemed to be everywhere. Oyster beds paved the Quinnipiac River for three miles, from its mouth at New Haven Harbor to the salt marshes at North Haven. Oysters grew in New Haven Harbor's Morris Cove and, to the east, in the Thames River and at the mouth of the Hammonasset. To the west, from the cluster of islands that protects it at its mouth to the heart of the city upriver, Norwalk Harbor seemed one big oyster bed. Oysters lived off Shippan Point at Stamford, and thrived near City Island and in Eastchester Bay. West of Throgs Neck, oyster banks spread across the flats at College Point and in Flushing Bay. Almost any place where the Sound's shallow salt waters were freshened regularly by rivers and streams, oysters could be found.

The work was there if you wanted it, but—in the western end of the Sound, anyway—few wanted it. Raking oysters was thought to be degrading work, at least until 1814 or 1815, when half a dozen City Islanders began harvesting the bivalves for a living. The City Island men ranged as far as Shippan Point and the mudflats of Brooklyn's Newtown Creek, opposite Manhattan. In those days, the wedge of water from Throgs Neck to Norwalk on the north and Port Jefferson on the south was considered an extension of the East River. When the City Islanders decided that raking oysters was a dignified way to earn a living, it marked the start of the "East River" trade, which would grow with the century into a position of dominance in the American oyster industry.

Oystering was coming to life elsewhere on the coast, as well. On the wild and often harsh promontory of Milford Point, which curves across the mouth of the Housatonic, fifty or sixty men patched together crude huts of shipwreck lumber and seaweed thatch to form a colony of oystermen, all but destitute at first but soon accumulating the foundation of wealth.

A number of coastal towns had not only the shellfish but the supporting businesses that allowed oystering to grow into an industry—South Norwalk and Stamford, for example, and, most prominently, New Haven and its surrounding villages, especially Fair Haven. Native oysters grew abundantly in the Quinnipiac, in Morris Cove, and in New Haven Harbor proper, and were supplemented in the outer harbor by oysters imported from more southerly oyster grounds. Harvested oysters were stored in cool cellars until the weather turned cold. They were then opened, packed in kegs, and loaded into saddlebags and wagons, drawn by teams of two or four horses, to be peddled in Hartford and in Springfield, Massachusetts, and north in Vermont and Canada. Wagon-loads of oysters were sent to Albany, then barged west to cities in central New York. New Haven became one of the most important oyster depots in the United States.

Even as oysters were being hauled inland, to cities that never saw the tide rise or smelled the salt air, oystering on the Sound through the first decades of the nineteenth century was less a burgeoning industry than an occupation of families who needed to supplement other sources of food and income. One man, working alone, could store away enough oysters to last his family through the winter—good food, free for the taking. Connecticut law made the state's native oyster beds off-limits through the summer spawning season until November 1, but as opening day approached, families throughout the countryside within twenty miles of the Sound began mending boats and rakes, checking and gathering bags and baskets, loading wagons, and hitching boats to hay carts to be hauled to shore, in preparation for a great oystering free-for-all.

The village of Fair Haven, a wide neck on the west bank of the Quinnipiac, near the river's mouth, was at that time the heart of the New Haven oyster region—large native oysters, "as big as a shoehorne," were still abundant throughout the river and the adjacent harbor—and on October 31 Fair Haven became the terminus of the shoreward journeys of farmers from anywhere within a day's jaunt. Although oystering still contributed to the subsistence economy of the nearby countryside, in Fair Haven it was serious enough business to make the bumpkins' annual migration unwelcome competition. A farmer who carted his dilapidated boat to Fair Haven was wise to guard it carefully, to keep the town boys from hiding it or damaging it to the point of unseaworthiness.

The season opened at midnight. As October 31 ebbed, women and children gathered at the shore to watch the fun. The men put on their

Oyster boats
Oystermen on Long Island Sound worked in sloops, square-ended skiffs, steam-powered draggers, and other vessels. In the mid-1800s, some fifteen to twenty New Haven oystermen still used dugout canoes, the last dugouts to be seen anywhere from Maine to Chesapeake Bay. Pictured here is a sharpie, a sailboat designed by Connecticut oystermen to ply waters that were barely submerged. This sharpie is on the Five Mile River in Rowayton. The building in the background is an oyster house.
Courtesy of the Rowayton Historical Society.

oilskins, lugged their oars, paddles, tongs, and rakes, and assembled with their boats — skiffs and canoes and square-enders and sharpies. They waited along both sides of the river and the harbor. They twitched with nervous anticipation and adrenaline. The men hunched down in their vessels and squinted in the lantern light at their watches as midnight approached. Everyone drew silent. The great church clock in New Haven was invisible in the dark but its bell's peal rang out clearly, and when the first clang reached the river, the boats burst from opposite shores like small-vessel navies entering into combat. Before the bell could ring twelve times, the boats were on the beds, and men —

green farmers and seasoned oystermen alike — were raking and tonging oysters.

The experienced men, for whom oystering was more than a once-a-year chance to fill the cellar, knew where to find the richest lodes. They rowed straight for those spots and refused to yield. The best beds drew a crowd, the boats beam-to-beam, and were quickly scraped clean. Fights and quarrels broke out as spectators on shore cheered the combatants. If your goal was to put away food for the winter, an honest effort on that first day usually sufficed. Thousands of bushels were packed up, ready to be stored in cellars under blankets of seaweed insulation. The farmers then loaded up their families and their gear, and returned to their homesteads for another year. It was no doubt an exciting day, enlivening dull coastal towns with an infusion of people and energy. But the tradition was also a relentless overharvesting, by farmer and oysterman alike. And by the 1860s it had resulted in the inevitable: the native oysters that were the first foundation of the local oyster industry were gone. Their disappearance must have hurt the individual oystermen, who raked their own oysters and peddled them near home, and it definitely hurt the inland farmers, who now would have to pay cash for a source of food that heretofore had cost them only their labor.

But the larger oyster businesses, which had been operating successfully throughout New Haven Harbor, were insured against the depletion of native stocks, and had been for decades. In 1810 or thereabouts, Fair Haven companies began supplementing local supplies by sending schooners to acquire oysters on the Housatonic River. Every few years the boats ranged further — to the Hudson River, then Newark Bay and Raritan Bay, then Delaware Bay, and finally, with one Captain Merritt Farran pushing south, to Chincoteague, Virginia, and, about 1823, into Chesapeake Bay. Most of the imported oysters were shipped north out of New Haven before they ever tasted the Sound's waters. But about a quarter of the imports were bedded down in the harbor, particularly along the sand spit that points in toward the mouth of the Quinnipiac from West Haven, an excellent growing ground that was covered at high tide and exposed at low. The oyster houses hired more than twoscore men to stay on the beds around the clock to keep thieves away.[1]

The sand spit was New Haven's best grounds for transplanting oysters, but the New Haven houses also bedded their oysters in shoal areas in Milford Harbor, along West Haven, throughout New Haven Harbor and Morris Cove, and east around Lighthouse Point to Branford Harbor. Newcomers to the area, such as a French visitor sent to study American oystering in the 1850s, were confronted with curious reminders of where the transplanted oysters lay: "As far as the eye can see, the bay is covered with myriads of branches, waving in the wind, or swayed by the force of the currents. It looks as if a forest were submerged, the tops of the trees only rising above the surface of the water."[2]

The New Haven industry reached its peak from the 1850s to the 1880s, a period that saw New Haven's population grow from 20,000 people to more than 60,000. It was a lively era, with the broad, shallow harbor and the Quinnipiac River — itself still a viable estuary — dotted with boats and lined with the wharves and warehouses of 125 planters, dealers, and shippers. Fifteen or twenty local oystermen paddled about in dugout canoes, the last dugouts to be seen anywhere from Maine to Chesapeake Bay. More common were the square-ended skiffs that replaced the dugouts as the canoes deteriorated; one hundred or so tied up along the Quinnipiac. New Haven's sailboats were all sharpies — one hundred fast, roomy vessels, developed in Connecticut, with flat bottoms that let the oystermen squeeze over barely submerged beds. The offices and unloading docks of oyster dealers jutted into the water along both sides of the river. Two large barrel and box factories in Fair Haven supplied packing material. Packing houses and shucking houses crowded the waterfront, and 475 people found work as planters, rakers, washers, shuckers, fillers, measurers, and packers. For laborers, the pay was poor: shuckers, for example, earned about twenty dollars a month. They were mostly local girls who "only work to provide themselves with pin money," as an observer reported in 1880. "It is an occupation no refined girl would choose, nevertheless, for the whole person becomes at once spattered with mud and water, and the hands are inevitably bruised and lacerated beyond repair."[3]

In their prosperity, the Fair Haven businesses were bursting beyond the bounds of New Haven Harbor — way beyond. Oysters were so abundant in Chesapeake Bay that it made sense not only to send vessels south but to open branch houses on the bay as well. Soon, well-established Fair Haven names — Maltby, Mallory, Hemingway, Rowe — were operating out of Baltimore. They expanded inland, too, as far as St. Louis and Chicago. Fair Haven companies exported oysters to the Pacific coast, Great Britain, and Germany. They also hosted Japanese oyster growers who hoped to learn the industry. One Fair Haven company, from 1852 through 1856, earned annual profits of about $25,000 — a sum reported with some admiration fifteen years later. In 1856, another firm, Levi Rowe & Co., owned twenty vessels, employed one hundred openers, and shipped one hundred and fifty thousand gallons

Bridgeport Natural Bed
These oyster boats are working Bridgeport natural bed,
a four-square-mile area off Bridgeport that was the Sound's largest
and most productive natural oyster bed. At the bed's peak, as many as
450 sailing ships — with enough deck space to cover more than
three acres — could be seen maneuvering across it at once.
Courtesy of the Rowayton Historical Society.

of oysters. Other houses shipped as many as fifteen hundred bushels of oysters a day. When the New Haven train left each afternoon for the interior of New England, one and sometimes two cars were reserved solely for oysters. The industry's shorefront property and vessels were valued at $130,000. A total of $480,000 worth of oysters were sold out of New Haven each year.[4] The era of Captain Merritt Farran pushing intrepidly into Virginia waters in 1823 to haul back six hundred bushels was long gone. Yet although the New Haven oyster industry had evolved considerably from the years when rubes from the farmlands competed for native oysters with the local wharf rats, greater changes were already starting to occur — changes that hit oystering on Long Island Sound simultaneously, revolutionizing it and helping to send it sinking toward near-oblivion.

In the first half of the nineteenth century, a four-square-mile strip of the Sound outside Bridgeport Harbor, from Point No Point to Black Rock, consistently produced abundant native oysters. But, as with most of the natural beds elsewhere on the Sound, the Bridgeport oyster bed was depleted by 1850 — and all but forgotten. For seventeen years oystermen let the bed sit. Then in 1867, mossbunker boats casting their nets in shoal water dragged up a load of oysters. Word got out and soon an oysterman named Chard became the first man to throw a dredge on the revitalized area. Bridgeport natural bed — as it was called — would soon become the center of the Long Island Sound oyster industry.[5] The second big change occurred in 1874. To escape the crowds oystering in New Haven's shoal waters, H. C. Rowe of Fair Haven moved beyond the New Haven lighthouse to plant oysters in the Sound proper, at depths of twenty-five to forty feet. Before Rowe pushed forth, no one believed oysters could live beyond their natural grounds. After Rowe, oyster plantations were established as far as four miles outside the harbors, bays, and islands that had marked the industry's physical limits for seven decades.[6]

The third major change took a decade to become established. Its innovator was Captain Peter Decker of Norwalk.

> In 1869, I invented a steam drum with gearing attached to make easy the hauling of oyster dredges. One of these drums was placed about the sloop *Peri* owned by my brother, Cap-

tain Abram Decker. In 1870, the burning of a factory in South Norwalk left a small engine without use, and it was bought and placed on board the *Peri* to wind the drum and thus haul the dredges.

The following year I put a like hoisting apparatus on my own sloop, the *Early Bird,* a vessel of eight and one-half tons measurement. Both sloops still used sail to propel them. The next year a propeller was added, but sails were still used to supplement the power of the boat.

The steamboat was not exactly a newfangled invention in the early 1870s. But oystermen had thought their heavy dredges would make a steamer impossible to maneuver—which, in fact, was precisely what happened several years later when a big steamer built on City Island attempted to drag six dredges from an unusually broad stern. By then, however, Captain Decker had already devised a solution: "About the year 1874, I put in a large wheel, boiler and engine, discarded sails, retained the same hoisting gear, put out a single dredge well forward on each side, and the problem of oyster dredging was solved."[7]

Decker's modifications became standardized in 1877, when a Norwalk shipbuilder, William H. Lockwood of William H. Lockwood & Co., decided that rather than work with an existing sailboat, he would design and build a steamer—the *Enterprise*—specifically for oystering. Among Lockwood's few customers in those early years was William H. Merwin, a Milford oysterman. In the spring of 1879 he enjoyed a success that doomed the Sound's sailing fleet. A Rhode Island oyster company had dispatched a sloop, with room for fifteen hundred bushels, to New Haven to buy seed oysters. Local oystermen were solicited, first-come, first-served. Sloops from Fair Haven responded, as did Merwin and his steamboat. But a dead calm arrived with the Rhode Island sloop, and the local sailboats could not haul a dredge. Merwin alone was not dependent on the wind. He loaded the sloop with twelve hundred bushels in two days. By 1880 seven steamboats were oystering on the Sound. Their captains included Joshua Levinness of City Island, Wheeler Hawley of Bridgeport, and H. C. Rowe of Fair Haven, whose Lockwood-built vessel was reputed to be the Sound's finest oyster boat.[8] The proof that a skilled captain could maneuver a cumbersome steamboat across the Sound dragged oystering from the age of sail into the Industrial Revolution. Many of the Sound's beds of native oysters had already been dredged bare — good stewardship of the oyster grounds was hardly an inherent characteristic of the trade. But steam-powered vessels would allow oystermen to work with an intensive efficiency unknown on the Sound's rather limited beds.

The steamboat oystermen and their rivals under sail competed not only for oysters large enough to go directly to market and then onto tables, but also for seed oysters. Harvesting seed was a new part of the Sound's industry. The seed oystermen worked private and public beds across outer Bridgeport Harbor, along the lower Housatonic, and off Milford, scraping year-old oysters the size of fingernails to be sold and transplanted — husbanded like a crop — until they reached market size four years hence. The oystermen who dredged private beds used steam power. But the bulk of the Sound's seed oysters were harvested by a thousand "natural growthers," who worked state-owned oyster grounds and were restricted by Connecticut law to laboring under sail. The seed beds covered only nine square miles. (Delaware Bay's oystermen, for comparison, ranged across an area twelve times larger, while Chesapeake Bay watermen worked beds that were almost a hundred times larger — 885 square miles, an area nearly as big as the Sound itself.) But Connecticut seed consistently set well in the north, and through the end of the nineteenth century and the early years of the twentieth, the state produced virtually all the seed transplanted in the Sound and throughout New York and New England.[9]

On the Housatonic — where seed paved the western side of the river for three miles from its mouth — oyster companies anchored seventy-five to one hundred vessels at once, each attended by up to half a dozen skiffs. They darted back and forth, scooping up bushel after bushel of seed, loading the small bivalves onto the mother ship, returning to the bed, until the ship held all it could and was dispatched to growing grounds elsewhere. Then another vessel slipped into position to keep the skiffs working. No time was wasted. The oyster companies stationed a ship on the river to house the men.[10]

Its fleet of ships and busy skiffs notwithstanding, the Housatonic could not match Bridgeport natural bed. The bed covered about four square miles and ran from seven feet deep nearest shore — about a quarter of a mile out — to thirty feet deep on its far edge. Bridgeport natural bed was the largest and most productive on the Sound. The first oystermen to work it were phenomenally successful. Three Bridgeport men — Captain Samuel Byxbee, Joseph Coe, and William M. Saunders — hauled three hundred bushels in one drift with the tide across the bed. Captain Joshua Levinness dredged a thousand bushels in three drifts. A Captain Barnes loaded the deck of his fifty-ton sloop in one drift. A revival that rich could not be kept secret. When word spread, as many as four hundred and fifty sailing ships — with enough deck space to cover more than three acres — could be seen maneuvering across the bed at once.

It must have seemed like bedlam from the shore. The boats were scattered thickly across the grounds, in constant motion. The men hauled the dredges as many as six times in one drift of a thousand feet, yelling all the while, and at times collapsing on deck, exhausted from the exertion. But the captains were masters at maneuvering. They al-

A Load of Oysters
This boat is loaded with oysters after a day on one of the Sound's oyster beds.
Virtually every town and harbor from Hell Gate to the Race supported
an oyster industry in the last half of the nineteenth century.
Courtesy of the Rowayton Historical Society.

lowed their vessels to drift with the tide at staggered intervals, following parallel paths back and forth, staying on course and at a proper speed, and avoiding collisions. A sloop that could hold one hundred to three hundred bushels generally needed two or three days to load up. But sometimes ships were aided by the luck of a favorable wind and a thick accumulation of oysters and could haul a hundred bushels in two hours. A sloop called the *Ann Gertrude* once needed but five days to fill her huge hold with 1,029 bushels.[11]

The Sound's oyster industry was entering its era of greatest prosperity. From Hell Gate to Mount Sinai on the south shore and to the Pequonock River east of the Thames on the north, there was hardly a harbor, tidal inlet, or river mouth where men in skiffs and sharpies, sloops, and steamers did not dredge oysters. Natural beds along the Queens shore, from Little Neck Bay west, produced seed oysters for planters cultivating those crowded, rocky waters. Oystermen from College Point worked Flushing Bay. Whitestone and Little Neck oystermen staked out Little Neck Bay. As many as a hundred small boats at once, with a crew of one or two, maneuvered between Sea Cliff and Throgs Neck, hauling oysters with dredge-like clam rakes.

The great number of cargo ships and excursion vessels that steamed through—near the turn of the century three hundred and fifty ships a day passed Hell Gate—probably made the already-tricky waters near the Stepping Stones, Gangway Rocks, and Execution Rocks even more dangerous for the vulnerable oyster skiffs. But by constantly spitting their cinders into the Sound the steamers also created the ideal hard bottom that oysters needed. These steamboat-channel cinder grounds eventually extended almost to Norwalk and allowed a thick, three-mile bed to grow off Eatons Neck.

The busiest Long Island harbor was Cow Bay—now Manhasset Bay—and the busiest oyster town was Port Washington, whose wharves were a regular destination of sloops dispatched by New York City oyster dealers, who advertised in huge black letters on their vessels' broad mainsails. From the hills coddling the village and the bay, countless small oyster boats could be seen skittering across the water. A man named George Mackey had set the first oyster plantations in Cow Bay, in 1835. By 1880, two hundred of Port Washington's three hundred and twenty registered voters were oystermen. Oyster Bay likewise was crowded with oystering vessels in the latter decades of the nineteenth century: thirteen sloops and one hundred rowboats operated out of Bayville, seven sloops out of Cold Spring Harbor, twenty-three sailboats out of Oyster Bay village itself, and so on, through Centreport, Huntington, Stony Brook, Port Jefferson, and Mount Sinai — the last harbor before the Long Island shore stretches for more than forty miles of unbroken sand bluffs that peter out at Orient Point.

Oystering accounted for at least a small part of the local economy on the north shore of the Sound in towns much further east than Port Jefferson and Mount Sinai. Both native and transplanted oysters were harvested from the Poquonock River in Groton and from the Niantic River in Waterford. Madison and Guilford supported an oyster industry, and Stony Creek and the Thimble Islands produced "native oysters of extra quality," according to an observer in 1880. Rhode Island oystermen in search of seed sent sloops each spring to Stony Creek, where "an air of unusual thrift is observable about the oyster houses on the shore, which do not, as is too often the case, disfigure the pleasant scene."

After H. C. Rowe pioneered the use of the deeper Sound waters off New Haven for oyster plantations, fifty acres were considered the minimum necessary to make transplanting pay off. Many oystermen accumulated more than a hundred acres, broken into one-acre squares and delineated with buoys. Rowe himself farmed about fifteen hundred of the thirty-five hundred acres under cultivation at New Haven in 1880. Watchtowers rose from Long Wharf, the West Haven sand spit, Lighthouse Point, and off Branford Harbor to guard against theft.

All of the Sound's south shore oyster communities, and the north shore oyster towns from Norwalk west, took part in what oystermen called the East River trade. Its chief function was to ship a steady supply of plump oysters to the New York oyster market, an assemblage of scows and barges that crowded the Manhattan shoreline along the Hudson and East Rivers. As far west as the Bronx, riders on the railroad line that ran along the coast could peer out the windows and see men raking oysters from the shoals at Port Morris, the mouths of the Bronx River and Westchester Creek, and across the narrow strip of water to College Point. Oystering supported fifty families — or two-thirds of the population — on City Island. From Pelham through Rye, oystermen peddled their catch from wagons in shorefront villages. "A considerable colony of oyster-planters" lived at Port Chester and Byram, and the inlets and creeks of Greenwich—Old Greenwich, Greenwich Cove, Cos Cob, Mianus—were coated with planted oysters. At Five-Mile River, in Rowayton, "the little creek-mouth [was] perfectly filled with oyster-boats."

The north shore terminus of the oystermen's "East River" was also the East River trade's busiest oyster port. In 1880, the Norwalk River fleet consisted of two steamers, a dozen sloops, thirty smaller sailboats and sharpies, and numerous skiffs. A hundred families in South Norwalk derived part of their living from oystering, supplementing it, when the beds were closed for spawning season, with fishing, farming, and hotel-keeping. Oystermen unloaded their catch at a maze of wharves that led to several large onshore warehouses, or at the more than two dozen floating oyster houses, locally called "arks."[12] With its seed oysters keeping much of the Northeast in business, and its market oysters in demand throughout the country, the Sound's oyster industry settled onto a plateau of peak production between 1885 and 1910. Connecticut oystermen controlled more private beds than in any other state—almost 87,000 acres. In 1898 the Sound's industry pushed to its apex—more than fifteen million bushels were harvested, worth more than $1 million.[13] Bridgeport natural bed alone produced up to a million market-sized oysters a year at the turn of the century.[14]

Amid the prosperity and abundance, though, were signs that oystering, particularly in the harbors and river mouths that served as the sewers that supported the region's industrialization and urban growth, would prove incompatible with manufacturing. By 1880 oil refineries had destroyed oyster beds on the Sound's far western reaches. And oysters would no longer grow on the Thames because of waste from factories along the river and its tributaries. As the century ended, oystermen working the grounds near the mouth of the Housatonic, and off Bridgeport and elsewhere in the western part of the Sound, began noticing that the shells of their oysters were stained green. The source of the discoloration was copper, which had washed downstream in the waste from the brass mills. The only recourse for the oystermen was to dredge the oysters, haul them across the Sound to Long Island, and transplant them in cleaner water. After three or four years the green tinge would disappear.[15] But the green shells and oyster beds tainted with oil and heavy industrial pollutants were relatively easy to respond to, because the contamination was visible. During those same years, a bigger problem arose unseen, and its consequences were tragic.

On October 20, 1892, some students at Wesleyan University in Middletown began to get sick. The first cases were mild, but within a week the illnesses grew, in number and in severity. Fevers were high and prolonged—104 degrees for as long as ten days. The stricken students lost weight and had little appetite. Abdomens became bloated and pulse rates dropped. Periods of constipation alternated with bouts of diarrhea. Twenty-three young men took sick. Thirteen of the twenty-three cases were considered "very severe," and four of them died. "[I]t became very evident that some of the cases at least, were those of typical typhoid fever," a college investigator wrote. At first, college officials suspected two wells near the school's athletic fields. One of the wells was just thirty feet from an abandoned cesspool. The college had cautioned against using the wells, and city water was piped to the campus, but some students nevertheless continued to drink from them. Investigators learned, though, that town residents also drank from the wells, as did spectators at athletic events, yet none of them had taken ill. Besides, several of the students who were sick said they had not drunk well water. The wells were therefore eliminated as a possible source of the typhoid. No source could be found in the students' residences—some lived in the college's two dormitories, some in two fraternity houses, some in private rooms in town. Nor were any but men infected: "The ladies among the college students, about fifty in number, were wholly exempt from the disease," which ruled out contamination in the classrooms or other college buildings.

Investigators soon found a connection among those who became ill—almost all of the cases were men who were members of three of Wesleyan's seven fraternities. The plumbing in the fraternity houses was ruled out as a source. So was the food. There were no common links among the sick men's roommates, so they could not have been the source of the illness. A shipment of new football uniforms was even investigated as a potential source of the typhoid, but the uniforms — even if they had been infected — were shared by all seven fraternities, not just the three whose members became ill.

The investigators knew the approximate incubation time of typhoid fever, and so they worked backward from October 20, looking for a day on which the students might have been exposed to the disease. They learned that the seven fraternities had held initiation suppers on the same day. "The date of these suppers, October 12th, it will be noticed, is just exactly the proper date to explain the outbreak of typhoid on the twentieth of October, and its disappearance after the fourth week following the suppers, about November 10th," an investigator wrote. The fare at the suppers came under scrutiny. One by one, ham, lobster salad, chicken salad, fruit, milk, cream, water, ice, even celery was investigated and eliminated as a source. All that remained were oysters. "As soon as attention was turned to the oysters . . . the problems began to be solved at once," Wesleyan's investigator wrote. The oysters explained why only men had gotten sick: the college's women had held no special suppers on or near October 12 and in any case had eaten no raw oysters. Of the seven fraternities, two had not served oysters at their suppers; one had purchased raw oysters from a dealer in Hartford; another had obtained oysters from a Middletown dealer and served them cooked. The three others had all gotten their oysters from that same Middletown dealer and had opened their initiation meal by serving oysters on the half shell. Those who ate them included the twenty-three students as well as four Wesleyan alumni and two Yale University students who were guests at the suppers. All twenty-nine got typhoid fever.

The Middletown oyster dealer had bought his shellfish from an oyster house in Fair Haven, which had transferred them from the deeper waters of Long Island Sound to the fresher water at the mouth of the Quinnipiac River, where they had remained for a day or two before being sold. "The object of this treatment is partly to thus 'fatten' the oysters and partly to wash them," the investigator wrote. "Close to the oyster beds where this fattening occurs are the outlets of a number of private sewers. At a distance of some three hundred feet from the beds where the oysters were fattened was an outlet from a private sewer from a house in which were two cases of typhoid fever. The patients were a lady and her daughter. The cases were severe, the lady dying on the twenty-first of October, and the daughter convalescing only after five weeks' sickness. . . . When the grounds were surveyed it was further noticed that at the rising tide an eddy was found to be setting along the shore from the region of the sewer outlet up stream, in the direction of the oyster beds."

Oysters feed by filtering particles from the water they live in. Anything suspended in the water, and small enough to be sucked in by the oyster, gets concentrated in the oyster meat, including bacteria and viruses. The Fair Haven oysters had been fattened and washed by sewage contaminated with typhoid. Investigators later learned that six students at Amherst College in Massachusetts had also eaten Fair Haven oysters on the same night at the same kind of event—a fraternity initiation supper—and had contracted typhoid fever. And a young Boston man who had been in Middletown at the same time and had eaten oysters from the same Fair Haven batch also came down with typhoid. In all, thirty-six people got typhoid fever by eating oysters taken from sewage-tainted waters in the great oystering community of Fair Haven.

The Wesleyan incident marked the first time that an illness was linked conclusively to eating raw oysters that had lived in polluted waters. The report concluded, "Oysters may serve as a means of transportation of typhoid wherever they are fattened in the vicinity of sewers; and wherever they are placed in the mouths of fresh water streams for this fattening process, there will always be the chance of contamination from sewage. Few of the fresh water streams in the vicinity of our large cities fail to have sewage emptying into them."[16]

The Sound's oysters had been growing fat by feeding on the waste of Connecticut's and New York's exploding population—on the sewage that prosperous cities supported by prosperous industries were dumping into the Sound and its tributaries. And that sewage, and the bacteria and viruses it contained, were transported to oyster eaters across the country. In 1924, fifteen hundred people in Chicago, New York, and Washington contracted typhoid fever after eating contaminated oysters; one hundred and fifty died. The oysters were traced to three sources: New York City, New Haven, and Norwalk.[17] Public confidence in the oyster industry collapsed, and the oyster industry itself went down with it.

The damage that sewage could inflict on human health was of course well-known by the late nineteenth and early twentieth century. Yet for decades, the cities whose populations were doubling and doubling again, and the factories that seemed to be expanding infinitely along the Sound and its tributaries, poured out ever-increasing amounts of sewage and industrial waste. The destruction of an ecosystem meant little. Industrial America could provide everything her citizens needed and wanted, an attitude implied in the 1914 Chase Company memo instructing an employee to "please change the location of the Naugatuck River." This attitude was made explicit in the reaction of the author who quoted the memo approvingly in the industrial history section of a four-volume *History of Connecticut,* published in 1925: "Thus does modern business require nature to accommodate itself to its needs."[18]

But there were some who recognized that what was good for industry was not always good for America. H. C. Rowe, New Haven's successful oyster pioneer, expressed it with commonsense conviction in the oystering chapter of the same *History of Connecticut.* "From 1880 to 1910," Rowe opined, "Connecticut has led the world in the production of a valuable food at a time when the world is approaching overpopulation and when mankind have devoted their energies to destroying the bountiful provisions of nature, as forests, buffalo, and other animals, and fishes, valuable resources which men would carefully conserve if they were governed by intelligent foresight." Long Island Sound's oyster industry suffered disastrously because men were not governed by intelligent foresight. And after the wastes of urban society had done their damage, nature piled on further injury. In the first decades of the new century, the rate of oyster reproduction fell dramatically. A succession of hurricanes and storms — particularly the fierce hurricane of 1938 — stirred up sand and mud, smothering the beds and tearing apart the oyster fleet. Salt marshes were drained, filled, built on, and constricted by bridge and road abutments, eliminating an enormous source of food for oysters. And predators — particularly the meek but oyster-ravenous starfish — crept across the

Sound's shallows like an invading horde to devour entire oyster beds. By the time H. C. Rowe was summarizing oystering's past, in 1925, Connecticut's annual oyster production was less than 20 percent of what it had been at the start of World War I.[19] Like an endangered species seemingly fading toward oblivion, the oyster industry declined over the years until only those few still in the business knew for sure that it had not become extinct.

SEVEN

Sprawling Suburbs

The waning decades of the nineteenth century brought a change in the way people in New York and Connecticut lived. Suburbia was born, and with it came new sources of pollution that would push Long Island Sound toward an ecological crisis. The growth away from the urban center of New York began in the middle of the nineteenth century, when commuter railroad lines were strung from New York City to provincial villages on the Sound's north shore, reaching through Westchester and into Fairfield County, Connecticut, and bringing the metropolis closer than anyone could have dreamed. Outposts on Long Island's North Shore — Port Washington, Glen Cove, Northport, Port Jefferson — were joined to each other during the century's latter decades and connected with Manhattan after 1899, when the state legislature gave the Long Island Rail Road permission to tunnel under the East River. Yet as long as the railroad was the only link, the suburbs remained merely spokes pointing from the hub. Commuters were limited in where they could live by how far they could walk from the train station, and villages yielded to countryside within about a mile. For the suburbs to really grow, something else was needed — something to allow people to get to the station from farther away. Henry Ford provided it, and the local, state, and federal governments did all they could to accommodate it.[1]

Ford's Model T hit the market in 1908. But, just as the brass industry and its consequences remained small until Eli Whitney's process of manufacturing interchangeable parts was applied to it, the automobile remained a curiosity of the rich until 1914, when Ford revolutionized its construction with the creation of the assembly line. From 1910 until 1924, while wages were rising, the price of a Model T fell from $950 to $290. In 1925, workers were assembling one Model T every ten seconds — or 9,000 cars a day. Between 1908 and 1927, when Ford halted its production, sixteen million Model T's lined the streets of North America, amounting to half the cars on the road. Ownership of an automobile had been transformed into an essential part of middle-class living, which had become the way of life of the suburbs. Automobile registrations rose by more than 150 percent between 1920 and 1930, and the suburbs of the ninety-six biggest cities in America grew twice as fast as the cities themselves. In New York, Nassau

County's population almost tripled while Westchester County grew from 350,000 people to 520,000, and Connecticut's nineteen fastest growing towns were all suburbs.

The great wave of automobiles demanded better thoroughfares than the gravel roads that had been satisfactory stages on which the wealthy owners of the first automobiles could show off. Paving materials improved, and the function of roads themselves evolved into primarily arteries for auto traffic. And a new kind of road was invented, one whose only purpose was to accommodate autos. The first was the Long Island Motor Parkway, built by William K. Vanderbilt between 1906 and 1911. Also in 1906, Westchester County embarked on an ambitious system of automobile-only roads, when it began constructing the Bronx River Parkway. It was — and remains — a pleasant, meandering road that links the Bronx with quintessential suburban communities such as Scarsdale and Bronxville. So successful was the Bronx River Parkway — a road, as the name suggests, that was as much park as thoroughfare, meant not only for commuting but for recreation — that within a decade of its completion in 1923, Westchester had begun work on the Hutchinson River Parkway, the Saw Mill River Parkway, and the Cross County Parkway.[2] The Hutchinson River Parkway was extended from its terminus at the Connecticut border (where it was renamed the Merritt Parkway) and snaked through Greenwich, Stamford, and New Canaan, and on for an additional thirty-five miles to the Housatonic River. On Long Island, Robert Moses was duplicating Westchester's success by building the Southern State Parkway, the Northern State Parkway, and the Meadowbrook Parkway.

The new roads were government projects, paid for by public funding but lobbied for by real estate interests, whose property outside New York City would turn to gold if only people could get to it. Only 12 percent of the families in New York City owned their own homes in 1920, and only 46 percent nationwide. But the countryside was on the threshold of the era of home building, and the American dream was about to be redefined to include a one-story house with a backyard, a next-door neighbor, and a garage to shelter the family car. Between 1922 and 1929, nearly 900,000 houses were built each year in the United States, a rate that was twice as great as any previous seven-year period.[3]

Early Sprawl
Development started to spread along the Sound's coves and harbors in the early
twentieth century, as shown by these two photos, taken twenty-one years apart
at Savin Rock in New Haven. In the top photo, shot in 1911, only three or
four houses dot the landscape, and salt marsh grass still sprouts from the
mudflats. In the bottom photo, taken in 1932 when the tide was about
one-quarter up, about twenty houses crowd the bluff, a guard rail
runs alongside the road, indicating increased auto traffic, and the
salt marshes are gone. Courtesy of Thomas G. Siccama, Yale
University School of Forestry and Environmental Studies.

On Long Island, the shore of the Sound had been graced with the great homes of great industrialists and businessmen. Louis Comfort Tiffany's Laurelton Hall, overlooking Cold Spring Harbor, encompassed 82 rooms and 25 baths. His neighbor, railroad tycoon Otto Kahn, spent $9 million on a 126-room chateau in Cold Spring Harbor. The Woolworths built a mansion for the same amount in Glen Cove, where H. L. Pratt of Standard Oil also settled. At Sands Point, Jay Gould's son, Howard, constructed an estate that was later sold to Solomon Guggenheim. These luxurious edifices sprawled across equally luxurious expanses of land. But after the Gatsby era, the spectacularly rich could no longer maintain their extravagances. Their palaces and mansions and chateaus became not monuments to the Gilded Age but real estate to be grabbed up, subdivided, developed, and sold to people made newly mobile by the auto.[4] "Long Island is built up for half its length to accommodate those who make New York the metropolis of America," *National Geographic* reported in 1923. "Even Connecticut, as far as Stamford, Greenwich, and New Canaan, is peopled with those who work in Gotham by day and sleep in the country by night." A committee appointed by President Herbert Hoover reported, in 1932, that the automobile "had erased the boundaries which formerly separated urban from rural territory and has introduced a type of local community without precedent in history."[5]

In 1932, however, the real estate development revolution had not even begun in the outlying areas of Long Island. The founders of that revolution were just establishing themselves. Abraham Levitt and his sons, William and Alfred, started in the early 1930s as relatively small-scale builders of upper-middle-class homes, first in Rockville Centre, and then near the Sound in Manhasset, where the houses in a 200-unit subdivision called "Strathmore" sold for as much as $18,500. Their first post–World War II development was bigger—2,250 houses built in Roslyn, at the head of Hempstead Harbor—but was aimed at the same economic stratum: they sold for up to $23,500. The Levitts, however, knew they were on the cusp of a boom, and so while construction of the Roslyn development was getting under way in 1946, they moved south to Hempstead and began buying potato farms, eventually assembling four thousand acres.

The Levitts were the Henry Fords of home building. They mass-produced houses of 750 square feet, turning them out in almost assembly-line fashion, to be erected on 60-by-100-foot lots. The price was an affordable eight thousand dollars. For that, buyers received not only the house but the right to participate in a new way of living, with the Levitts as social engineers of a community whose every detail they planned and carried out. "The Levitts planted apple, cherry, and ever-green trees on each plot . . . and the development ultimately assumed a more parklike appearance," wrote Kenneth T. Jackson in *Crabgrass Frontier: The Suburbanization of the United States.* "To facilitate devel-opment as a garden community, streets were curvilinear (and invari-ably called 'roads' or 'lanes'), and through traffic was shunted to pe-ripheral thoroughfares. Nine swimming pools, sixty playgrounds, ten baseball diamonds, and seven 'village greens' provided open space and recreational opportunities. The Levitts forbade fences (a practice later ignored) and permitted outdoor clothes-drying only on specially de-signed, collapsible racks. They even supervised lawn-cutting for the first few years—doing the jobs themselves if necessary and sending the laggard families the bill." Not only was such orderliness and tranquil-ity what the Levitts wanted, it apparently also satisfied the desires for home and hearth of the new postwar suburbanites. Levittown ulti-mately grew to 17,400 houses and 82,000 residents—the largest pri-vate housing development in history. The era of tract houses obliterat-ing the natural landscape had arrived.[6]

Cars, in the meantime, kept pace with suburban sprawl, both in numbers and in speed. Autos produced in 1940 were three times faster and more powerful than those made in 1920. And government contin-ued to build and improve roads to accommodate the vehicles, spawn-ing the superhighway on October 1, 1940, when the first portion of the Pennsylvania Turnpike opened.[7] It would become the first link in the 42,500-mile interstate highway system established during the Eisenhower administration following a 1954 study of America's high-way needs by a committee chaired by Lucius D. Clay, a director of General Motors. The Clay committee focused immediately and unwa-veringly on the potential for an interstate system, and recommended that the nation's transportation needs be met solely by cars and trucks.

According to Jackson, "not a single word was said about the impact of highways on cities and suburbs, although the concrete thoroughfares and the thirty-five-ton tractor-trailers which used them encouraged the continued outward movement of industries toward the beltways and interchanges. Moreover, the interstate system helped continue the downward spiral of public transportation and virtually guaranteed that future urban growth would perpetuate a centerless sprawl. Soon after the bill was passed by the Senate, [urban planner and historian] Lewis Mumford wrote sadly, 'When the American people, through the Congress, voted a little while ago for a $26 billion highway program, the most charitable thing to assume is that they hadn't the faintest notion of what they were doing.'"

What must have been Lucius Clay's dearest dream soon became true. Americans more than ever relied on automobiles. In 1930, there was one car for every five people in America; by 1960 the ratio was one for every three people, and by 1970, one for every two people. In 1925, twenty million cars and trucks were registered in the United States; in 1955, more than sixty-four million; and in 1975, Americans drove more than one hundred and thirty-two million cars and trucks.[8] Locally, those numbers were indicative of a tremendous growth in population. Fewer than 350,000 people lived in Westchester County in 1920; by 1970, the population was almost 900,000. Nassau County had 126,000 residents in 1920; in 1970, it had almost 1.5 million. Those five decades saw Suffolk County's population grow from 110,000 to more than 1 million. Fairfield County grew from 320,000 to almost 800,000. The sprawl away from New York City dramatically changed the landscape of these and other suburban counties—a change that continued for the rest of the century. After 1960, undeveloped land gave way to the bulldozer and the backhoe at an unprecedented rate. More land was built on between 1960 and 1990—houses, shopping malls, corporate headquarters, highways—than during the previous three hundred years.[9]

The decades of growth almost tripled the amount of sewage flowing into the Sound from treatment plants at New Rochelle, Mamaroneck, Rye, and Port Chester on the north shore, and Glen Cove, Great Neck, Huntington, Oyster Bay, Port Jefferson, and Port Washington

Shoreline Development
In 1911, Shell Beach in East Haven had grassy dunes, derelict pilings, a handful
of houses, and ample sand, as the top photo shows. Townhouses and a sea wall
were later built along the beach, and by 1994, when the bottom photo was
taken, the beach had eroded considerably. Courtesy of Antoinette Wannebo
and Stacy Ritter, Yale Forestry and Environmental Science Project.

on the south shore—from twenty-five million to sixty-five million gallons a day. And with the increased sewage came an element not normally thought of as a pollutant but which, in the amounts that reached the Sound year after year, slowly overwhelmed the Sound's ability to function as an ecosystem: nitrogen. Along with oxygen, hydrogen, and carbon, nitrogen constitutes the bulk of living material and is exceedingly abundant in nature—both in the air, which holds 80 percent of the Earth's supply and is the greatest nitrogen reservoir, and in plants, animals, and the soil's organic humus. Living things, not excluding the plants and animals in the Sound, need nitrogen and are able to take it directly from the Earth's soil, or indirectly from soil via water. Some nitrogen reaches the soil from the air through a process called nitrogen fixation, carried out by bacteria and algae living in the earth and on the roots of plants in the pea family—clovers, soybeans, peas. The soil also retains nitrogen through a cycle of growth and decay: plants take up nitrogen from the soil, and when they die and decompose they release their nutrients back into the soil; or animals eat the plants, and their wastes are returned to the soil.[10] It is always being used and always in demand, so only small amounts escape from the soil into water.

For decades, the influx of nitrogen into the Sound was slow and inconsequential—an estimated 40,000 tons a year. Forests, meadows, salt marshes, swamps, and the Sound itself all absorbed and recycled the nitrogen that existed naturally in the environment. But the growth of cities and industries, the emergence of the automobile as the dominant form of transportation, and the spread of the suburbs more than doubled the amount of nitrogen that reached the Sound—by adding nitrogen directly, through sewage, and by impairing the land's ability to absorb nitrogen. Development attacks the landscape's autoimmune defenses against pollution. Builders cover the land with impermeable structures, driveways, sidewalks, and roads; development compacts soils, wiping out their natural sponginess. When rain falls on an acre of woods, it percolates through the trees, shrubs, and soil, which sift out organic matter and nutrients as the water seeps into brooks and streams. But if that acre is cleared for development, the forest's ability to filter is obliterated, and the denuded land will release a thousand times as many particles into the waterway as forested land would.[11]

"When you increase impervious surfaces, you increase the chance of nitrogen reaching coastal waters," said Joseph Costa, the manager of an Environmental Protection Agency study of Buzzards Bay, the Massachusetts estuary that wedges up into the shoulder of Cape Cod. Even an acre of well-managed farmland, with its nutrient-rich manures and fertilizers, will release a hundred times less soil than land cleared for a housing development.[12]

This phenomenon has been measured again and again in the Chesapeake Bay watershed. From 1950, 160,000 tons of sediment washed down Maryland's Patuxent River toward the bay every year. By 1980, however, 21 percent of the woodlands in the river's drainage basin had been developed for other uses, and the river was a conveyor belt for 710,000 tons of sediment a year. A suburban shopping mall produces an estimated 572 pounds of nitrogen a year; the nitrogen released annually by a development of 2,400 houses jammed onto 400 acres amounts to 2,130 pounds.[13]

The problem is not limited to densely developed suburbs. Houses built in areas with large-lot zoning—the kind of zoning that is dominant in much of Westchester, Fairfield, Nassau, and Suffolk counties—can pollute on a similar scale. When Maryland's Howard County, hoping to deflect development to another part of its jurisdiction, changed the minimum lot size in its undeveloped, forested western region from one acre to three acres, it made the area especially attractive to wealthier people. Wood lots and farmland were quickly sold off to developers and built into upscale, three-acre subdivisions. The new houses were on septic systems—which remove only 15 to 43 percent of the nitrogen in sewage—and the Patuxent's nitrogen flow jumped twentyfold. When the houses were linked to a sewage treatment plant that discharged into the river, the nitrogen influx shot up 110-fold.[14]

Nitrogen swept downstream is just one problem that development and erosion cause. All along the Sound's coastline, the buildup of sediments has changed local ecosystems, and not for the better. In the eighteenth and nineteenth centuries, the residents of towns along the Sound built dams on dozens of tidal creeks, outfitted the dams with tidal gates, and built mills on these newly created ponds. The gates were opened as the tide rose and closed when the ponds filled with seawater. When grain needed to be ground or lumber sawed into boards, the gates were opened and the rushing water powered the mills. The inflow freshened the mill ponds with seawater and estuarine life; the outflow flushed it, sending sediments into the Sound itself. But eventually, transportation improvements, particularly the railroad, made it easier to haul in grain and lumber than to produce them locally, and the mill ponds and tide gates outlived their need. The gates fell into disuse, and over time people stopped bothering to open and close them. But the suburbs did not stop growing, nor did the flow of sediments downstream cease.

In Darien, Gorham Pond — as it is called on charts; neighbors call it Gorham's — was for two centuries the heart of the town's commercial life. After its mill closed, the town paid a family to open and close the tide gate regularly, to keep the pond refreshed and flushed. But the last of the family died in the 1940s and the tide gate remained shut. Within years, mudflats began to appear in Gorham Pond and the water stagnated. Complaints in the 1950s prompted the town to raise the dam, which raised the level of the pond and submerged the mudflats. But sediments continued to flow down the Goodwives River, and by the 1990s Gorham Pond was almost silted in again. Pete Griffith, who lives on the shore of Gorham Pond and who has been working on the issue for the homeowners' association, said that raising the tidal gate regularly was no longer practical because it required a backhoe to lift it. Phragmites — the tall, common reeds that invade disturbed wetlands, crowd out other plants, and provide little benefit to wildlife — began to colonize the mudflats.

The neighbors, the town, and several environmental groups began collaborating on a plan to revive Gorham Pond. They hope to repair the dam and tide gate; until then, using a backhoe, they are opening the tide gate for three days and nights every full and new moon, when the tide range is the greatest. They are hoping to get permits, first, to dredge the area of the pond closest to the gate, and later to dredge the entire pond. And the town will clean out two upstream sedimentation basins, so they can again trap particles before they reach the pond. "The reason for the increase in sedimentation is absolutely the increase in blacktop and concrete in the town of Darien," Griffith said in an interview. "Gorhams Pond just happens to be the place where every drop of rain that falls in Darien will end up."

Developed land not only has less ability to absorb pollutants, it also contributes pollutants. Dogs and cats can be a significant source of bacteria and nitrogen; the streets of Washington, D.C., for instance, get covered with an estimated seven million pounds of pet droppings a year, most of which gets washed into storm drains that empty into the Potomac River and, eventually, Chesapeake Bay.[15] Suburban homes are showplaces for lawns, whose stunning verdancy is generally a result of liberal applications, often by commercial lawn care companies, of chemical nitrogen fertilizers. Nitrogen that occurs naturally in the soil is taken up by plants for growth only as it is needed, but chemical nitrogen dissolves easily in water, and anything not used immediately by the grass is washed away in the first rainstorm. Chemical nitrogen fertilizers have been on the market only since World War II. In the first twenty-five years after they were introduced, production increased by 1,050 percent. Most synthetic fertilizer, of course, is applied to crops. (Chemical nitrogen fertilizers have done what agribusiness has demanded: agricultural production in the United States rose by 38 percent between 1950 and 1970, while acreage in use fell by 4 percent. But the higher output carried a price: the use of synthetic fertilizers and pesticides increased over the same decades by almost 300 percent.) Yet front yards hardly starve for attention. In the northeast United States each acre of fertilized lawn is covered with an average of 134 pounds of nitrogen a year.[16]

Water has always been a chief conveyor of nitrogen to Long Island Sound. Much nitrogen reaches the Sound in rain and snow, which hold traces of more than a dozen elements. If there were no air pollution in the northeastern United States, precipitation would sprinkle nine-tenths of a pound of nitrogen on each acre annually. But rain and snow have been absorbing an additional nitrogen burden since the dawn of the industrial era, and especially since the end of World War II, and have been dumping it across the land in the form of acid rain. In the northeastern United States, the snow and rain that fills the reservoirs, and waters the gardens, and washes the streets spreads ten times more nitrogen than if the precipitation had remained unpolluted — almost nine pounds of nitrogen a year on every acre in the region (and as much as twenty-two pounds per acre on mountains, where the clouds come into contact with the land).[17]

In searching for blame for the Sound's problems, one need look not only at the suspects usually fingered for causing acid rain in the Northeast — the coal-burning power plants of the Ohio Valley. A visit to the shore of the Sound in the 1980s or '90s often revealed plumes of black smoke rising from the four stacks at the oil-fired power plant operated by the old Long Island Lighting Company in Northport, or from Northeast Utilities' Manresa Island power plant, at the mouth of Norwalk Harbor. But the largest source of nitrogen in acid rain — as much as 45 percent — is transportation and automobiles, especially the big, powerful gas guzzlers that started rolling off Detroit's assembly lines after World War II. In the late 1940s, auto manufacturers began to make cars that were faster and stronger still, able to break onto busy highways as quickly as a hare and accelerate while climbing hills, and each time power rose, the amount of nitrogen pumped into the atmosphere rose with it.[18]

The average horsepower of the typical American car jumped from one hundred to two hundred and fifty between 1950 and 1968. That surge of power required automobile engines to run at higher cylinder compression ratios — 50 percent higher — and thus at higher temperatures. Heated more than they had been in the less-powerful engines, oxygen and nitrogen combined to form nitrogen oxides, which were pumped into the atmosphere through tailpipes. Although air pollution regulations cut emissions of nitrogen oxides per car, the steadily increasing number of cars easily overtook the pollution controls. In 1971, the Environmental Protection Agency, heady with the potential of the new Clean Air Act, predicted that in 1985 there would be 70 percent less nitrogen oxides in the air than in 1975. In fact, the amount rose by more than 4 percent.[19] Now, autos cloud metropolitan New York with almost 200,000 tons of nitrogen a year.[20] (Water pollution is not the only problem caused by nitrogen from autos and power plants, nor is it necessarily the most important. It is also a key component of photochemical smog, which forms when nitrogen, ozone, and volatile organic compounds combine in the presence of heat and sunlight.)

Acid rain was virtually an unknown factor in the pollution of the Sound until May 1988, when the Environmental Defense Fund released a study called "Polluted Coastal Waters: The Role of Acid Rain."

It reported that nearly one quarter of all the nitrogen entering Chesapeake Bay originated as acid rain. The group's scientists had not looked at the Sound in as much detail, but a preliminary analysis showed that the proportion was about the same in the Sound as in the Chesapeake. EDF said that approximately 3,400 tons of nitrogen fell directly on the Sound; another 46,000 tons fell on the land throughout the Sound's drainage basin, of which about 8,700 tons reached the Sound itself. In other words, according to EDF, acid rain accounted for more than 12,000 tons of nitrogen polluting the Sound every year.[21] "The EDF report was-eye opening," said Jonathan Garber, who heads the ecosystems branch of EPA's Environmental Research Laboratory at Narragansett, Rhode Island. "Even after considerable scrutiny, the research community was unable to dismiss their estimates based on either their methods or the other data available at the time."

Acid rain had not been included in scientists' reasoning about nitrogen sources because no one had known how much of the nitrogen that fell across the Sound's watershed actually reached the Sound. The Sound's drainage area covers 16,000 square miles and extends through the Connecticut River valley beyond Vermont and New Hampshire to part of Quebec. Massachusetts, Vermont, and New Hampshire, in fact, make up 65 percent of the Sound's watershed. A particle of nitrogen that falls on a Vermont pasture must survive a long journey and many chances to be waylaid if it is to reach the Connecticut River and then the Sound. "Before the EDF report, most estuarine scientists had calculated the amount of nitrogen entering estuaries only by direct deposition to the water surface," said Jonathan Garber. That calculation usually came out to less than 10 percent — far lower and far less significant than the nearly 25 percent figure from the Environmental Defense Fund.[22]

The most efficient way for the nitrogen in acid rain to reach the Sound — aside from falling directly into the Sound or one of its tributaries — is to land on a paved area, from which the rain flows into a storm drain that empties into a stream or into the Sound itself. This transport method is not perfect: the speed of the stream and the season of the year help determine how far the nitrogen progresses. A sluggish stream might give algae or microorganisms that feed on nitrogen a chance to eliminate the nutrients before they reach the Sound; a quick stream might carry the nitrogen to its mouth before it can be used. In fall and winter, when daylight is short and temperatures cold, algae are not growing and reproducing and thus have little need for nitrogen.[23] Generally, most of the nitrogen that falls on a street or parking lot or driveway will be added to the annual burden of nutrients that fertilize the Sound and ignite hypoxia.

The same seasonal factors also affect nitrogen-rich acid rain that falls on a forest, meadow, or lawn. A dormant tree is unlikely to be a great wintertime absorber of nitrogen. Microbes that live in the soil also feed on nitrogen but they, too, need little in winter. During the growing season, a woodland or other naturally vegetated landscape is a tremendously efficient nitrogen sponge. But with biological systems continually cycling and recycling, a nutrient taken in by a plant can still be freed and sent downstream. "A molecule of nitrogen that falls in rainfall on a forest floor in April may wind up in a leaf," explained Peter Groffman, an assistant professor of natural resources at Rhode Island University, and Carole Jaworski, the coordinator of the Rhode Island Sea Grant Advisory Service, in an article in Sea Grant's *Nor'easter* magazine. "When that leaf falls to the forest floor in October, it will decompose and may release its nitrogen back to the soil where it can then wash into a stream or coastal waters. Similarly, nitrogen immobilized by soil microorganisms can be re-released to the soil when the microbial cells die. Over long time scales (decades), there is concern that the appetite of plants and microorganisms for nitrogen could be 'saturated' by the increased loads of nitrogen in precipitation. If this occurs, then vegetation will be an even less reliable 'sink' for rainfall nitrogen."

Another complication enters the equation if the acid rain falls on sandy soils, which cover most of Long Island. The water might filter down through the sand to an aquifer, which does not receive the sunlight necessary to support plant growth. The aquifer then would provide an efficient ride for the nitrogen to reach the Sound. But aquifers often feed marshes, which are among nature's best nitrogen filters.[24] Unfortunately for the Sound, the fifteen thousand acres of salt marsh in Connecticut and the twenty thousand on Long Island's north shore represent only half the marshland that buffered the Sound three hundred to four hundred years ago.

And then there is sewage. Nothing—not acid rain, not suburban sprawl, not urban runoff—disrupts the Sound's ecosystem like sewage. Every day of every year, eighty-six sewage treatment plants empty 1.047 billion gallons of sewage into the Sound and its tributaries. Four New York City sewage treatment plants alone—Wards Island, Tallmans Island, Bowery Bay, and Hunt's Point—account for seven hundred million gallons a day spewed into the narrow wedge between Throgs Neck and Hell Gate. Their flow, if combined, would make them the Sound's fourth largest tributary, smaller only than the Connecticut, the Housatonic, and the Thames. Near Flushing Bay, the heart of that strip, the water is 1.5 percent sewage.[25] Every time it rains, 10 percent of the amount treated by those four facilities—70 million gallons—flows raw into the Sound. Even in dry weather, more than 37 million gallons of raw sewage leak out of the city's sewer system— all of it laden with nitrogen.

Four centuries ago that nitrogen never came close to the Sound. It was locked underground in petroleum, or held in the self-contained cycles of upland ecosystems; much of it did not even exist until chemical companies synthesized it in laboratories. Now it is the element that is both the symbol and the result of modern society's divorce from the natural processes that nurture the Earth—a divorce that has brought Long Island Sound to the brink of disaster.

EIGHT

Strangling the Sound

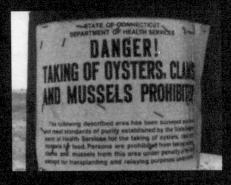

T he scientists concerned with nitrogen's effect on Long Island Sound often use the term *over-enrichment*. Nitrogen in the amounts that flow down rivers and pour from sewage plants and wash off streets and fall from the sky is too rich for the Sound. Long Island Sound is being slowly overfed to death. And its demise would be nothing less than an ecological catastrophe.

Acre for acre, estuaries like the Sound are almost unrivaled in their fertility. Only coral reefs and tropical rainforests are comparable. In the sheer mass of organic material that lives and dies there — and provides nourishment for plants and animals throughout the food web — estuaries are richer than grasslands, temperate or boreal forests, and tundras. By one estimate, modern farms yield just slightly more than half the organic material of an estuary. The open ocean is a biological desert in comparison; estuaries produce twenty times more organic material per acre than oceans.[1] Of the total number of fish consumed by humans worldwide, more than three-quarters depend on estuaries for at least part of their growth and development. "Farmers long ago learned that you don't put the well near the barn where you put the manure," said Hal Stanford, of the National Oceanic and Atmospheric Administration. "We are just beginning to learn that about estuaries."[2]

An estuary is where salt water from the ocean meets and mixes with fresh water draining off the land. It is an arm of the sea coddled by the land. Estuaries are secure from the waves that pound the ocean's coast, but are renewed continually by tides and currents and rivers — the word *estuary* comes from the Latin verb *aestuare,* to heave, boil, surge, to be in commotion.[3] The foundations of an estuary's biological richness — the array of life that starts with the marsh grasses and encompasses bacteria, diatoms, larval crabs, lobsters, striped bass — are the physical and chemical processes that stimulate life. Sunlight is essential. It must be dispersed to virtually all of an estuary's plants and animals, so shallow waters are important. Long Island Sound has an average depth of seventy-nine feet.[4] Chesapeake Bay, a more productive estuary than the Sound, averages about twenty-one feet deep, including the tidal portion of its tributaries, and 20 percent of the bay is less than six and a half feet deep. Much of Haverstraw Bay, the most vibrant part of the Hudson River estuary, is only six feet deep.

The tides freshen and renew the estuary. They deliver nutrients and oxygen to the estuary's bays and harbors and marshes. They scatter the larvae of a multitude of fish and crustaceans. They expose the mudflats to the sun's warmth, or cool them from its heat. The freshening power of flooding and draining is a lesson that people have learned and applied to rice cultivation, where the regulated inundation of paddies mimics the tides.[5] The tides also infuse the estuary with oxygen, carrying it from the oxygen-rich ocean or roiling the surface so it mixes in from the atmosphere. The waves and winds that chop the water into whitecaps also add oxygen, as does the mass of vegetation in an estuary, through photosynthesis. Oxygen concentrations fall naturally in an estuary in summer. As the water grows warmer, its ability to hold oxygen diminishes. But the deeper water stays cooler, so a relatively deep estuary like the Sound stratifies into two layers, warmer water floating on top of cooler water. The stratification is strong; the two layers do not mix. So when the occasional thunderstorm or cold front moves through and churns in oxygen at the surface, it does not reach the bottom layer. Yet while fresh oxygen is confined to the surface, the estuary's organisms can move freely from top to bottom. The plants and animals that make up the estuary's plankton still consume nutrients, grow and reproduce, and die and sink, using up oxygen as they decompose in the oxygen-starved bottom. But the stratification prevents nutrients that are released from the decomposing organic material on the bottom from returning to the top, where they would feed more plankton. The nutrient supply gradually drops, and so does the growth of plankton that would continue to suck oxygen from the bottom. It's a natural shutoff valve that keeps the summertime oxygen depletion under control.

Change comes in late summer and fall. Winds pick up, and temperatures drop. Salty water pushing in from the sea cools the lower layer; the atmosphere cools the upper layer. Eventually the temperatures of the layers almost equalize, and the stratification breaks down. From top to bottom, oxygen-rich water infuses the estuary. Oxygen-rich is a relative term, however. Even in the best of times the amount of dissolved oxygen in sea water is minuscule. In winter, when Long Island Sound is saturated with oxygen, concentrations peak at approximately eight milligrams per liter, or 0.08 percent. (For comparison, the air we breathe is about 20 percent oxygen.) In summer, under the burden of man-made nitrogen, oxygen concentrations can plummet to zero. But until recently it was unknown how far oxygen levels fell in hot weather before the Sound region became heavily developed. In other words, no one knew how much of the Sound's ecological crisis was man-made and how much was natural.

To answer that question, researchers needed an estimate of how much nitrogen had reached the Sound each year when the region's sole human inhabitants were Algonquians and when, for practical purposes, the only conveyors of nitrogen were the Sound's tributaries. The key to that calculation was finding waterways that could be presumed to be carrying the same amount of nitrogen as they had four centuries ago — creeks or rivers that were free of sewage and runoff from development and farms. Paul Stacey of the Connecticut Department of Environmental Protection made the search, and he found two streams that met these qualifications: Burlington Brook, which flows through the town of Burlington, into the Farmington River, and then to the Connecticut River and the Sound; and the Salmon River, a tributary of the Connecticut that cuts through East Hampton and Glastonbury. The United States Geological Survey had been monitoring nitrogen flow in those streams for about five years. Stacey studied the USGS data and learned that the streams carried an average of 0.68 milligrams of nitrogen per liter of water, a reading that was among the lowest in the state. Each liter of water flowing from the mouth of the Connecticut River, for example, carried twice as much nitrogen. Stacey then applied the two streams' nitrogen flow rate to all of the Sound's tributaries.

He discovered that, four centuries ago, about forty thousand tons of nitrogen a year had flowed into the Sound from its tributaries. Stacey had that number plugged into a computer model of the Sound and came up with another estimate: in a typical year before the Sound's watershed was settled by European colonists, dissolved oxygen in the western end of the Sound never fell below about 5.5 milligrams per liter, which was plenty to keep even the relatively shallow waters, such as those in the far western Sound, habitable for marine creatures. Forty thousand tons: the amount of nitrogen the Sound had adapted to over ninety-eight centuries, and the amount needed to keep dissolved oxygen at healthy concentrations.

Nutrients from a Salt Marsh
Salt marshes, like this one with its salt hay flattened into typical cowlick patterns,
provided the nutrients that made the Sound a rich, healthy estuary when this
picture was taken near New Haven in 1911. Courtesy of Thomas G. Siccama,
Yale University School of Forestry and Environmental Studies.

Just as nitrogen is used and recycled on land, it undergoes the same
process in estuaries: algae need nitrogen to grow; larval fish, small invertebrates, and plankton eaters consume the algae; lobsters and larger
fish eat the algae-eaters; and the waste from the fish and lobsters is
consumed by the algae.[6] In Long Island Sound, the most explosive
growth period of algae happens in late winter and spring, a bloom of
critical importance to the estuary. As winter wanes, the days lengthen.
Ice in the Sound's harbors and bays plows into the salt marshes, mow-
ing the broad flats of *Spartina* grasses into a copper-colored stubble,
and grinding the grasses into smaller and smaller bits. The tides wash
this organic matter into the deeper water, where it decomposes and
fertilizes the algae, the most abundant of which are the diatoms.

Diatoms are the estuary's basic food crop. They thrive in coastal
areas, where winds keep the surface waters well-mixed, helping to give
the diatoms the sun's full benefit by suspending them near the top. Diatoms come in many shapes — some are bladder-, needle-, or disk-like,
some resemble subtly curving worms. In February, fed by the nutri-

The Harvest
Salt marsh grass is so rich that farmers harvested it for their animals, as shown
in this photo taken in September 1912. Courtesy of Thomas G. Siccama,
Yale University School of Forestry and Environmental Studies.

ents released by decomposing grasses and stimulated by increasing
sunlight, the diatoms and other phytoplankton (a survey once found
one hundred and twenty-five species in Long Island Sound) reproduce
at a tremendous rate. The diatoms can double in number every day.
More than forty million individual phytoplankton cells may cram into
three cubic feet of water; eighty cubic feet may hold a billion individual plants.[7]

As spring progresses, the food chain extends to another estuarine
organism of critical importance, the copepod. If diatoms are the estuary's vegetable crop, copepods are its animal protein. The abundance
of these tiny, shrimp-like crustaceans is awesome, matched only by in-
sects among the multicellular members of the animal kingdom. Their
most important food — and their main source of energy for reproducing — are the diatoms. Like crabs and lobsters, copepods must shed
their chitinous outer skin to grow. They live for barely more than a
couple of months, from hatched egg to adult. The adult males, their
usefulness having been exhausted after mating, are lucky to linger for
another few days. The adult females live longer, feeding and produc-

ing eggs for several weeks after reaching adulthood. Copepods graze on diatoms in what can only be considered a feeding frenzy, given the copepods' furious reproduction in the months immediately following the diatoms' surge. Being a step up on the food ladder, there are necessarily fewer copepods than diatoms. From April through August a cubic meter of the Sound's water may hold between ninety and one hundred and twenty-five animals, some as big as one-sixth of an inch or longer.[8]

As long as the amount of nitrogen flowing into the Sound was relatively low, the mass of plankton remained under control and oxygen levels stayed high enough to sustain the winter flounder, blackfish, and lobsters that crowded into the Sound. They all relied on that perfect mechanism of self-regulation that shut off the supply of nitrogen to the deeper waters and prevented oxygen concentrations from plummeting. But as the number of people who lived in the watershed grew and spread across land that had never supported anything but forests and farms, the amount of nitrogen reaching the Sound escalated as well. Four centuries of ever-increasing development and population had swollen the Sound's burden of nitrogen to 91,000 tons a year, a 128 percent increase over the estimated 40,000 tons that flowed to the Sound before European settlement. The additional 51,300 tons of nitrogen included 29,600 tons from sewage plants and factories, and 8,800 tons from storm water runoff.[9] That flow subverted the Sound's natural safety valve, because the supply of nitrogen was steady, year-round, and overwhelming. The system that the Sound had evolved for surviving the summertime oxygen depletion no longer worked. Nothing remained to stop oxygen concentrations from crashing.

Scientists were noting abnormally low oxygen levels as long ago as the early 1950s. But the possibility of disaster was only occasionally remarked upon. A rare warning came in 1971, when Donald Squires of the University of Connecticut spoke of hypoxia as "one of the most pressing problems" in the western Sound. The researchers who measured dissolved oxygen over the three decades following 1950 worked independently of each other, however, and few scientists — and virtually no one else — thought to form the independent parts into a cohesive picture. The data were there and the trend they outlined was disturbing, but hardly anyone was seeing it.

Sewage Contamination
Development sent so much sewage into the Sound — raw and treated,
from sewage plants and in runoff — that shellfish beds were closed
for health reasons. Courtesy of Save the Sound.

The first comprehensive study of dissolved oxygen in Long Island Sound was conducted by Yale professor Gordon Riley during the summers of 1952 through 1955. Riley wanted to know how summertime readings compared with the saturation level of eight milligrams of oxygen per liter. He found that, in the eastern third of the Sound, dissolved oxygen bottomed out near 6.7 milligrams per liter, or about 85 percent of saturation. In the central basin, off New Haven, the minimum level was far lower, about 3.9 milligrams per liter, or about 50 percent of saturation. And in the western third of the Sound, the lowest level he recorded — possibly near Execution Rocks, between New Rochelle and Manhasset — was 3.1 milligrams per liter, or 40 percent of saturation. As long ago as the early 1950s, in other words, the western Sound was on the verge of plunging across the threshold of hypoxia.

Over the next twenty-five years, that level breached that threshold regularly. A crash in August 1970 sent dissolved oxygen falling below 1 milligram per liter, killing mossbunkers and lobsters in Hempstead Harbor and near Execution Rocks and New Rochelle's Davids Island. A year later, spring and summer readings were taken at eight locations, from Throgs Neck to Hempstead Sill. In the spring, oxygen concentrations were at their highest, 7 or 8 milligrams per liter. But by early August no reading exceeded 1.9 milligrams per liter, and the waters of Hempstead Sill held just half a milligram. Signs of trouble were becoming apparent further east as well, with readings below 4 milligrams per liter along the Connecticut coast, from Bridgeport to New Haven, in July and August of 1972. East of New Haven the water was much healthier, containing from 5 to 7 milligrams per liter.

During that summer the Sound's central basin was the site of what scientists called a "benthic crash"—a large-scale killing of bottom-dwelling animals. The precise cause of the die-off is unknown—perhaps unusually heavy erosion scoured the bottom, exposing anaerobic muds, which were fatal to the various bottom animals; or maybe the Sound was hit by what now can be fairly considered a more typical hypoxic crash. Whatever the cause, researchers headed out from their National Marine Fisheries Service laboratories at Milford in April 1973 to assess the damage. They found that, compared with the summer of 1972, there were 86 percent fewer benthic animals and 55 percent fewer benthic species. In other words, almost nine out of ten *individual* animals, and more than half of all the *kinds* of animals, were wiped out. The effects spilled over to all areas of the Sound that have mud bottoms. Five years later the recovery remained incomplete. The pattern was the same in August of 1977. Dissolved oxygen sank to 1.3 milligrams per liter just east of Hell Gate, 1.7 near Execution Rocks, 2.3 south of Greenwich, and 3.4 off Smithtown Bay.[10]

And so it continued into the 1980s. Although hypoxia and anoxia—the complete absence of dissolved oxygen—are not problems that can be seen, swimmers and sailors knew something was wrong and was getting worse. Each year they complained more insistently that the Sound was not as clean as they remembered it from past years. It was murkier. The curtains of seaweed seemed denser. Sewage spills and beach closings had become more common. It had become well known that storm water running off streets was as polluted as raw sewage. By the middle of the decade, people who lived near the Sound, who fished its reefs, who used its winds to race their yachts, who had learned to restrict their swimming to high tide because the inundation made the water seem cleaner, had begun to think seriously that the Sound might have reached the point where conditions would never improve.

A scientific consensus also was forming. In 1985 the National Oceanic and Atmospheric Administration included the Sound in its program of "Estuary-of-the-Month" seminars in Washington, D.C., at which there was agreement that hypoxia was threatening the Sound and that the cause was sewage: not raw sewage, because the 1972 Clean Water Act had virtually ended the practice of discharging untreated waste, but treated sewage, in particular the tons of nitrogen contained in the 1.047 billion gallons of treated effluent that was dumped into the Sound every day. But even the experts at the seminar were mostly unprepared to say what the effects had been, never mind predict what they would be.

Among those scientists were Donald Rhoads, an ecologist who was then at Yale, and Barbara Welsh, who had spent a year and a half at Yale on a fellowship working in Rhoads's laboratory as a visiting faculty member in geology and geophysics. Welsh had been part of the University of Connecticut's marine sciences department at Avery Point in Groton since the early 1970s, and had developed expertise in the ecology of the shallow bays and harbors that lined Long Island Sound — small estuaries that were themselves suffering from pollution. For the Estuary-of-the-Month seminar, she was asked to address problems in the Sound's deeper water; Rhoads's topic was the bottom sediments. Their thinking at the time, Welsh told me, was that hypoxia was born on the bottom. They believed that the organic matter that had built up in the sediments was the trigger that set off hypoxia in the Sound. This was how it worked elsewhere — in Albemarle and Pamlico Sounds, in Mobile Bay, in Chesapeake Bay, where the stranglehold of hypoxia and anoxia routinely spread like tentacles along the main stem of the estuary and choked the life out of fish and shellfish. In July of 1985, in fact, when I interviewed Rhoads about conditions in the Sound, much of our talk was about Chesapeake Bay, which was important to the Sound, he said, because it gave scientists something to compare the Sound with — though the comparison was not encouraging.

He said that his research showed that the bottom sediments of the western end of the Sound were starting to look like the sediments of the bay. Don't be fooled, Rhoads cautioned, by the Sound's high annual lobster catch. The figures may be deceiving. When oxygen levels drop, the lobsters will search for healthy water and herd into it in great numbers. The lobstermen then home in on them. That is not a sign of a well-balanced ecosystem, Rhoads said. It is "bliss before disaster." The herding of lobsters into a small area because of habitat loss will inevitably lead to a crash in the lobster population: either the fishermen will catch them or, in fierce competition for a limited food supply, the lobsters will die off. It was a serious condition, an indisputable sign that the ecosystem's health was suffering. But Welsh and Rhoads also believed that because the sediments ignited the hypoxia, the low-oxygen zone would hug the bottom, rising two or three feet up into the water, but not much more.

At the seminar in Washington, Welsh also discussed what might happen if a severe oxygen drop killed a large portion of the Sound's marine life. The decomposing animals, she speculated, might themselves deplete oxygen and trigger a further drop. It was a situation that everyone at the seminar was familiar with because of a 1976 incident involving the spread of decomposing surf clams and intensified hypoxia through the New York Bight. But when Welsh raised the possibility of such a chain reaction in the Sound, its remote likelihood elicited chuckles.

"I called it a biological firestorm," Welsh recalled. "That got people's attention — they thought that was pretty funny, and I backed off [and thought]: 'Well, I know it probably couldn't happen in the Sound, but I mean, after all, if we keep dumping sewage in there, why, who knows? That's the end point of what could happen.'"

NINE

The Brink of Disaster

The Environmental Protection Agency chose a hot day in the middle of August 1985 to announce the start of a study of water quality in Long Island Sound. A pioneering, $25 million study of Chesapeake Bay had been finished the year before, and, given its disturbing findings, Congress decided that it would be wise to make similar, if less-expensive, explorations of other estuaries. Congress created the National Estuary Program and appropriated money to research not only Long Island Sound but also Narragansett Bay in Rhode Island, Buzzards Bay in Massachusetts, and Puget Sound in Washington. The Long Island Sound Study would be a cooperative effort that included the EPA, the Interstate Sanitation Commission, New York State and Connecticut, the National Oceanic and Atmospheric Administration, the National Marine Fisheries Service, the State University of New York, and the University of Connecticut.

Those agencies were all represented on that August day, first at a press conference at the U.S. Merchant Marine Academy at Kings Point on Long Island, and then on board an EPA research vessel for an afternoon tour of the narrow, island- and rock-studded waters of the western Sound. The Sound study, according to Mickey Weiss, a marine biologist who was then co-chairman of the study's citizens advisory committee, would try to consider the Sound as an ecological region rather than as a political entity controlled by competing jurisdictions. The study would focus on the two problems revealed by the bits and pieces of research done over the years: dissolved oxygen might be sinking to unhealthy concentrations, and the assumption that heavy metals and toxic compounds like PCBs would be contaminating sediments in urban, industrialized areas. The sense that day was that the Sound study would be an intensive, deliberate course of research that would reveal the extent and depth of the pollution, and that policymakers would use the information to make wise decisions about how to clean it up. "The problems are the same as those fifteen years ago," University of Connecticut's Donald Squires told me that afternoon. "The difference is, we know a hell of a lot more. I'm not certain if it makes it easier or more difficult. I think the latter."

No research was conducted that day, not even any of the demonstration trawls or dissolved oxygen measurements that scientists often use effectively as publicity tools. Not until a year later, in August 1986, did Barbara Welsh begin any systematic measurements of oxygen concentrations, which she conducted between Throgs Neck and New Haven. And although oxygen levels were low, Welsh saw nothing that might have given Squires, or anyone else, an inkling that the problems had been growing significantly worse by degree over the past fifteen years. As late as December 1986, few people were thinking of the possibility of disaster.

"I haven't heard anything that makes me think there is a catastrophe in store," Mickey Weiss told me then. "The problems are a little less critical than that, and we have some time to deal with them. Hopefully we can avoid a crisis." It took the grim epiphany of 1987 for the realization to hit that the problems *were* critical, and that the time to deal with them had arrived. By the third week of July, vast blooms of algae had turned the Sound an opaque reddish-brown, oxygen levels were pushing down toward zero, toxic hydrogen sulfide was being loosed from the sediments, and fish and lobsters were dying in uncounted numbers. The science fiction scenario that scientists had thought comical two years earlier — Barbara Welsh's biological firestorm — was sweeping through the waters from City Island to Greenwich, Connecticut.

In late July of that summer, I went out to find John Fernandes, a Portuguese immigrant who for almost thirty years had made his living catching lobsters out of Port Chester, New York. He kept his boat in a tiny and crowded marina next to a restaurant on the Byram River, about a hundred yards upstream from Port Chester Harbor. To get there, you drove under Interstate 95 and skirted a garbage transfer station, a sewage treatment plant, Port Chester's public works yard, some oil storage tanks, and a couple of manufacturing plants. It was about as far from the world of yacht clubs and sailboat racing that one could be and still be on the Sound.

I found him on the narrow road that ran above the river, walking slowly in the sweltering afternoon, his thin face looking weary. A lean man with strong, wiry arms, Fernandes was wearing rubber boots, blue work pants, and a white tee shirt soaked with sweat. On his head was a battered baseball cap. As I approached him, a blue Mercedes pulled up and parked near us, in front of the restaurant, Pearl of the

Dead Lobsters
John Fernandes, who lived in Rye and fished for lobsters out of Port Chester,
was one of the first to discover the harsh effects of hypoxia. In July of 1987,
he hauled a holding pen to the surface and found that three hundred
pounds of lobsters were dead. Courtesy of *The Journal News*.

Atlantic. The driver was Salvadore Carlos, like Fernandes a lobsterman
and a native of Portugal, but also the owner of the restaurant. Carlos
is short, round, and muscular. His bald spot shone in the sunlight. He
was wearing gray slacks and a blue windowpane shirt, a couple of gold
chains around his neck, a gold watch, and a slim gold bracelet. Carlos
knew who I was because I had stopped by several times in previous
weeks to ask about the fishing.

"How are the lobsters?" he asked Fernandes.

"The lobsters are dead," Fernandes said.

The summer lobster run had started well, with Fernandes pulling each of his four hundred traps every four days and catching two pounds per trap. "This year would've been my best summer, the way it was going," he said.

But the reward had waned as the summer progressed. A day's catch was often too meager to bother lugging to the fish market. So Fernandes began storing his lobsters in a wire bin, near his dock or in rocky, inshore waters. When he had accumulated several hundred pounds, he would retrieve the lobsters and sell them. Which is what he was hoping to do one July day when he slipped his boat between the rocks to his holding pen, and discovered that all his lobsters were dead. It was money gone for good, for Fernandes and for virtually every other lobsterman working the western Sound.

"We don't know what was lost that didn't enter traps," Phil Briggs, a lobster specialist with the New York State Department of Environmental Conservation, told me then. "The actual stuff that was dead in holding crates and that came up in pots is inconsequential when compared with what was lost and never caught. It's tough when a person loses three hundred pounds or more. It's even tougher when he can't catch another three hundred pounds to replace it."

"They're fearful for their livelihood right now," he added, "and I don't blame them."

The next day I went with Skip Crane, a marine scientist and an educator with the Long Island Sound Taskforce, as he piloted the Research Vessel *Oceanic* from Stamford to Lloyd Neck, on Long Island, a distance of about four miles. The trip was unremarkable except for the dozen or so lobster boats that blocked our southward progress. The crew of each boat was working hard on this hazy July morning, hauling traps along lines of buoys. Crane had to maneuver nimbly to avoid entangling the buoys in the *Oceanic*'s propeller.

The hypoxia apparently had not yet crept as far east as Stamford–Oyster Bay. Lobsters were plentiful here, perhaps more plentiful than usual. Fishermen working these waters would later report catching eight pounds of lobster per trap, an excellent although not unheard of average. But considering that Fernandes and Salvadore Carlos and the other men from Port Chester, barely seven miles to the west, were catching nothing, it was enough to give observers pause. The lobsters being caught off Stamford were perhaps animals that normally would have been trapped further west had they not fled in desperate search of oxygen.

"One wonders," Barbara Welsh remarked later that summer, "if that sort of harvesting effort going on was a depletion of the stocks." There was no way of knowing for sure, of course. When fishermen pull traps crammed full with lobsters, it may be because of their skill, or because the lobsters are in the middle of a good, natural run. But Welsh's implication was clear. What Skip Crane and I witnessed that morning as we approached Lloyd Neck might have been Donald Rhoads's "bliss before disaster."

The number of commercial lobstermen on the Sound has fluctuated in recent years between about eight and nine hundred, the number tending to rise after word spreads of an abundant catch and to sink with the perception that the effort is increasing but the pay isn't. No matter how great the reward compared to the effort, however—no matter if they are enjoying the fruits of "bliss before disaster" or struggling to pay the cost of fuel—the lobstermen work hard. They fetch bait early in the morning. They haul traps heavy with spider crabs and seaweed. They deliver hundreds of pounds of lobsters to retailers and wholesalers, driving in some cases to Fulton Market near the southern tip of Manhattan to sell their catch. They fish in the hottest, sultriest days of July and August, and only the most bitter winter weather will keep them ashore.

You don't find lobster fishermen at the yacht clubs or expensive private marinas. Marina customers, owners of sleek and gleaming vessels, don't want them around, with their inelegant, dingy boats, their salty language or foreign accents, the smell of dead fish as they load their bait. The fishermen squeeze in where they can, at the rare yard that allows them the room to stack extra traps, barrels, boxes, rope, and other gear. On City Island one fisherman keeps his boat near a seedy restaurant and beyond a mudflat that at low tide reveals an amazing array of trash—an old radiator, an old bicycle, waterlogged planks of various lengths. Other fishermen find room in the industrial ports like Bridgeport or the blue-collar harbors like Norwalk or Port Chester, docking near bridge abutments and old bulkheads. Such circumstances are a fact of life for the lobstermen. They don't want to improve their surroundings because it would probably mean their docking fees would rise. These are not yachtsmen, after all — they are workers who start early and return late, tired and cold, or tired and hot, and probably are just as happy when no one is around to look at them askance, or to hobnob, or, worse, to pry into the circumstances of their trade. As a newspaper reporter, I certainly got no warm welcome when I showed up, deferential in body language, staying on the dock and off the boat unless invited on (which I rarely was), trying to phrase questions that would elicit more than a grunt.

Some lobstermen, like the guys who dock on City Island, are almost unbelievably competitive and unpleasant in their insistence that I understand the truth: that no one else catches lobsters as well as they do — not as a group, because there is little loyalty to others on the island, but as individuals: Each brags that he is the best and everyone else is worthy only of scorn. One mocks another for calling himself the "Lobster King." Another says he controls the entire area and the others work only because of his largess. He brags of ramming boats and pulling shotguns when territorial boundaries — which are illegal — are ignored. Still others elsewhere, like the men from Portugal who work out of Port Chester, are pleasant and soft-spoken, even in the late-afternoon dockside conversations I imposed on them when anybody who had spent a hot day on the water pulling lobster traps should rightly be too tired to answer questions.

"How much are you getting for your lobsters?" I asked.

"The price is up but it don't do me any good because I don't have any," John Fernandes responded.

"People tell me they wouldn't eat lobsters from the Sound," I said.

"People are scared of eating fish, and I don't blame them," Fernandes said. "But if we're going to be scared we have to be scared of everything — they put chemicals into the ground and they get up into the plants. I eat lobsters almost every day. It hasn't done anything to me yet."

I asked Salvadore Carlos, "Has anything this bad happened in the past?"

The last two years there have been a total of about six good weeks each year, he told me. "Last year was the first year I had a problem holding lobsters for a week or more. Some died on me. This year was a total loss."

Nearby, Joe Baglieri pulled lobsters out of a blue barrel, one by one, and stretched thick rubber bands over their claws. With his black beard, hook nose, and huge girth, he could be a pirate counting his loot. Loot, however, is hardly the word for his trove.

I asked him, "How did it go today?"

He said he hauled two hundred traps and caught twenty pounds of lobster. Last Monday was his best day of the season — three hundred traps, a pathetic seventy pounds.

"The traps come in full of mud, loaded with mud. It's like a slime, a real thick slime," Baglieri told me. "It's some mess. Lobster fishing stinks."

It is not cheerful talk. For someone like John Fernandes, who moved to the United States from Peniche, Portugal, and worked construction until he had saved enough money to buy a boat and take up the trade he had left behind, the hypoxia threatened to wrench him away from an area that had been productive enough to provide him with three decades of gainful employment. He was planning to head to Florida soon, he told me, to take up long-line fishing for tarpon, at least through the winter. No longer could he count on making his living from Long Island Sound. It was a sad and bitter truth, underscored by the irony that the spot John Fernandes had chosen almost thirty years before was one of the finest lobster grounds in the Northeast.

Long Island Sound marks the approximate midpoint of the American lobster's inshore-Newfoundland-to-offshore-North-Carolina geographic range. The Sound as a whole is a fertile lobster ground, but the waters of the western half are especially rich. Two researchers at the University of Connecticut, Lance Stewart and William Lund, Jr., discovered this fact during work they performed in the late 1960s. Dividing the Sound into three areas — western, middle, and eastern, each defined and dominated by large, gyre-like currents — they found that four to five times as many larval lobsters live at the surface of the middle and western sections as in the eastern Sound, or in comparable waters more commonly associated with lobsters, such as Block Island Sound and the Atlantic off Massachusetts. They found the most fecund waters to be near Northport, Eatons Neck, Mount Misery Shoal, and Stratford Shoal. In June and July, when populations peak, the surface of the Sound is crowded with billions of lobster larvae.[1]

The larval lobsters progress to adulthood through four stages and — along with creatures like lion's mane jellyfish, comb jellies, copepods, and the larvae of crabs and oysters — are part of the Sound's animal plankton. During the first three larval stages, lobsters are unable to swim and are at the mercy of the currents. In the eastern end, where on the surface the ebb tide is stronger than the flood, some are swept into the Atlantic through the Race. But the gyres in the middle and western sections hold together better, and a larval lobster that develops there will stay put. Many live bunched together in long plankton slicks formed by smaller currents, like galaxies of life in a slowly swirling universe.[2] For larval lobsters, this is heaven, and they feed voraciously throughout their fourth stage, when they look and swim like adult lobsters but are only an inch long.

The abundance of plankton is important to the larval lobsters in the Sound for a reason other than nutrition. In summer the organic matter grows so dense that sunlight fades away to blackness at fifty or sixty feet below the surface. This coincides with the descent of the small and vulnerable lobsters into deeper waters, where the darkness conceals them from predators. They grow quickly, molting up to ten times in their first year, and soon become the formidable crustaceans that most predators, save man, strive to avoid.[3]

The lobsters live the rest of their lives on the bottom, settling contentedly into almost any habitat — mud or sand or rocky areas with natural or man-made reefs such as sunken boats and barges, which are especially attractive to lobsters and a host of other animals. They feed on crabs — rock crabs are especially choice lobster food in the Sound — as well as marine worms and dead fish. Though lobsters will attack and eat other lobsters in captivity, such cannibalism is rare in the wild. Nor are lobsters prey to many other species — cod, black sea bass, striped bass, spiny dogfish, and blackfish are among the few species that can prevail against their armor.

Lobsters grow slowly after that first year of quick metamorphosis. To grow, lobsters — like crabs and other animals with hard exoskeletons — must slip out of their split shells, add weight and bulk, then form a new, roomier shell. They usually molt twice a year until they are ready to breed. Females must shed their shells again to mate, which in the Sound takes place in late spring and summer. After a year or more of carrying the sperm, the female extrudes fertilized eggs, and they become attached like berries to the underside of her shell. The next year, usually in June or July but sometimes as late as August, the eggs hatch.[4]

Outside the Sound, lobsters are as migratory as birds. In the Atlantic south of Long Island, for example, many lobsters head from inshore waters to the edge of the continental shelf in fall and then return to Long Island in spring and summer, a round-trip journey of perhaps one hundred and twenty miles. In the eastern Sound, up to 10 percent of the adult lobsters migrate through the Race to the edge of the shelf. But elsewhere in the Sound food is so plentiful there is no reason to leave, and biologists believe that the Sound's adult lobsters stay close to where they settle as larvae. In a tagging experiment off Eatons Neck, Phil Briggs of New York's Department of Environmental Conservation found that more than 90 percent of the tags returned to him were taken from lobsters caught near where he originally tagged them.[5]

Lobster fishermen in the western Sound treat the scientists' theories with scorn. They think lobsters reach the Sound by scuttling out of New York Harbor, up the East River and through Hell Gate and Throgs Neck, finally fanning out into the rocky waters off Great Neck and Manhasset, congregating around the islands and breakwaters off Westchester County. At least one biologist, Mark Blake of the Connecticut Department of Environmental Protection, hedged when I asked him about that theory. It's possible, he said. We don't really know.

Wherever it comes from, a Long Island Sound lobster needs at least five years for its carapace — the shell that covers its back — to grow to the legal size of three and one-quarter inches. By contrast, a lobster that has just grown to legal size in the Atlantic off Maine will be seven years old. Many of the Sound's lobsters begin breeding before they reach two and three-quarter inches long, and virtually all breed at least once before reaching legal size. In the Atlantic, only 6–12 percent of the population will have bred by then. The reason is water temperature. The Sound, which dips into the low thirties in winter, becomes a warm, nutrient-rich stew, almost eighty degrees, in summer — far warmer than the Atlantic ever gets, and a more congenial place for lobsters to grow. The Atlantic remains well-stocked with lobsters only because fishermen catch a smaller percentage of the population than they catch in the Sound.[6]

In the Sound, lobsters are almost like livestock being raised for slaughter. A lobsterman on the Sound can haul a trap crammed with up to twenty undersized lobsters for every keeper. These "shorts" have gorged themselves on the bait, and since the lobsterman must by law toss them back, he is, in effect, feeding lobsters now so they will be big enough to keep later. But unlike the Atlantic's lobsters, the Sound's animals have virtually no chance once they reach legal size. Ninety percent are caught within a year of becoming legal, an efficiency which biologists say is unheard of elsewhere and which makes it that much more critical for the lobsters to breed before they reach legal size.[7] For the lobstermen, the efficiency exacts a price: the typical Sound lobster weighs only a pound or a pound and a quarter. Among the rarer sights on the Sound is a lobster pot with a two- or a three-pounder inside.

Not all shorts get their freedom, of course. Some lobstermen hoard them in underwater cages and then sell them, hoping the innocent-looking fishermen watching this activity from a nearby boat are not undercover conservation police. Some fishermen also illegally keep egg-laden females, scraping off the "berries" with a wire brush that obliterates the evidence. Such infractions earn more than a slap on the wrist. One City Island man lost his license — and, essentially, his job — when he was caught selling undersized animals once too often. Another City Island fisherman who was nailed selling shorts was fined ten thousand dollars and had the fruits of his illegal labor confiscated and returned to the Sound via Mamaroneck Harbor. The cheating can be attributed to the competition. In 1980, commercial fishermen licensed by New York and Connecticut to work the Sound caught 1.4 million pounds of lobster. By 1983 the total shot up to 2.8 million pounds, and a year later it rose to 3 million pounds. But the catch from the 1980s was a pittance compared with what was to come in the 1990s. The average annual catch in 1996, '97, and '98 was 10.5 million pounds, with a peak of 11.6 million in 1997.

Generally, biologists are wary of attributing a higher catch to a higher population of lobsters, but, after analyzing the figures, Phil Briggs and others said they had no problem making that connection for the 1980s and 1990s. Explaining it is another matter. Still, it led to a real and easily explained increase in the commercial licenses New York and Connecticut issued. Until recently, the states provided a license to anyone who paid the fee (Connecticut, for example, charged $100 through most of the 1980s and increased the fee to $150 for the 1991 season). So as the catch rose, word of the abundance spread, and new fishermen got into the business: if so many lobsters were out there waiting to be caught, the thinking went, lobstering must be an easy way to make a living without the tyrannies of a boss or a nine-to-five schedule. In 1995, though, the states imposed a limit on the number of licenses they would issue. The federal government had earlier done the same with the commercial lobster licenses it issued for federally controlled ocean waters — those that are at least three miles from shore. The concern in New York and Connecticut was that the federally imposed limit might prompt lobstermen who were shut out of the offshore waters to move into Long Island Sound. So the two states decided in 1995 to close the fishery to everyone except those who had held a license at any time from 1980 through 1995. In 1999, 941 licenses were issued to lobstermen who worked the Sound — 419 in Connecticut and 522 in New York. Of these totals, a handful are issued to fishermen who work trawlers and catch lobsters incidentally; others are issued to people who buy them but hardly ever use them; and about three-quarters are issued to fishermen who make the bulk of their living catching lobsters.

How much money those lobstermen make is another question. More than one knowledgeable non-fisherman has told me that the full-time commercial lobstermen make good money — not that anybody is willing to quantify what they mean by "good money." Those who aren't lobstermen don't really know; those who are cry poverty. The truth probably is that they make good money but that they work hard for it. At a dockside rate of $3.40 a pound, which was the average in New York in 1987, the 1.3 million pounds caught in the state were worth $4.4 million. One man hauling five hundred pounds in a week would gross $1,700. By 1998, however, the dockside rate had actually fallen to $3.26, so that same five hundred pounds would gross just $1,630. And over those same eleven years, the cost of diesel fuel doubled. So a lobsterman who wanted to increase his take-home pay over those years had to work considerably harder.

Of course, for several weeks in the middle of the summer of 1987, working harder on the western end of the Sound accomplished little.

On those hot and muggy days men like John Fernandes were working hard to catch what turned out to be dead lobsters. True, diminished expectations had already become part of the job. Fernandes told me that, as the years went by, his catch and his earnings had leveled off — at best — while the number of hours he fished had risen. But 1987 was different. The look on his face was that of a man who every day confronted the reality that the waters of Long Island Sound, roughly from Throgs Neck east to Bridgeport and south to Port Jefferson, might no longer be capable of providing him with a living. An area of about three hundred and fifty square miles was being transformed at the height of summer into a dead zone.

The relief was palpable among the researchers in 1987 as oxygen levels rose and fish returned in September. Although UConn's Donald Squires had said that the oxygen collapse was not "a Long Island Sound is dying kind of thing," and although Barbara Welsh had later agreed, few others had been willing to make such a confident assertion. Perhaps to prepare us for the worst, no matter how slim the possibility, many scientists had been saying that they were not sure whether the intricate mesh of organisms in the Sound had been unraveled permanently and disastrously by the collapse in oxygen levels. That had been a fear — remote but worrisome nonetheless. But measurements made on September 2 showed that the shallow water over Hempstead Sill held five milligrams of oxygen per liter; a week later deeper areas of the western Sound were similarly restored.

"We haven't seen that since the first week in July," Barbara Welsh told me. "Our divers saw the first fin fish that we've been observing in the Greenwich area. They were sort of heartened to see something swimming around out there."

The research trawler operated by the Connecticut Department of Environmental Protection — the vessel that in July and August had caught no fish — searched in early September for species that feed near the surface, where the water would be highest in oxygen. It pulled to deck typical surface feeders like bluefish and butterfish "in more or less normal numbers," according to Penny Howell, a fisheries biologist for the department. Then, in fifty feet of water, the trawler caught a range of fish that Howell said showed an "encouraging diversity" — fluke, squid, weakfish, windowpane flounder, hogchoker, winter flounder,

Fishing for Eels
Karen Chytalo, a biologist with the New York State Department of
Environmental Conservation, fishes for eels near a marsh on Long Island's
north shore. She was collecting eels to be tested for hazardous substances such
as PCBs and heavy metals. The work was part of a number of coordinated
studies that New York, Connecticut, the U.S. Environmental Protection
Agency, and several other agencies and universities were conducting
simultaneously. Courtesy of Save the Sound.

scup, smooth dogfish, mackerel, horseshoe crab, lobster, and saurel.
The hypoxia of 1987 had ended. Cooler, stormier weather lay ahead,
and dissolved oxygen would continue to rise into winter. Still, there
was certainly no guarantee that it would not return in 1988. It was naive
to think it wouldn't. The summer of 1988, in fact, started out primed
for disaster. The heat and the still, muggy days that are prerequisites
for hypoxia were abundant. Welsh spent the bulk of these glaringly
hot days on a small boat, making measurements, watching, waiting.

"It's hot and flat out there," she told me. "It's *really* hot and flat."

I caught up with her one sweltering evening, in the parking lot of
a hotel in Stamford, shortly after she had come in off the water. She
was about to return to her home in Waterford, Connecticut. Sitting in

a pickup truck with the door open, she looked exhausted. She reviewed the previous weeks for me, sounding at times hopeful, at other times worried. There had been an algal bloom in late June, but it had triggered no crisis because the waters still had plenty of dissolved oxygen. The bloom knocked concentrations barely below five parts per million, which was close to the normal summertime range. In early July, Welsh had submerged a remote-controlled vessel with a video camera into the waters around Execution Rocks and saw sand lances, flounder, lobster, anemones: "a lot of life on the bottom." She had been encouraged on the fourteenth of July because the waters off Port Chester still showed no signs of acute distress. But then, later in the month, a sheen of reddish-brown algae began to spread between Nassau County and Westchester County. It was a year and a week after the disastrous bloom of 1987. It grew as rapidly, and then died and disappeared as rapidly. And when it was gone, oxygen levels dropped with it. Although they fell below three parts per million, they never got as low as in 1987. By now, she told me that evening, everything west of New Haven was in the middle of a "general hypoxia," with dissolved oxygen levels ranging from one and a half to three milligrams per liter. The lowest readings were over Hempstead Sill, where her instruments recorded less than one milligram per liter.

I asked her why the Sound this year had seemed to escape the fish and lobster kills of 1987. She reminded me that in 1987 the anoxia had moved up and out of the Sound's deep center trough to connect with oxygen-depleted waters in the harbors and bays, leaving fish with nowhere to flee. So far in 1988, she said, that link had not happened. Mobile animals still had an avenue of escape. Another crucial difference, she said, was that when the cloud of algae began growing in 1988, oxygen concentrations were higher by about one milligram per liter than they had been when the 1987 bloom spread over the western Sound. And so when the 1988 bloom collapsed, dragging oxygen levels down with it, oxygen bottomed out at approximately one milligram per liter higher than it had in 1987. That was enough to keep the hypoxia from intensifying into anoxia.

"That's a very fine line," Welsh said. "Because when the oxygen gets down so low that it gets too close to zero, what happens is the hydrogen sulfide coming out of the sediments takes over and uses up the rest of that oxygen. And then we get hydrogen sulfide up in the water column, and hydrogen sulfide is a natural product of decomposition, and it's toxic. So you go from a condition of simply depriving animals of oxygen, something they need to breathe, to actually being toxic — [and] lethal — very, very quickly." That change, from a condition that forced fish to flee from the area but also gave them time to flee, to a condition that poisoned them, was what turned the Sound in 1987 from merely being uninhabitable to being deadly. She also reminded me of 1987's sewage spills, first a large breakdown at a treatment plant on Hempstead Harbor, and then smaller spills in Larchmont and Mamaroneck. Perhaps, she said, the Sound in 1988 was beneficiary of dumb luck. There were no sewage spills, so the line between a stressed environment and an environmental disaster was never crossed. Or perhaps, she speculated, the outrage and worry of 1987 — the headlines and broadcast reports and talk that the Sound was dying — had struck the people who run the sewage treatment plants with a greater sense of responsibility. Perhaps they thought twice before opening the bypass valves to let raw sewage thunder into the Sound's waters.

All this was small comfort. The Sound in 1988 had dodged a repeat of 1987 by a difference of one milligram of oxygen per liter. And as anyone who lived near the Sound knew, a summer in which there were no sewage spills was an aberration. Welsh had been trying to show me that conditions in 1988 were cause for optimism, albeit extremely cautious optimism. But she could not hide her concern about the uncertainty that faced the Sound. For one thing, although there had been no reports of dead fish or lobsters, she was not at all sure that the decimation was not soon to arrive. And although it never did, Welsh was adamant that dissolved oxygen levels of one milligram per liter were no cause for glee.

"Our margin of safety," she said, "was ever so slim."

However narrow the margin, the Sound's lobstermen were unaware of it. In 1988 lobsters were abundant, and the lobstermen were gleeful in their good fortune. They reported excellent fishing, and I had never seen them happier. To their way of thinking, if the catch was high, the Sound must be healthy. It mattered little — if they even were aware — that biologists were suggesting that a good lobster catch might be a sign that the animals had been driven out of hypoxic areas and into oxygen-rich pockets where fishermen could home in on them. Lobsters were abundant, and as long as they were abundant the lobstermen were not interested in hearing that their big catch might be a symptom of a major problem. Abel Miguel, who docked in Rye, and John Fernandes, Salvadore Carlos, and Joe Baglieri, all from Port Chester, reported doing well in 1988, and several said they had had more success than in any year since the early 1980s.

Miguel told me that he and his two mates fished a thousand traps, pulling a third of them each day. The traps yielded up to twenty-five shorts each and averaged four legal-sized lobsters — eight thousand keepers in a six-day workweek. With the supply that high, the cost would be far below the average of $3.31 a pound. But even if he was selling lobsters for $2.50 a pound, and if each of his lobsters weighed only a pound, he was still grossing $20,000 a week. As we talked, Miguel loaded crates of bait onto his boat — the remainder of filleted flounder, un-iced and peppered with flies. He grinned, the ripeness of the fish notwithstanding, and it was no wonder: "There's not too many years like this," he said.[8]

Fernandes also had a good summer, although, working alone, he could not match Miguel and his crew. When I tracked him down at the dock near his boat on the Byram River, he remembered our conversations from the previous year and spoke before I could ask a question: "I haven't seen one dead lobster yet." Fernandes was smiling. He climbed into his boat and took two 7-Ups from a cooler, offering one to me. He said he started lobstering in May, having spent the winter, as he had planned, long-line fishing in Florida. "I was in touch with lobstermen here and they were not catching anything in the spring at all," he said — at least nothing big enough to keep. But luck changed in summer and so Fernandes returned north. He fished three hundred traps, one hundred fewer than in 1987. Pulling them every three days, he averaged a pound per trap during a five- or six-week run that peaked in the middle of July.

"It has been a year of good production also," he said. "There are so many lobsters out there that we throw out because they're not legal. That's a good sign. It means the lobsters didn't die."

Fernandes was finishing his last chores of the day. He knelt on the dock and hauled a basket loaded with lobsters out of the Byram. Upriver, just beyond a bend, a sewage treatment plant was releasing about four million gallons of rudimentarily treated wastewater a day. The effluent had turned the Byram into a virtually lifeless sinkhole. The water from which Fernandes hauled his holding pen was a weird opaque green. He had been storing his lobsters there for several days. One by one he dropped them into a plastic bin until it was filled to the brim with writhing lobsters, eighty pounds worth. That they could even survive in the Byram proved to Fernandes that the Sound must be healthy. "You see how lively these things are? And the water here is not the best water." (Westchester County converted the Port Chester plant to a secondary-level facility in 1989, seventeen years after the Clean Water Act mandated secondary treatment.)

He took a couple of sheets of a Portuguese-language newspaper, dipped them in the river, and laid them over the bin. He filled another bin and covered it. Then he looped a rope through the handle of one and dragged it along the dock and up the ramp to his van. Then the other. He was on his way to Fulton Market, where he would sell them for $2.70 a pound — $432 worth of lobsters. He said he had gotten a better rate in the past but only when he was catching fewer lobsters. He climbed into the van no longer the sullen, worried man of the summer of 1987: "This year was a pleasure to work. When you go out and pull the traps and see dead lobsters, it breaks your heart. You lose your appetite to work. But this year was wonderful. This year I'll have a profit."

John Fernandes and Abel Miguel were catching lobsters, and so to them everything was fine. Barbara Welsh was finding dissolved oxygen readings well below the hypoxia threshold but had uncovered no evidence of fish kills, and so 1988 was bad but not as bad as 1987. It was not until several months later that Penny Howell of the Connecticut Department of Environmental Protection added another important piece of research and offered an interpretation of what actually had gone on in July and August of 1988. Howell tallied and analyzed the results of the fish trawls made by the department's Bureau of Marine Fisheries over the previous three summers. She compared the number of fish caught by the trawler in 1986 — before the hypoxia — with the catch in 1987 and in 1988; and she compared catches at Hempstead Sill with catches off New Haven, where oxygen concentrations were two or three milligrams per liter higher. The differences were pronounced and disturbing. The vessel averaged thirty trawls a year in each location, from April through November. Off New Haven the average catch per trawl, from 1986 through 1988, went from 422 fish to 341 to 533; off Hempstead, the average catch went from 345 fish to 151 to 197. So in the central Sound, under hypoxia's onslaught, the catch dropped 19 percent initially, but overall it rose more than 25 percent over the three-year period. But in the western basin, it suffered a first-year drop of 56 percent before settling at a 43 percent decrease overall. In short, the waters over Hempstead Sill were supporting marine life in far lower numbers than off New Haven. The fish population in the western basin was more than two and a half times smaller.

When pieced together with Howell's data, the lobstermen's tales of record catches became not a cause for delight but, perhaps, evidence of the herding phenomenon, bliss before disaster; and Welsh's observation that hypoxic water in the Sound's center trough had not linked up with hypoxic water in the harbors and bays became a reason merely for the absence of any fish kills. Howell's data clarified the meaning of what the lobstermen had experienced and Welsh had measured: hypoxia had turned a rich, vibrant habitat into an area that was at times almost devoid of marine life. In 1988, scientists saw with disturbing starkness that the Sound could be seriously, unmistakably polluted and yet manage to pass through the summer without the drama of a major fish kill. And they were to witness it again the following year.

July and August 1989 were, if anything, as bad as 1987. Hypoxia was spreading; in 1987, fifty square miles of the Sound had measurements of less than one milligram of oxygen per liter, while in 1989 there were fifty-one square miles. But in 1989 the portion of the Sound that had less than three milligrams of oxygen per liter had expanded eastward. In 1987, the waters from Throgs Neck to Bridgeport–Port Jefferson, an area of three hundred and fifty square miles, were below three milligrams per liter; in 1989, hypoxia gripped the Sound as far east as New Haven–Shoreham, an area encompassing five hundred and seventeen square miles.

Penny Howell, her colleague Dave Simpson, and their Connecticut Department of Environmental Protection research crew concentrated on hypoxia's effect on specific habitats. Sharpening their focus to the time of the worst hypoxia, they made four twenty-minute tows over Hempstead Sill, in water forty feet deep. Their net yielded dead lady crabs and dead spider crabs, twenty-eight live lobsters, most of which were very small, and a number of live mud worms. As for flounders, blackfish, hogchokers, fluke, mackerel, and other fish, the haul yielded none: "*Literally* none," Howell said. In one trawl they pulled in two adult bluefish and about twenty snappers: all died as the net was being lugged on board.

"That doesn't normally happen," Simpson said. "The stress of being caught in low-oxygenated water killed them."

From July through September the net again and again came up virtually empty. In the oxygen-rich waters to the east, each tow yielded an average of four hundred fish. But farther west, where the water contained less than one milligram of oxygen per liter, each tow hauled in just two or three fish — .006 percent of the catch from the healthier waters of the eastern Sound. Dissolved oxygen readings of around one milligram per liter were measured through September 12; even in 1987, concentrations had shot up to five milligrams per liter by September 2. These were startling numbers. The fish kills of 1987 were comparatively ephemeral.

"Marine systems aren't supposed to be voids," Howell said. "There's supposed to be something there."

Autumn is the time of year when many fish are migrating south as northern waters turn colder, feeding in the rich coastal areas as they go. An area with an insufficient supply of oxygen will block them like a brick wall — as the western Sound apparently had through September. Not until October, when four tows yielded about ten thousand fish, did life return. As Simpson explained, "When oxygen is put back into the system, the fish come right in." At my urging, Howell and Simpson offered several speculative explanations of what the research meant. They are scientists given to conservative interpretations of data collected painstakingly — especially when the state of Connecticut is underwriting the research — but the information they had at hand, while not constituting indisputable truth, was still too provocative to ignore.

"I don't believe that large numbers of fish are being killed outright by hypoxia," Simpson told me. "Most do have a chance to escape. Every summer's a little different; if hypoxia comes on quickly and moves right to the shore [as it did it 1987], they're not going to escape. But an impact on a population level that we could measure, I don't expect to see that. It's the loss of habitat for some period — six weeks to ten or more weeks every year, and the larger the area that's impacted the worse things are going to be."

Howell said that the waters east of New Haven might be harboring significantly higher numbers of fish because the area had become a refuge for animals escaping the polluted waters to the west. Or, she said, the central basin might have become a kind of holding basin for fish whose normal migration was blocked by the barrier of hypoxic water. Hypoxia might have been forcing the central Sound to support not only the fish that should have been there but also those that should have been farther west. To take it a step further, hypoxia not only was making the western Sound uninhabitable, it also might be dangerously intensifying competition among fish in the central basin for limited food and living space.

"Removing habitat for a couple of very important months a year . . . does have that impact — it removes grazing area," Simpson said. "That range land isn't available to feed, and so they have to go somewhere else and, in Long Island Sound, concentrate more feeding activity in a limited area."

As Joel O'Connor, an EPA biologist in New York who has studied the effect of hypoxia on fish for the agency, explained, "The concern is, if it occurs regularly it could at least impair habitat in that it changes the communities of the benthic organisms that they depend on for food.

"The effect of hypoxia pretty much has to be reinforced pretty regularly, and the long-term effects result from continued low dissolved oxygen. If you relieve the stress this year it would not take many years to recover. But of course we're not going to relieve the stress this year."

If fewer fish than normal were hanging around off Nassau, Fairfield, and Westchester counties in 1989, that might also have explained why, despite the severely stressed waters, the only reported fish kill in the western Sound was a small one near Hempstead Harbor in the middle of July. One hundred fish, crabs, and lobsters, encompassing eighteen species, were wiped out. Dissolved oxygen measured 0.8 parts per million.

"Whoever happened to be in the water right then got knocked

right out," said Karen Chytalo, a biologist for the New York State Department of Environmental Conservation. The death toll probably was limited to one hundred fish, Howell said, because only one hundred fish were in the vicinity.

"It's another year where all the animals have left the area," Howell said. "'87 turns out not to be once in a lifetime."

One morning in August 1989 I met Howell at Greenwich Point Park, where she and two colleagues were seining as part of a survey that would locate important spawning areas for winter flounder. Howell also was hoping the work might yield information about how juvenile flounder were holding up under hypoxia. The winter flounder, unlike most fish, lives year-round in the Sound and so is considered a potentially good indicator of problems. "They're sitting ducks," Howell said. If their systems are stressed because they live in areas where oxygen levels routinely plunge, or if they are forced to expend more energy than usual to find food, their growth and, ultimately, their ability to survive might be hindered.

It was typical August on the Sound — hot, no hint of a breeze, hazy. The almost-flat waves murmured rather than crashed. Tufts of cordgrass poked up along the shore. I had taken off my shoes and rolled my pants up to mid-calf so I could stand in the water. Penny and I watched as the others lugged the net out of the water and picked through its contents on the wet sand. It was the sixth tow of the morning. The haul yielded little that differed from the previous five.

"Looks like you got a bunch of nothing in this one, too," Howell said.

About one hundred and fifty silversides were writhing in the net. But there were no flounder. An area that in 1988 had averaged nine young flounder per haul on this day averaged barely more than one — by morning's end, eight flounder in seven tows. When they caught one, Howell would scoop it up, measure it, and drop it back in the shallow water. The olive-drab fish was the precise color of the wet sand, and when it was submerged it would lie flat on the bottom and let the sand quickly cover it until it vanished. There was, of course, no way of knowing for sure if hypoxia had caused the drop-off in the number of flounder. Yet we knew that the waters off Greenwich were among those with the lowest oxygen readings anywhere. We knew the

Seining for Flounder
Two researchers from the Connecticut Department of Environmental
Protection — Eleanor Mariani and Charlie Thompson — haul a beach seine
to shore in Greenwich in August of 1989, as part of a survey of young winter
flounder. Seven tows yielded just eight juvenile winter flounder in an area that
a year earlier had averaged nine per haul. Courtesy of *The Journal News.*

trawler had been catching nothing. We knew there were virtually no
flounder today. We knew that the Sound was in the grip of a problem
that seemed to be choking it to death.

I asked Howell about the future.

"That's probably the hardest thing about dealing with the hypoxia," she said. "We know it's bad because the fish don't live in it. But
we don't know what else it does to them." She paused. The beach
looked southwest toward Hempstead Sill and Long Island, invisible
in the summer haze. "One thing we can guarantee," she continued, "if
the Sound continues to have dissolved oxygen levels below one part
per million, maybe even two parts, [it] will have no fish. They just
can't survive."

By 1989, Barbara Welsh had moved from the research vessel to the
laboratory. The responsibility for the long hours and painstaking
cruises necessary to get accurate, useful readings of dissolved oxygen,
temperature, and salinity now fell to researchers from the State University of New York at Stony Brook and the Connecticut Department of
Environmental Protection. Freed from the job of measuring "what,"

Welsh had taken on the task of figuring out "how" — making sense of her data and observations, many of which did not fit within her comprehension of how estuaries, even those under severe stress from pollution, were supposed to work. At the core of that knowledge, expressed back in 1985 at the time of the Estuary-of-the-Month seminar in Washington, D.C., was the notion that drastically low levels of oxygen were a phenomenon of the bottom waters: hypoxia, it was thought, was triggered in the sediments, was limited to the two or three feet of bottom water that were close enough to the sediments to be affected by them, and would grow gradually less severe farther from the bottom.

That was generally how hypoxia worked in Chesapeake Bay and Mobile Bay, for example. Both bays are essentially river beds and river valleys flooded by the sea. In each, a narrow central channel — the beds of the Susquehanna River and Mobile River, respectively, which were drowned when sea level rose with the melting of the last ice sheet — forms a deep spine flanked by broad shoals. Both estuaries run north–south and are fed from the north by rivers that pour prodigious amounts of freshwater on top of the salty water that creeps in from the sea. Like Long Island Sound in summer, both bays stratify — they physically divide into two horizontal layers. In the bays, the stratification is caused by differences in the saltiness of the water.[9]

In Mobile Bay, the bottom layer may have ten parts of salt per thousand more than the top layer — a significant difference considering that even the undiluted salt water of the ocean contains only thirty to thirty-five parts of salt per thousand. The stratification is strong, but it is regularly broken down by natural phenomena, and the hypoxia breaks down with it. In the more southerly reaches of Chesapeake Bay, and in the bay's York River sub-estuary, tides push so much salt water in from the sea that the layering dissolves. In Mobile Bay, heavy rains flood the estuary, overwhelming the fresh-on-salt layering. Both bays are shallow enough in places to allow winds to stir in oxygen from top to bottom. In Mobile Bay, as in Pamlico and Albemarle sounds off the Carolinas, hypoxia occurs in patches and the estuary is so shallow that the wind actually blows the hypoxia around, refreshing one part of the bay while stressing another. Although Chesapeake Bay has deep areas where the hypoxia is more persistent, in general in Chesapeake and

Mobile bays, and Albemarle and Pamlico sounds, the severe, choking drop in dissolved oxygen happens near the bottom and is set off by the sediments.[10]

Barbara Welsh was familiar with those conditions and had been taught by experience to look for them. But Long Island Sound showed something different. Most prominently, the lowest oxygen readings were not in the bottom waters at all. For instance, near Execution Rocks, as the thick curtain of algae strangled the western end of the Sound in 1987, Welsh recorded less than 1 milligram of oxygen per liter at a depth of twenty-eight feet. As she measured progressively deeper, oxygen concentrations stayed the same. Not until her probe reached nearly to the bottom, in almost one hundred feet of water, did the readings change, nudging slightly higher, to about 1 milligram per liter. At the same time, off Greenwich, Welsh found the lowest oxygen reading — about 1.5 milligrams per liter — in twenty-eight feet of water; but at thirty feet, concentrations shot up to 3 milligrams per liter and stayed that high down to the bottom, a depth of sixty-six feet. Clearly, the fuse igniting the hypoxia did not lie in the sediments.[11]

Another important difference between Long Island Sound and the other estuaries was in the way the Sound stratified. Stratification was one of the keys to hypoxia — while nitrogen was continually being poured in at the surface, fertilizing the oxygen-depleting algae, the stratification stopped oxygen from being mixed down into the water from the surface layer. Welsh's data showed that, unlike Chesapeake Bay or Mobile Bay, differences in salinity from top to bottom were not the key to stratification in the Sound. The bottom waters, in fact, were only slightly saltier than the top waters.[12]

"We're the weakest stratified, which is why I started asking these questions about these other bays, because we shouldn't have this problem," Welsh explained. "It's because these bays have much more fresh water inflow than we do." Only in the eastern end of the Sound, where the Connecticut River gushes out eighty-four thousand gallons a second, is the infusion of freshwater large enough to set up that typical fresh–salt stratification. But while the difference in salinity is tiny, Welsh saw, the difference in temperature was great. The surface waters of the Sound, in fact, were as much as eight degrees Celsius warmer than the bottom waters.[13]

The place in an estuary's water column where the salinity changes is called the pycnocline. It is the barrier between the two layers, separating the lighter, fresher water on top from the denser, saltier water on the bottom. The greater the difference in salinity between top and bottom, the stronger the stratification and the stronger the barrier formed by the pycnocline. But in the Sound the pycnocline is weak because the bottom waters are not much saltier than the top. It is so weak, in fact, that Welsh thought it should not be capable of barring oxygen from mixing into the bottom layer, yet oxygen obviously was not breaching that barrier.[14] Welsh remembered that her lowest oxygen readings came not at the bottom but rather right below the pycnocline. Other measurements showed that the amount of biological activity in this same region of the water was high—although the water was murky, just enough light was seeping down to spur the growth of tiny plants and bacteria. It was here, as these microscopic organisms died and decomposed, that oxygen was being removed from the Sound. The bottom sediments had little to do with it, which is why oxygen concentrations near the bottom were often slightly higher than they were just below the pycnocline, and why hypoxia did not gradually fade toward the surface.

This meant that although the Sound was physically broken up into two layers, biologically it had three. The top biological layer was where oxygen mixed in through the surface. Here abundant sunlight streamed through the water, feeding plants and animals with ample energy to thrive in enormous numbers. The middle layer was just below the pycnocline, where the light began to fade but still penetrated well enough to spur the plant growth that led to the water column's highest rate of oxygen removal. And the third layer, which held the greatest volume of water, extended to the bottom, a dark region where few plants could grow. Yet because this region was so large, the amount of oxygen removed from the water there was also large, even though biological activity was nowhere near as furious as in the middle layer.[15] Having seen all this through her measurements, Welsh thought back to another obvious difference between the Sound and Chesapeake and Mobile bays. The bays were formed by narrow, deep river beds and their shallow valleys. The Sound was starkly different.

"We go virtually shore to shore with a deep, U-shaped valley," Welsh explained. "We're very, very different in shape. We have two sills that we acknowledge — the Hempstead Sill and the Mattituck Sill — but in fact, as you go from the western end to the eastern end, we're a deep, U-shaped, glacially carved valley, from side to side. It takes a little while for stuff to get down through here and it can be intercepted in the water column and used." Which is precisely what was happening. In Chesapeake and Mobile bays, the sediments were the fuse that set off the oxygen depletion, because the sediments, in relationship to the volume of water, occupied more of the estuary. In the Sound, the sediments played a smaller role than the water itself.

The significance of Welsh's findings was that in Mobile Bay, in Pamlico and Albemarle sounds, and in the shallower areas of Chesapeake Bay, hypoxia comes and goes. The wind, the rain, the tides wipe it out as infusions of water break down the difference in salinity. In Long Island Sound, salinity is far less important. Temperature, the shape of the Sound's basin, and the large volume of water below the pycnocline are the crucial characteristics. And together they form a system that, when 51,300 tons of additional nitrogen are mixed in, is prone to begin early in summer, lead to severe oxygen losses, and last almost until fall. And the only reason the annual crashes have not been more devastating is that Long Island Sound — what Welsh calls "this nice, deep arm of the sea" — started with strength that has been far greater than anything we've been able to pile on top of it. "What the Sound has done — what this robust and marvelous system has done — is save us from our own sins," Welsh said. "The Chesapeake Bay has not been so saved. But we can't continue to clobber [the Sound] like this."

There is no telling how the Long Island Sound Study would have progressed had the crisis not revealed itself in 1987, '88, and '89. What is indisputable is that those three summers concentrated attention and interest on the Sound as never before. Research became urgent. Politicians seized the issue. Citizens became involved not merely as shrill advocates but as participants in debates about sewage treatment technology and limits on growth and development — debates that grew hotter as the understanding of the Sound's crisis and the magnitude of the solutions grew deeper. The goals of the study changed. Hypoxia remained paramount. The fate of the Sound's fish and wildlife was deemed to be equally important. Toxic contamination was found to be far less critical than hypoxia and was relegated to a second rank of concerns, along with the bacterial contamination that keeps beaches and shellfish beds closed, and floating debris, which is more a litter problem than a pollution problem.

The study generated a variety of emotions, but it was also an impressive and heartening attempt to learn and then convey, without flinching, the seriousness of the problem and the ecological cost of ignoring it. The Sound study itself told it as straight as possible in two reports released in 1990. One report, an interim summary of the dissolved oxygen research, said that if the population around the Sound increased by as little as 5 percent, hypoxia would no longer be limited to just the western third of the Sound. Fully half the estuary would suffer disabling hypoxia every year. And, it warned, although there was no way to predict the ecological consequences of that expansion, the connections among the parts of the ecosystem were so sensitive that the destruction of plants and animals might easily be disproportionate to the spread of hypoxia.[16] The other document, the Sound study's annual report, was equally bleak: "If the nitrogen load to the Sound increases substantially in the future, summertime dissolved oxygen at the western Narrows could be reduced to nearly zero, representing total anoxia and the severest possible conditions for living marine resources."[17] Those assessments catapulted the Sound study into action and resulted in accomplishments that led finally to more emotion — euphoria when the cleanup of the Sound at last started, tempered by a deeper commitment to finish the truly difficult work that lay ahead.

TEN

Sewage

It was obvious from the earliest days of the Long Island Sound Study that if the Sound was going to be restored, sewage treatment plants would have to be improved. Other sources of nitrogen would have to be reduced as well, of course. Combined sewers, which carry both storm water and sewage and are designed to discharge untreated waste into the Sound during a heavy rainstorm, would have to be eliminated. Acid rain would have to be curtailed. Land-use controls would have to be imposed to manage development, storm water, and the use of nitrogen fertilizers. But those were relatively small parts of the problem. Any plan to ease the burden of nitrogen choking the Sound would have to be founded on treatment plant improvements. Indeed, an undercurrent of the Sound study was that the government officials who were guiding it would need as much hard data as possible from scientists to justify the expense of renovating sewage plants. And that expense might be considerable: in the spring of 1988 Robert Smith, chief of the bureau of water management for the Connecticut Department of Environmental Protection, testified before Congress that nitrogen removal might cost more than six billion dollars.

Throughout the twentieth century, whenever sewage-clogged streams and bays became intolerable, communities along the Sound looked to technology to save them (alternatives to waterways for sewers were never considered). But the pollution control technologies they chose were too inadequate, too limited, or too poorly maintained. Starting in 1927, Westchester County, for example, installed sewers throughout the towns and villages in the watersheds of two of the Sound's smaller tributaries—Blind Brook, which drains into Milton Harbor, in Rye, and the Mamaroneck River, which empties into Mamaroneck Harbor. The sewers carried almost eleven million gallons of wastewater a day to facilities, in Rye and Mamaroneck, that employed a method barely one step higher on the treatment scale than simply piping raw sewage into the Sound: the sewage flowed through a screen that filtered out particles bigger than a quarter of an inch in diameter, and then chlorine gas was injected into the wastewater to kill pathogens.[1] This rudimentary treatment method no doubt improved Blind Brook and the Mamaroneck River, but it was far from leading edge technology. By choosing it, county officials were simply transferring the problem to Long Island Sound. That problem — low levels of dissolved oxygen — might not have been apparent yet off Rye and Mamaroneck, but it would soon grow into a nuisance elsewhere, and two cities — Norwalk and New York — would try to do something about it.

In 1931, Norwalk built a treatment plant that was a notch better than the two Westchester County facilities, a simple plant that relied on gravity. The new facility incorporated large tanks, not just pipes and screens. As wastewater roared from the main sewer into the tanks, traveling as fast as two feet per second, it slowed to a much calmer rate of six inches per second, thereby allowing gravity to do its work. As the water flow dropped to a placid swirl through the tanks many of the particles of solid material that had been carried along in the swift water settled to the bottom — similar to a mountain brook splashing over a rock into a deep pool — "Nothing more than a glass of water with sand in it," as one sewage treatment engineer described it. The remaining wastewater, ranging in color from soapy to dark gray, was disinfected with chlorine and allowed to pour into Norwalk Harbor. The solid particles — the sludge — that built up on the tank bottom were removed and burned. Using this simple, physical process, 30 percent of the organic material in raw sewage was rendered harmless — material that, if it were dumped into Norwalk Harbor or the Sound, would have sucked oxygen out of the water as it decomposed.

In the same year that Norwalk's plant began operation, New York City started to build an enormous facility on Ward's Island, at Hell Gate, to treat sewage from Manhattan and the Bronx. Water pollution generally, and dissolved oxygen in particular, were far worse in the narrows separating Manhattan, Queens, and the Bronx than just about anywhere farther east on the Sound. The Metropolitan Sewerage Commission had recommended that a treatment plant be built on Wards Island as far back as 1914. In 1937, dissolved oxygen bottomed out at less than one milligram per liter near Riker's Island and in Flushing Bay. When the Ward's Island plant finally came on line in 1937, it tried to attack the problem by employing Norwalk's treatment process and then adding another step — a method called activated sludge, or secondary treatment.[2] The activated sludge method uses the same screening, chlorination, and sedimentation process as primary treatment; then, when the wastewater emerges from the settling tank, it flows into another tank, into which some of the organic sludge that had settled to the bottom of the primary treatment tank is injected. Air is then pumped into the whole mixture. The air allows a host of micro-organisms to reproduce and feed on any organic particles that have not already settled out of the wastewater. If the process is carefully regulated, it removes more than 80 percent of that organic material, a vast improvement over primary treatment.

At Ward's Island, workers opened the floodgates from the sewer lines on October 16, 1937. Wastewater flowing at a rate of sixty million gallons a day rushed into the plant and through its screens, languished in its tanks, and then poured out into the western end of the Sound. With Ward's Island on line, ninety-two million gallons of sewage from New York's Sound shore communities were being treated at some level—screening in Westchester County, primary sedimentation at Port Jefferson, Glen Cove, and elsewhere on Long Island, activated sludge at Ward's Island. Yet New York State was also contributing another eighty-one million gallons of raw sewage to the Sound every day—and would continue to do so for years.[3] An aerial photograph taken in 1947 shows a clearly delineated barrier: clean, tide-driven water that had originated further east in the Sound is pushing grossly polluted water down the East River between Manhattan and Queens.

More plants would be built in the years before World War II—the Works Progress Administration was responsible for public works projects, including sewage facilities, throughout the country. By the 1980s, eighty-six treatment plants were emptying 1.047 billion gallons a day into the Sound or its immediate tributaries. They employed an impressive range of technologies—activated sludge, trickling filters, sand filters, rotating biological contactors, extended aeration. But as impressive as they were in theory, in practice they were allowing the Sound to sink slowly toward ecological catastrophe. For one thing, older cities, like New York, Norwalk, Bridgeport, and New Haven, were using combined sewer systems—pipes that collected not only household sewage but also rainwater washing off the streets and sidewalks. The systems were perfectly adequate in dry weather: anything that was washed into the sewers flowed into the plant for treatment. But wet weather proved a disaster. Sewage plants are vulnerable to flooding—the equipment gets ruined, the micro-organisms that per-

Raw Sewage
A grayish mass of raw sewage coated the East River near Hell Gate
on September 21, 1947. The tide pushed the pollution up toward
the Sound. Courtesy of the Interstate Environmental Commission.

form much of the treatment process get washed away, and it takes
weeks to grow them again. The combined systems were designed so
that any time it rained hard enough to double the normal dry-weather
flow, floodgates were shut. Instead of coursing together through the
treatment plant, rainwater and raw sewage would pour directly into
the Sound. While there has been much talk by regulators about shut-
ting them down, New York City and seven Connecticut communi-

ties — Shelton, Bridgeport, Derby, New Haven, Norwich, Norwalk, and Jewett City — still have combined sewer systems.

Another flaw was maintenance. Sewer lines laid in the 1920s and 1930s began to crumble as the decades passed, and the sewage they were supposed to carry simply leaked into the groundwater, which eventually flowed into the Sound. In Westchester County, sewers in the communities that feed the sewage treatment plant in Mamaroneck — White Plains, Scarsdale, Harrison, New Rochelle, Rye, and Mamaroneck — were so deteriorated by 1984 that every rainfall contaminated beaches on Mamaroneck Harbor. In New York City, an estimated 5 percent of all the city's sewage leaked from the sewers before it reached a treatment plant.

And although the United States, through the Clean Water Act of 1972, decreed that all sewage must be treated at least to the secondary level (the standard attainable through the activated sludge process, among others), as late as the mid-1980s four treatment plants were still using a gravity-powered primary sedimentation method that was little better than the one installed at Norwalk fifty years before: New Haven (twelve million gallons a day), Port Jefferson (eleven million gallons a day), and Westchester County facilities at Port Chester (six million gallons a day) and Mamaroneck (eighteen million gallons a day). In the 1980s, Westchester actually asked EPA to absolve it of responsibility to provide secondary treatment at its Mamaroneck plant (EPA said no). New York State's annoyance at Westchester's delays prompted it to take the county to court, to force it to obey the law. Port Chester became a secondary plant in 1989, but Mamaroneck continued operating at the primary level until 1993. Thus did Westchester County follow its precedent, set in 1912 on the Bronx River, of doing the least possible to solve water pollution problems.

Westchester County's attitudes and actions were hardly the exception. Communities throughout the Sound's watershed historically did as little as possible to protect local waterways, with virtually no acknowledgment that the solutions they were relying on might damage a neighboring waterway. The Long Island Sound Study was an attempt to break from that history by gaining a deeper knowledge of the Sound's ecology and how it was suffering, and by reacting cohesively to the damage with solutions that recognized the Sound's existence almost as a living organism. Those solutions would have to advance beyond removing nitrogen at sewage plants, but they would amount to little if nitrogen removal failed.

Ridding sewage of nitrogen would not be easy. Nitrogen removal had many prerequisites, chief among them a dedication by the engineers and technicians who would have to run increasingly sophisticated treatment systems. It was hardly news that not everyone employed in a sewage plant was a selfless servant of ecological needs. Barbara Welsh had said as much in 1988, when she suggested that the mass fish mortality of the previous year was perhaps prevented by public pressure resulting in a newfound diligence among treatment plant operators. Yet even a sincere desire to protect the Sound would be inadequate if it were not accompanied by a higher level of skill. "The days of somebody's pal getting a job in the sewage treatment plant are going to be in the past," said Joseph Lauria, vice president at Malcolm Pirnie Inc., a consulting firm that redesigned and rebuilt Norwalk's plant.

The technology necessary to save the Sound demanded qualifications stronger than political connections or blood relations. It demanded smart, dedicated public servants committed to improving sewage treatment methods, people who would be willing to tinker with the process and, if necessary, to make mistakes (and who would be forgiven those mistakes if they were committed in a sincere effort to improve through innovation). Because mistakes at a sewage plant often meant enveloping the neighborhood in foul odors, new efforts demanded the support of the community. In Stamford, Mayor Thom Serrani encouraged new experiments, and the person who carried them out was Jeannette Semon, who ran Stamford's treatment plant. As Joseph Lauria said with obvious admiration, "Jeannette is a very innovative lady."

Stamford's sewage plant sits behind a brick wall, between a dead-end inlet called the East Branch and the road that leads to Shippan Point, where Sound-front property may be as valuable as anywhere in Connecticut. The plant's neighborhood is industrial. There are oil tanks, a railroad siding, and a sand-and-gravel company at which a huge crane scoops rock from barges and sifts it onto a storage pile. On a tropical August morning, the grinding, groaning, hissing,

Nitrogen Removal
Jeannette Semon, who runs Stamford's wastewater treatment system,
stands on a catwalk above one of the Stamford plant's tanks. Semon
pioneered the removal of nitrogen from sewage at plants
along the Sound. Courtesy of *The Journal News.*

pounding racket of industry saturated the air. It was the ideal atmosphere for the unusual sensory experience to come, one that abounded
in the kind of sights, sounds, and smells not usually encountered. I
was at the treatment plant, along with Mayor Serrani and two Congressmen who were up for re-election in November, to get a feel for its
workings and to learn about Jeannette Semon's innovations. Semon is
Stamford's supervisor of liquid wastes. She has an enthusiasm for the
intricacies of sewage treatment that seems humorously eccentric until
you realize that a similar eccentricity among other engineers would
make the Sound a healthier place. As tour leader, she took nothing for
granted. Starting at the beginning, she held up a laboratory bottle that
contained a cloudy liquid and said, "You can't really see raw sewage
floating up on the beaches. This is raw sewage. It's described in text-
books as a musty-odored, gray material."

She led us down a flight of steel steps to the lower level of a brick
building, into which a river of raw sewage roared. "Musty" did not

quite do justice to the odor. The smell was almost tangible as we pushed through it to look at the screen that constitutes the first treatment step. Wastewater rushed through the screen, carrying everything that had gone down the toilets, bathtubs, sinks, washing machines, and dishwashers of Stamford and Darien. A mechanical rake scraped the screen clean, the debris to be collected and burned.

"We get rocks, bricks, logs, diapers, condoms, tampax — anything you can imagine," Semon told us. "The one thing we don't see here is hypodermic needles. But we have had money come in here — all types of things."

We did not linger. We were eager to ascend back to the heat, glare, and humidity of an August morning. The Congressmen — Joseph DioGuardi, a Republican from New Rochelle who would lose that November, and Christopher Shays, a Republican from Stamford who would win — looked dazed. We walked toward another part of the complex, where dozens of herring gulls bobbed in the air over a circular vat. Semon identified it as the primary settling tank, where particles suspended in the wastewater were allowed to sink to the bottom. A mechanical arm sweeping the tank's radius skimmed grease off the surface. The gulls were scavenging the grease.

Beyond the settling tank was a much larger tank, rectangular and divided into eight compartments. These were the secondary treatment tanks. An aerator pumped oxygen in, and the wastewater churned in thick swells, like dark whipped cream. Sludge was folded into the mixture, carrying bacteria with it. The oxygen and sludge were combined in just the right proportions to allow the bacteria to multiply enough so that the sludge would be inadequate to nourish them. Consequently, the bacteria would begin grazing on the sewage's organic particles, leaving behind wastewater stripped of more than 80 percent of its organic material. That was the theory and practice of the activated sludge treatment method. Another strange smell — far weaker than the smell at the screen — squatted above the tanks.

"You get some odor — that musty odor," Semon said. "Nothing can be done about that. This is a well-operated treatment plant."

A treatment plant's processes are, in essence, nature's processes, harnessed within tanks and pipes. So far we had seen nothing special, only the conventional workings: the activated sludge method had been first used on the Sound in 1937, at Wards Island. It was in the secondary tanks, however, that Jeannette Semon was manipulating the activated sludge to rid the wastewater of most of its nitrogen. "We're way beyond secondary standards," she said.

She had not started her tinkering as an academic exercise. Semon was serving as chairwoman of a Long Island Sound Study work group whose task was to examine how treatment plants could best remove nitrogen. The group knew that its success or failure might determine the Sound's life or death. What's more, the cost of rebuilding treatment plants to remove nitrogen might reach six billion dollars. If engineers were not motivated by the well-being of the Sound, it was hoped that the threat of staggering costs would prod them to try innovations like Semon's.

To Semon, the double need — ecological health and balanced budgets — was an engineering challenge she was ready to accept. The seventeen million gallons of wastewater that rush into the Stamford plant every day contain almost twenty milligrams of nitrogen per liter, or forty-nine hundred pounds. Were this some ordinary facility operated by ordinary engineers, the nitrogen flowing in would equal the nitrogen flowing out. The reality, though, is far different. Semon wrings about 70 percent of the nitrogen from the wastewater, releasing fifteen hundred pounds a day into the Sound, or between five and ten milligrams per liter. Achieving the reduction required no huge capital expenditures, no construction of tanks, no extensions of the network of pipes and sluiceways.

"All we did was change the way we operate," Semon said.

The nitrogen in sewage is locked up in ammonia, which is a combination of nitrogen and hydrogen. Freeing it requires crews of bacteria, which act like teams of subcontractors, each performing a task that leaves the nitrogen in a form that the next crew can work on. The first task is to break down the ammonia by a process called nitrification and requires two specific bacteria to do the work. They need a good supply of oxygen, so to grow them Semon turns up the aerator in one of the eight secondary treatment tanks. The first crew of bacteria — microbes called nitrosamonas — converts the ammonia into nitrite; then the second crew — bacteria called nitrobacter — changes the nitrite to nitrate.

But nitrification is not enough. Although ammonia has been transformed into nitrate, nitrate is still a form of nitrogen, and it would contribute to hypoxia if it were dumped into the Sound. Therefore, another task remains: denitrification, which converts nitrate to nitrogen gas. This time, eight or nine different bacteria complete the job. Unlike the microbes that reduced ammonia to nitrate, these denitrifying bacteria will not grow if there is an abundance of oxygen. Where nitrosamonas and nitrobacter thrive on three to four milligrams of oxygen per liter, the denitrifying bacteria need to be oxygen-starved. To grow them, Semon turns down the aerator, pumping in a half-milligram of oxygen or less per liter. The bacteria chomp on the nitrate, turning it into nitrogen gas. The gas bubbles harmlessly out of the wastewater into the air, which is already 80 percent nitrogen. The nitrogen is now gone and, because the process does not involve any chemical treatment, no toxic residue remains to cause unforeseen problems.

Semon's subtle stroking of the plant is not perfect. The bacteria are living organisms, and their metabolisms operate at a higher rate in warm weather than they do during cooler months. In summer, Semon has cut the nitrogen outflow to between five and seven milligrams per liter, and at times has squeezed more than 80 percent of the nitrogen out of Stamford's wastewater. "I've gotten below five in summer with process modifications," she told me. "But getting below that five consistently is difficult." The bacteria are far less active in cold weather, and so she has had to be satisfied with a reduction to about ten milligrams per liter in winter.

The Stamford sewage plant's annual budget is two and a half million dollars; denitrification costs about ten thousand dollars. At a price equal to .004 percent of the budget, the nitrification–denitrification process would seem to be hard to resist along the Sound, at least as an interim step. The requirements are few. Semon said, "We had a well-operated plant, a stably operated plant. Basically it's a plain, old secondary treatment plant."

Yet engineers all along the Sound did, in fact, resist, because removing nitrogen from wastewater at a conventional secondary treatment plant had a prerequisite that few facilities could meet: the treatment plant had to be operating below the capacity for which it was designed. In Stamford, for example, Semon's facility was built to handle twenty million gallons a day; when she began her nitrogen removal program, the daily flow was actually 85 percent of that maximum, or seventeen million gallons. The extra room allowed her to keep sludge in the plant for the eight to fifteen days needed to grow the necessary bacteria — far longer than the day and a half of sludge retention that secondary treatment requires.

Semon's abilities as an intrepid tinkerer were hardly common. Other treatment engineers continued to live by the belief that if they had no room, they were paralyzed. And extra room was relatively rare; only twenty plants were operating below capacity. The Ward's Island facility, to cite perhaps the most egregious example, was designed to handle two hundred and fifty million gallons a day; the actual daily flow was more than three hundred and forty-four million gallons. (In the 1990s the capacity of the Ward's Island plant was increased to two hundred and seventy-five million gallons a day. But concurrently, the New York City Department of Environmental Protection began a program to cut water usage in the city, by installing water meters and providing low-flow toilets. The program worked so well that by early 2000, the flow at Ward's Island had fallen to two hundred and thirty million gallons, according to the DEP.)

And some facilities that had room did not embrace nitrogen removal with enthusiasm. In 1989, New York State officials considered Westchester County's plant at Blind Brook, in Rye, a good location to experiment with reducing nitrogen. But county politicians wanted no part of it. The Blind Brook plant sits near a park, in the middle of a residential neighborhood. Political leaders in Westchester feared that the trial and error needed to adjust the nitrification–denitrification process would encourage the growth of a smelly bacteria called nocardia. Like nitrosamonas, nitrobacter, and the denitrification bacteria, nocardia live on sludge. If a treatment plant gets rid of its sludge within a day or two, the nocardia have no chance to grow. But if the sludge is kept for longer than two days — as it must be to cultivate the nitrogen-changing bacteria — nocardia proliferate, wafting bad odors over nearby areas. Fearing the anger of Rye's voters, Westchester officials told New York State that they had no interest in trying to remove nitrogen at Blind Brook. It was only in 1991, when New York and Connecticut—through the Long Island Sound Study—declared that for the time being the flow of nitrogen into the Sound would have to be capped at 1990 levels, that Westchester began considering nitrogen removal at Blind Brook. Adam Zabinski, the county's director of wastewater treatment, told me that even with the state forcing them to act, Westchester officials were preparing for a political attack from those living near the treatment plant, because the nocardia would be uncontrollable.

"We fully expect that to occur—it happens to every place else where this has been done," Zabinski said.

The cleanup of the Sound, in other words, had been threatened by local politicians' fears that voters would resent neighborhood inconveniences. (Zabinski, who is dedicated and knowledgeable, eventually found a way to solve the nocardia problem.) Getting treatment plants to remove nitrogen was obviously something to be forced at a higher level. It might require that people tolerate bad odors. It almost definitely would need an outlay of public money. And it might necessitate controls on development that were far stricter and more comprehensive than local zoning codes. As it turned out, a neighborhood quarrel over bad odors at a treatment plant might have been a quick and easy skirmish compared with the bigger battles that nitrogen removal would ignite.

ELEVEN

The Cleanup

The consensus that Long Island Sound's sewage plants would need upgrading left many hard questions to be answered. Would, for instance, all treatment plants have to eliminate all nitrogen? Or should it be assumed that most of the nitrogen removal would come from the plants nearest the heart of the hypoxia — in Mamaroneck, Rye, Port Chester, and New Rochelle on the north shore, and in Port Washington, Great Neck, and Glen Cove on the south shore? How much did the massive treatment plants in Queens and the Bronx contribute to the problem? Was their wastewater carried away through the East River to New York Harbor or pushed east beyond Throgs Neck? What role did the Housatonic River play? Did its nitrogen-loaded flow sweep west past Stratford, carrying with it the wastewater of Bridgeport, Norwalk, and Stamford? Did a sewage plant's contribution to hypoxia depend on its location or on the amount of sewage it treated? Did it matter if nitrogen was removed in summer but allowed to flow into the Sound in winter?

Researchers knew from the outset that only trial and error would uncover the answers, and that there were two ways to proceed. One way would provide absolute, indisputable results. It would require an immediate outlay of money — hundreds of millions, if not billions, of dollars — to upgrade treatment plants, and then the patience to wait years to watch how those changes affected the Sound. If the Sound did not improve — if the wrong treatment plants were upgraded or if the improvements did not go far enough — modifications to the strategy could be made and more patience expended. Until the right solution was hit upon, the Sound might remain a functioning estuary. Or it might not.

The second way would be to simulate the real-life bricks-and-mortar upgrades on a computer model. Modeling is a comparatively quick and inexpensive way to test cleanup scenarios and then modify them based on the results that the computer spits out — "a mathematical representation of what occurs in the real world," as Charles App, an environmental engineer with the U.S. Environmental Protection Agency, put it. Researchers could try an almost endless number of cleanup possibilities — removing nitrogen from treatment plants in New York City, for example, or removing three-quarters of the nitrogen from Nassau and Westchester and half from the city—and, if the underlying data were solid, determine if the cost of the upgrades would be money well spent or flushed down the toilet. The model would allow policy-makers to decide which sources of nitrogen were most important in triggering hypoxia, and which should be attacked first to ease hypoxia the quickest.

A computer model relies completely on the information it is fed. The model the Sound researchers were hoping for had to accurately predict, in time and intensity, the onset of hypoxia, its strength, and its fade, and all of the factors that influence hypoxia. From April 1988 through September 1989, researchers from the University of Connecticut, the State University of New York at Stony Brook, and the New York City Department of Environmental Protection collected data at seventy-four locations, from Governor's Island in New York Harbor, to Block Island, Rhode Island.[1] They measured the water's saltiness, temperature, dissolved oxygen, and clarity. They took samples and analyzed them for nitrogen, carbon, phosphorus, silica, alkalinity, chlorophyll-a (a measure of the amount of algae in the water), and hydrogen sulfide. They measured photosynthesis rates of the Sound's algae. They determined how fast the Sound's bottom sediments removed oxygen from the water, and the rate at which nutrients moved in and out of the sediments. They measured tides, water levels, and the speed and directions of currents.

One model, built by HydroQual Inc., a consulting company in Mahwah, New Jersey, followed the fluctuations in water quality in the Sound. HydroQual's engineers started small, with a "steady-state" version of the Sound, a numerical portrait based on averages of all the data from all locations and at all times of the year. It was quickly replaced by what Charles Dujardin, HydroQual's project manager, called a "time-variable" model, which charted the changes that the Sound went through week by week. The time-variable model successfully mimicked the drop in dissolved oxygen through July and August and the subsequent rise as cooler weather arrived.

The next steps were more complicated. Instead of simply predicting changes through the year, the water quality model represented how nitrogen, organic material, and algae interacted to reduce dissolved oxygen. It divided the Sound into twenty-one sections, running east to west, from the Battery to Block Island; and it sliced the Sound horizontally into a bottom layer and a top layer. When combined with the time-variable model and then put into action, the water quality model calculated changes in dissolved oxygen from location to location and from week to week.

At the same time, the National Oceanic and Atmospheric Administration was assembling a model to mimic how water circulates into, out of, and throughout the Sound. It was as crucial to an understanding of hypoxia and its solutions as the water quality model, because it would tell researchers, among other things, whether the treatment plants that did not discharge into the heart of the most polluted waters were nevertheless contributing to the annual oxygen decline. But NOAA's model was late. Scientists who constituted a peer review panel were questioning the quality of the data NOAA was using.[2] And by 1990 and 1991, officials were having a difficult time predicting when it might be ready — although they knew it would be years rather than months. Yet after the summers of 1987–89, there was an urgency to act. If the models did not yet justify major reductions in nitrogen, at least the Sound should not be allowed to deteriorate further. That seemingly simple decision — to not let the crippling hypoxia of the late 1980s get worse — precipitated the first divisive public debate of the Long Island Sound Study.

The U.S. Environmental Protection Agency deserves credit for making sure that the officials and scientists conducting the Sound study did their work in public. The support of the people who lived near the Sound was considered essential. Early in the process, the agency established a Citizens Advisory Committee, whose co-chairmen — one each from New York and Connecticut — would sit on the Sound study's management committee. New York's co-chairman was a superb political tactician named David Miller, who was a vice president of the National Audubon Society. Miller took his responsibility to represent the citizens seriously, and in May and June of 1990 he organized a series of "Listen to the Sound" public meetings in fifteen towns in the two states. The meetings were well-promoted and well-attended. They became the forum at which the isolated voices that had been calling for the Sound to be saved jelled into a coherent constituency. And the dominant theme at every meeting was that the biggest threat facing the Sound was the overdevelopment of its watershed: "More population means more sewage, more floatable garbage, more fertilizers, more auto exhaust, more oil leakage, more boats in marinas, more blacktopping, and more hardening of shoreline areas, which reduces the biological filtration properties of land," Susan Bellinson, the president of an environmental group called SoundWatch, said at the City Island hearing.

Speakers supported large-scale improvements to sewage treatment plants, but they challenged the notion that the improvements would be a panacea. "If we succeed in reducing the total pollution rate per person but continue to increase our total population, we will have spent millions of dollars to no purpose," said Robert Fromer of the Legal Environmental Action Fund, at the hearing in Mystic. And Albert Appleton, commissioner of the New York City Department of Environmental Protection, added: "If New York City and other municipal plants reduced their nitrogen loads by 75 percent, but each year development trends increased non-point and other sources by 3 percent, it cancels out the gains made. In less than twenty years, the Sound would be in the same state it is in today, even after we spent billions of dollars."[3]

The Listen to the Sound meetings placed the link between development and the collapse of an ecosystem into a regional perspective, perhaps for the first time. Until then, the forums for expressing concern with development's assault on the environment were strictly local. Testifying before planning boards during the real estate boom of the 1980s, residents in town after town tried to express the connection between too many buildings and the destruction of the qualities that prompted them to settle in their communities in the first place. The concerns rarely went beyond the neighborhood: too much traffic, not enough parking, overcrowded schools. But as the decade passed, the condition of the Sound and the link between development and pollution began to be raised more and more.

The problem for those worried about the Sound was that a local planning board was hardly the place to argue that waterfront condos could in any way contribute significantly to the pollution of the Sound. Development proposals were decided in isolation. Each one separately would produce a small but acceptable burden of pollution. No method existed for the planning boards to consider that the project before them was one of many being proposed at any one time or over any given period of years, and that the combination of small-but-acceptable burdens of pollution became large and unacceptable. It simply was not an issue that would be addressed on such a local level.

There was some recognition of this problem in the mid-1980s, after New York and Connecticut devised plans for managing coastal areas, to be administered in their respective capitals of Albany and Hartford. State officials promised to take a broader view in regulating how the waterfront could be used—and in fact they sometimes did, citing environmental reasons, for instance, in a decision to block construction of a large marina proposed for Clinton Harbor in Connecticut. But not until the Long Island Sound Study began to identify the causes of pollution did the Sound's advocates have a framework to encompass their arguments about the danger of overdevelopment, allowing them to carry it beyond the local planning board to the region at large.

One such development proposal was Davids Island, and it became a crucible for the anti-development environmental activism that cohered at the Listen to the Sound meetings. Davids Island is one of the many islands that dot the western end of the Sound. It is part of New Rochelle and sits less than a mile from that city's coast. From the 1860s until the early 1960s, the island belonged to the United States Army, which operated a military hospital there during the Civil War and later built Fort Slocum, a busy post commissioned in the late nineteenth century as part of New York City's coastal defense network. The army abandoned it to New Rochelle in the early 1960s, and the island has remained unused since, its sturdy brick barracks and officers' quarters inevitably yielding to the harsh leveling effect of neglect, vandalism, arson, sea weather, and rampant vegetation. Attempts were made to develop it—most notoriously by the power utility Consolidated Edison, which wanted to build a nuclear power plant there—but not until 1980 did a developer, urged and aided by New Rochelle officials, start to make progress.

The development company called itself Xanadu Properties Associates. Its plan was to build a bridge connecting the mainland with the seventy-eight-acre island, on which it would construct two thousand luxury apartments in buildings as tall as fifty-five stories. In addition, a marina for eight hundred boats would span much of the channel between Davids Island and Glen Island, a park owned by Westchester County. An enormous breakwater would protect the marina and provide a landing area for helicopters. There would be beaches, a yacht club, a health club. And the island would be completely private; only those who lived there would be allowed to cross the bridge.

Planning progressed with hardly any opposition. But then, in 1987, the developer made a tactical error. Xanadu, in its zeal to convince people that the project was faultless, released a massive environmental study that purported to show that the project would have absolutely no adverse effects on the Sound or on New Rochelle. The assertion was ludicrous on its face. People perhaps would have accepted a proposal arguing that the good outweighed the bad, but few could fathom that such a huge development would not hurt the region in some way. The environmental review also failed to mention hypoxia at all. The Long Island Sound Study had been proceeding, by that time, for a year and a half, and although all the details of hypoxia had yet to be learned, its extent and causes were starting to be understood. Xanadu's omission looked even more glaring in the summer of 1987, when oxygen concentrations collapsed and marine life died in the waters all around Davids Island.

Public opposition mounted, both in New Rochelle's shorefront neighborhoods and in neighboring communities such as Larchmont, Mamaroneck, and City Island. In its attempt to convince decision-makers, Xanadu instead unwittingly handed ammunition to its opponents when it revised its environmental review, in early 1988, to address hypoxia. The developer used data taken in May — before hypoxia gets started — to argue that the waters near Davids Island had healthy levels of dissolved oxygen; and it managed to summarize the Long Island Sound Study in less than a page. At a time when growing numbers of people were concerned with the health of the Sound, and when those concerns were concentrating on sewage and development as the causes of hypoxia, Xanadu insisted that the treated sewage from its development would have no effect. It was a blundering attempt to justify the intrusion of a dense urban area on a region that had had enough. Opposition spread beyond Westchester, into the Bronx, Queens, Long

Island, and Connecticut. The Xanadu plan for Davids Island died in early 1992. By then it had become more than just a bad idea that deserved rejection: it was a symbol of all that was causing the Sound's demise, and a rallying point for those who wanted to prevent that from happening.

In January 1991, the Audubon Society summarized the Listen to the Sound hearings in what it called "A Citizens' Agenda." The agenda divided concerns about the Sound into five topics, subdivided into thirty-five recommendations. Development was paramount, and the chief recommendation was broad and bold. The Citizens' Agenda wanted development decisions to be taken away from local planning boards and given to a regional Long Island Sound Coastal Area Commission, which would have the authority to set mandatory limits on coastal development. The commission would consider how each new project would make the Sound better or worse. And it would require builders to prove that new projects near the Sound were consistent "with sustainable development" — that is, "ensuring that human activities and development projects are in balance with the health of the ecosystem." The recommendation added: "Already, human activities have crossed that boundary and restoration efforts are needed. But the efforts society invests in restoring Long Island Sound can be totally undone by continuation of a development policy that does not put real limits on growth."[4]

In retrospect, the proposal for a regional development commission was unlikely to be adopted in New York and Connecticut, where home rule is only slightly less sanctified than the Ten Commandments. But as the centerpiece of a citizens' agenda for the Sound, it was a clear articulation that development-as-usual was no longer acceptable. "The idea of balanced development is a trick. I don't see how you can have balanced development," an Audubon Society biologist, Carl Safina, told the audience at a conference that Audubon held in Stamford in January of 1991. "All development leads to some erosion. The question is, how much will we tolerate." He added, to considerable applause, "I think we have too many people living here as it is."

It was impossible for the message to be ignored or misunderstood. The states and EPA acknowledged even before the Citizens' Agenda was published that they were hearing it. In November 1990 the Sound study's policy committee—the two EPA regional administrators and the environmental commissioners of New York and Connecticut who oversaw the broad goals of the study—directed that the Sound's sewage treatment plants would not be allowed to release more nitrogen than their 1990 outputs. The policy committee acknowledged that nitrogen reductions would follow eventually, but until decisions were made about where and how to cut it, the plants were to hold the line on nitrogen. That directive came to be known as the no net-increase policy, or the nitrogen cap. It meant that for every pound of nitrogen entering a plant above what it treated in 1990, a pound of nitrogen would have to be removed from the wastewater released into the Sound. The policy would not take effect until the release of the study's final report and cleanup plan. But when it did, it would formally acknowledge, by undeniable implication, that development causes pollution.

If the anti-development sentiment was not quite a torrent, it was a considerable flow, and the environmentalists and the Sound study officials who had created the flow were happy to be carried along by it. The real estate industry and its political allies could not help but understand what was happening. They did their best to foment a backlash against the nitrogen cap. The leaders were the administration of Westchester County Executive Andrew O'Rourke and the county's powerful construction industry. A nitrogen cap would be tantamount to a building moratorium, Anthony Landi, Westchester's Environmental Facilities commissioner, told me in February of 1991. The county's planning commissioner, Peter Q. Eschweiler, tried to argue that the region faced a choice between a clean Sound and its residents' social needs: "The people who make these decisions about no net-increase of nitrogen are playing to the gallery rather than being realistic. It's not that easy and it's going to be expensive," he said. "You have to prove to me why I have to divert money from human needs to the needs of the bay anchovy."

O'Rourke took up the construction industry's cause in a letter to New York Governor Mario Cuomo and Connecticut Governor Lowell Weicker in which he erroneously wrote that the no net-increase policy would cost the county more than $400 million. It would raise sewer taxes in the Port Chester sewer district, for example, from $375 a year to $1,500 a year, he said. And worse, even the treatment plant improvements would be "counter-productive," because the "benefits would not be felt for 50 to 100 years." O'Rourke's reference to $400 million, however, was not the estimated cost to Westchester of the nitrogen cap; Adam Zabinski, the county's director of wastewater treatment, had already said publicly that he could cap the flow of nitrogen at Westchester's Blind Brook plant, in Rye, for $200,000. The $400 million figure was the estimate for nitrogen reduction — a long-term project requiring major reconstruction of the plants. As for O'Rourke's assertion that it would take as long as one hundred years for the Sound to improve, that "fact" apparently was derived out of thin air; none of the scientists associated with the Sound Study had ever presented such a timetable.

The conflict became public in January and February 1991, when the Long Island Sound Study held meetings in seven towns to allow people to talk about the study's achievements and goals. The meetings were, for the most part, civil affairs; one of the meetings I attended, in New Haven, was downright soporific: hardly anyone could muster any questions or comments. Only at the meeting in Westchester County, in Rye, did the discourse take on the fervor of conflict, but with a paradoxical twist. Usually developers push for action by arguing that their environmental studies answer all the questions about a project, and so it's time to stop delaying and move forward. Environmentalists counter by asking: What's the rush? They argue that the approval process is moving too quickly; more environmental studies are needed, more data should be collected, more analyses made. But at the meeting in Rye, the positions were reversed. Environmentalists said time was running out on the Sound: the cleanup should not be delayed. Developers presented the "what's-the-rush" point of view: this study is moving too fast; we know far too little about the Sound to be recommending anything as radical as a nitrogen cap. Their fears were summarized by Albert Annunziata, representing the Building Trades Employers Association of Westchester and the Mid-Hudson Region. At the meeting in Rye he read from a letter that his association had mailed to Cuomo. The no net-increase policy would make it impossible to build anything in the Sound's watershed, he said: "This policy would spell disaster for the region's local economy."

The organizations that represent the construction and development industry in Westchester County had been shrill and not-always-reasonable participants in local environmental debates for years. As representatives of successful and wealthy developers, they used rhetoric that was stocked with cant about how development was important because hard-working laborers and tradesmen needed jobs. It was cynical and tough to stomach, but in the case of the nitrogen cap it was leavened by the sincere sentiments of others who also thought the cap was too much, too soon. The village of Port Chester, for example, had been struggling since 1985 to redevelop its depressed downtown. Village officials saw the nitrogen cap as a threat to economic revival. "We understand our local situation to need a critical mass of economic development to keep things going, to provide a tax base that's balanced," Thomas Farrell, Port Chester's development director, told me after the meeting. "This kind of proposal is only looking at one side of the question."

Those who supported the nitrogen cap made their points, too, at the Rye meeting, but the forcefulness of the developers and their allies made the environmentalists regroup. Their position in favor of the nitrogen cap became more adamant when, soon after the meeting, the researchers conducting the Sound study announced that they were six months behind schedule. Before the delay and its implications had a chance to sink in, there was another announcement: the computer model that NOAA was developing was not yet working properly. It could not answer an absolutely crucial question—how much did New York City's gargantuan sewage plants affect hypoxia—because the NOAA researchers were having trouble figuring out the flow of the East River.[5] The study's cleanup plan would be at least a year late. And because the nitrogen cap was scheduled to be imposed when the final report was finished, it would be at least a year late, too: sewage plants would be allowed to dump more and more nitrogen into the Sound until the end of 1992.

Environmental groups pronounced the delay unacceptable. Many of the largest and most powerful were represented on the study's Citizens Advisory Committee, which met in the spring of 1991 and voted to urge the study's policy committee to put the nitrogen cap into place immediately. Anything less would be a farce, said Jeff Kane, a committee member and the program coordinator for Citizens Campaign for the Environment. "Let's not back off the first concrete step the Sound study can really make," he said.

"The scientists have analyzed the data," said Kathryn Clarke, the president of the Long Island Sound Taskforce, who also served on the Citizens Advisory Committee, "and they are saying the western Sound is on the brink of collapse and we may see it die in our lifetimes unless decisive action is taken in the very near future."

David Miller of the National Audubon Society was the first to tip me off that the Sound study's policy committee was considering the environmentalists' advice to implement the nitrogen cap earlier than originally planned. I called the four people on the committee. Three of the four—the two EPA regional administrators, Julie Belaga and Constantine Sidamon-Eristoff, and New York State's deputy environmental commissioner, Robert Bendick—said that they believed that the lateness of the study made it imperative to put the nitrogen cap into place as soon as possible. "I, at this point, think it would be wise to go ahead," Sidamon-Eristoff said. "I think time is of the essence. Why not take steps now if you know what you can do and it's doable?" "I think we're all anxious to get going on this," Bendick said.

Only the Connecticut environmental commissioner, Timothy Keeney, demurred. He was not against the policy, he said, but he had not yet decided if it should be implemented now. He would make up his mind before the policy committee met on August 16 in Hartford to vote on the cap. If the developers and their allies had been agitated in February, they were now apoplectic.

Before the policy committee could put the nitrogen cap into effect, it needed a formal resolution to vote on. Writing it was the task of the study's management committee, which represented the second highest level in the study's hierarchy, the people who guided the actual research and analysis. The committee gathered at Rye City Hall on a rainy Friday morning, two weeks before the policy committee was to meet. It was a public meeting, and a quick glance around the audience made it plain that the conflict over development would arise before the session was finished. In the center of the room sat Dolph Rotfeld, an engineer who represented the Westchester County Builders Institute, and who had forcefully denounced the no net-increase policy at the Sound study's public meeting in that same room in February. In the back was Gerald Lloyd, who, although assumed by many to be something of a gadfly for the developers' point of view in his attacks on attempts to restrict development, was actually a vice-president of the Robert Martin Company, Westchester's largest developer. Also in the back were Gary Gianfrancesco, a Port Chester Village trustee who would make a development moratorium a theme of his unsuccessful campaign for the county Board of Legislators that fall; and Peter Iasillo, the mayor of Port Chester, who was fretting about the village's downtown redevelopment (to be done by the Robert Martin Company). In the days before the meeting, Iasillo had issued a one-page statement, purporting to be from a coalition of communities along the Sound, that said the nitrogen cap was difficult to justify until more data about the Sound and its hypoxia had been gathered and analyzed. In the front of the room sat Robert Funicello, a lawyer and former trustee of Mamaroneck Village, who, throughout the debate over Davids Island, had been an articulate and volatile spokesman for sending that development proposal to an early grave for environmental reasons. And to the side sat Al Appleton, New York City's Environmental Protection Commissioner. The word preceding the meeting was that the developers' representatives considered Appleton an ally because, they believed, he thought the no net-increase policy was premature and an unfair burden on the city.

From the start, a sense of urgency hung over the room, as if those who were eager to get the nitrogen policy in place felt that this important step — which would, essentially, mark the beginning of the cleanup of the Sound — would be delayed, that momentum would be lost and never regained. Richard Caspe, the director of the water division in EPA's New York office, chaired the meeting. At issue, he said, was the schedule of the Sound study — the cleanup plan would be late and so the nitrogen cap would have to be put into place sooner than anyone had originally thought. The cap was critical because it would be years before large-scale nitrogen reductions could begin, and further deterioration in the Sound might make recovery impossible. Then Appleton spoke. Any notions that he would side with the developers quickly dissipated. The nitrogen cap was important for reasons beyond the actual effect it would have on the Sound, he said. People perceive that the study is moving too slowly—that the Sound might be studied to death. "Part of the purpose of a policy like this," he said, "is to mobilize public support for action." Thus within minutes, two government officials—Caspe, who was representing Sidamon-Eristoff, a Bush administration political appointee, and Appleton, who was speaking for the city of New York—had aligned themselves with the limited-growth position of the environmental groups. It seemed likely that those who opposed the nitrogen cap would achieve little on this day.

Before the meeting could proceed very far, Mayor Iasillo stood and asked to be heard. He implored the committee to reconsider the policy because it was "a drastic measure that will have a brutal impact upon the local economy, particularly those in the construction industry who already have fallen on hard times." The burden of a clean Sound would fall on property owners, whose real estate taxes would inevitably rise. And just as inevitably, the public support needed to pay for sewage plant improvements would wither. "We want the Sound cleaned up," Iasillo said. "A clean Sound also helps the village of Port Chester. But we heard the word moratorium. . . . "

Caspe tried to reassure him. "We believe it will be done in a way that you can manage with it," he said. "You will be allowed to have some reasonable amount of development. To equate a freeze with a building ban is really taking it to a point that goes beyond where the policy really takes it. It doesn't mean it's going to be painless, but we're not going to ask you to do something you can't do."

With Iasillo still standing, Philip DeGaetano, of the New York State Department of Environmental Conservation's bureau of water quality management, explained how the nitrogen cap would work. First, treatment plant operators must figure out, by year's end, how much nitrogen their facilities released in 1990. That would be the maximum amount they could release in the future. Then, early in 1992, the nitrogen limits would be formally incorporated into the permits that regulate each sewage facility. At the same time, plant operators would submit plans to the states describing how they would meet the nitrogen limits. Some sewer districts might have to restrict new connections to their plants—in effect, banning development temporarily. But, DeGaetano said, the people studying the Sound believed local officials might be able to figure out other ways to meet the nitrogen cap.

Neighboring communities, for example, could agree to "trade" nitrogen rights. If, for instance, Westchester County cut the nitrogen flow at its Blind Brook plant, in Rye, the Port Chester plant could be allowed to increase its output by the same amount, which would allow some development in Port Chester.

DeGaetano also told Iasillo that demographers were forecasting a stable population in the near future: people would relocate within the area but there would be no great influx from elsewhere. And so the total amount of nitrogen flowing from the Sound's sewage plants might remain the same even though new houses would be built. Then, DeGaetano said, when the individual sewer district plans were finished and approved, the nitrogen cap would go into effect. By March of 1993, the flow of nitrogen into the Sound would be stabilized at 1990 levels. "There's nothing in what we're proposing that immediately puts a moratorium on a one-family house," DeGaetano told Mayor Iasillo.

Iasillo seemed unconvinced. "I hope you're right," he said, without enthusiasm.

The issue was now in the open, and Caspe allowed the pleas and responses to continue. The Westchester County Builders Institute's Dolph Rotfeld argued that as long as the Sound study remained incomplete, the nitrogen freeze was premature. Nothing should be done until the study was finished and analyzed, he said. Interim plans based on sketchy information might hurt more than help. Then it was Gerald Lloyd's turn. The prospect of a nitrogen cap was "terrifying the public," he said. The cap should be put into place only after researchers know precisely how any new development would worsen hypoxia. Government officials can claim that the no net-increase policy is not a moratorium, he said, but the result will inevitably be a moratorium. There is no other possibility, he said. Lloyd struck a nerve where Iasillo and Rotfeld had not. Caspe sounded as if he were in no mood to be lectured. "If you think that this is a construction ban and there's no way around it," he said, "perhaps you should find a good engineering firm, and they would find ways around it."

Appleton took his shot. "Pollution is free garbage disposal — it's using a public resource to subsidize a private activity," he said. "All we're really asking private activities to do is pay the true cost of doing business." He added: "We who are the public no longer want to use Long Island Sound to subsidize certain kinds of economic activities." Then attorney Robert Funicello spoke. On the contrary, he said to Lloyd, the public is not terrified. Long Island Sound is important economically, ecologically, and recreationally. The people who live near the Sound know that, which is why they overwhelmingly said at the meetings last winter that they wanted the nitrogen cap imposed immediately. And then Caspe closed the discussion: "I think we all think we have a pretty strong basis for doing it." By early afternoon the committee had molded a resolution that would cap the nitrogen flow from treatment plants, limit the amount of nitrogen that reaches the Sound in storm water, and protect fish and wildlife habitats. All that remained was for the four people on the policy committee to pass the resolution at their meeting in two weeks.

The developers and their allies, though, were not going to yield so easily. They saw their industry being made a scapegoat. And during the next fortnight, they showed that they had enough punch still to inject turmoil into the debate and to come close to derailing the nitrogen cap altogether. The construction industry's argument was that rebuilding sewage plants would be enough to save the Sound. Any other parts of a solution, especially if they involved restrictions on development, were not worth the price. "Let the sewage plants be updated — I don't care what kind of money it costs," said Arthur Colasanto, president of the Building and Construction Trades Council of Westchester and the Lower Hudson Valley, a labor union umbrella group. "But you can't say by virtue of the fact that the Sound is polluted that you can't have any construction. I'm born and raised in Rye and I remember when the water was crystal clear. But was the construction industry responsible for polluting the Sound? Everybody's been guilty. We want a clean environment but not at the cost of no growth and no development."

The unhappiness expressed by O'Rourke, Colasanto, the Building Trades Employers Association, and others must have roused Cuomo's office from a slumber that it had slipped into nine months earlier when Robert Bendick had originally given New York's approval for the nitrogen cap. Late in the afternoon of the day before the August 16 policy committee meeting, I called the Audubon Society's David Miller at his Albany office. It was a routine call, to see if he remained confident that the no net-increase resolution would be approved. Miller was on another call and said that he would have to phone me later: Thomas Jorling, the commissioner of the New York State Department of Environmental Conservation, had just backed out of the next day's meeting.

Within minutes I was on the phone with an EPA spokeswoman. "Tom Jorling could not resolve several complicated budgetary and policy issues," she told me. The meeting would be rescheduled, possibly in two or three weeks. I called Albany and talked to a DEC spokesman, Ben Marvin, who unwittingly made it clear that more was happening at the capitol than merely a discussion of "complicated budget and policy issues." Why did Jorling back out of the meeting, I asked. He read me a brief statement, his version of what the EPA spokeswoman had told me. What exactly were the "complicated budget and policy issues," I asked. Marvin seem flustered by the question. He blurted: "I'm not going to tell you!"

Other people I talked to that afternoon were clearly not confident that New York State would stand by the nitrogen cap. Anger crackled through the phone line when Miller called me back. He calmly recited a prepared statement: "Some things have come to light that they need to work out. For the benefit of the citizens of Long Island Sound I just hope New York will resolve their internal difficulties and come to the table and place a vote for Long Island Sound." Then he abandoned the statement and told me what he really thought.

"This policy does not have anything to do with development moratoriums, it does not have anything to do with widespread limits to growth or economic development," he said. Talk of a moratorium is misinformation being spread by Westchester County, he said, because of the county's "linkage to private interests that don't view it [the nitrogen cap] correctly. Let's get back to the basics. Unless we all agree to deal with pollution in Long Island Sound, the Sound isn't going to be cleaned up. When a couple of private interests are concerned about their profit margins in Westchester County, that should not negate the tens of thousands of people that want the Sound cleaned up."

Like Miller, Kathryn Clarke of the Long Island Sound Taskforce started by putting the most optimistic spin on the state's decision: "I guess we're finally getting down to it—people realize it's serious and they're starting to jockey. I'm relieved that we're finally getting into substantive discussions." Then, she added: "New York City is acting responsibly. I think that the DEC is acting responsibly. I think the irresponsible partner is Westchester County. Connecticut is clearly the leader but the problem is Westchester County rather than the state agencies. Their history with regard to sewage treatment and concern for Long Island Sound is dismal. It doesn't make them a good partner."

"New York State knows what the right thing to do is," Terry Backer, a former lobster fisherman who was working as the Soundkeeper, an independent environmental monitor, told me, "but they don't know what the political thing to do is."

Before the afternoon ended, Robert Bendick, DEC's deputy commissioner, called me to explain Jorling's decision. "There are a wide range of issues relating to the next step for the Long Island Sound committee on the agenda for tomorrow, many of which have budgetary implications and other implications for the department in terms of our delivery on those issues," he said. I reminded him that he, as a member of the policy committee, had voted for the nitrogen cap last November. "We've been through one heck of a big budget crisis since last November," Bendick said.

That did not explain why the decision to postpone the meeting was made with less than twenty-four hours' notice. Or why Bendick had told me earlier in the summer that it was appropriate to take action on the nitrogen cap. But, of course, he was not free to provide what was probably the true explanation — the letters to Cuomo from O'Rourke (the two had been on friendly terms since 1986, when O'Rourke, helping out a feeble state Republican Party, had run a badly overmatched campaign for governor against Cuomo) and others had made the governor wonder whether a clean Sound was worth the ire of the labor unions that had always strongly supported him.

Environmentalists were justifiably worried that Cuomo would abandon New York's previously expressed position in favor of the nitrogen cap. It was Cuomo, after all, who had appointed a commission, headed by National Audubon Society President and former state DEC commissioner Peter A. A. Berle, to study how the Adirondack Mountains should be protected. When the committee submitted a plan calling for strict limits on development, Cuomo barely acknowledged that the plan existed. And for years the developer pushing the Davids Island project had been telling people that the proposal would win approval because Cuomo, through his surrogates, was in favor of it. As if to cement the deal with political influence, the developer had hired Howard Rubenstein, a public relations man and a friend of Cuomo's, to represent him. When Cuomo's Secretary of State, Gail Shaffer, who oversees the state's coastal management program, decided that the Davids Island proposal should not be built because it was monstrously out of scale with the region, Cuomo said he supported Shaffer but then tried to take the responsibility for coastal management away from her.

So there was reason to fear that New York State might be abandoning the Sound for political reasons. Bendick, however, tried to reassure the skeptics. He said he did not believe that the postponement of the meeting would have major implications for the Sound study or the nitrogen cap. He said the state was not yielding to local pressure. He said the postponement would be brief. "We're just trying to make sure that all the pieces fall in place," Bendick said.

Miller and Audubon quickly issued an "Action Alert," urging environmentalists to call Cuomo's office: "The meeting was canceled, we were informed by reliable sources, due to pressure put on the Department of Environmental Conservation and the governor by those with development interests who believe this will halt that development." But the gathering momentum for the nitrogen cap seemed to have been stopped. Without New York's participation, the cleanup would stall. "Unless everyone's on board, there's no point in going ahead with it," Mark Tedesco of the EPA's New York office told me that afternoon.

And then like that, the tide changed. Connecticut's environmental protection commissioner, Timothy Keeney—who earlier in the summer had said he had not made up his mind about the nitrogen cap—announced that in lieu of the next day's meeting he would hold a press conference. He would announce that Connecticut was ready to implement the no net-increase policy on its own. The state was prepared to give local communities $15 million for a handful of treatment plants that could be improved relatively easily. Connecticut would establish what he called a "nitrogen bank," which would build up accounts of nitrogen savings at plants across the state and apply them to other plants where nitrogen removal was not possible, thus allowing some development to continue.

Audubon used Keeney's announcement to keep the pressure on New York: "Connecticut, always ahead of New York environmentally, has agreed to go ahead and implement the nitrogen load limits at their strategic STPs [sewage treatment plants] in spite of New York's foot dragging."

I don't know why Keeney decided to continue with Connecticut's plan, or why he chose to announce it at a press conference once the meeting was postponed. And I do not know what the reaction was in Albany. Cause and effect were inscrutable. But the next morning New York State officials began their day by trying to establish a new date for the policy committee meeting. And Andrew O'Rourke announced that he would instruct the men running Westchester's treatment plants to find ways of capping nitrogen without resorting to a building moratorium. Mayor Iasillo and the construction industry representatives were not particularly mollified, but no matter—the apparently inevitable progression toward the nitrogen cap, which, less than twenty-four hours earlier, had seemed flattened by an unexpected political weight, had resumed.

On September 6, the policy committee met at the Maritime Center in South Norwalk, in a third-floor meeting room overlooking the Norwalk River and, on the other bank, Norwalk's sewage treatment plant, from which six hundred thousand gallons of wastewater surged into the river every hour. It was a bright and breezy Friday, the sky washed bright blue, the optimism tangible. "We're about to move from a study mode to the beginning of some action for Long Island Sound," Julie Belaga, the head of EPA's New England region, announced.

David Miller presented the committee with a cardboard box, which he said contained petitions with sixty thousand signatures supporting the nitrogen cap. Then Jeff Kane handed Miller a brown paper bag. Miller pulled out four shocking-pink baseball hats, with the word "nitrogen" written in script across the front—nitrogen caps. As Belaga, and EPA's Constantine Sidamon-Eristoff, and Timothy Keeney, and Robert Bendick voted yes, each donned a symbolic cap—although equally symbolically, Bendick was reluctant to put his cap on until urged by the three others. But the hesitance notwithstanding, the nitrogen cap was now the formal policy of the federal government, New York, and Connecticut, and the Sound cleanup had begun. The opponents of the no net-increase policy did not disappear, but they did change their strategy. And that change turned out to be a signal that maybe environmentalists and the construction industry could agree on some parts of the Sound cleanup. If so, the cleanup's political support would be much more solid.

Audubon and other groups interested in the Sound — environmentalists, sportsmen, recreational sailors — had formed an organization called the Long Island Sound Watershed Alliance, which planned to hold a second Citizens Summit, this one on January 18, 1992, at Stouffer's Hotel in Harrison, New York. As the meeting day drew near, the construction industry continued to worry aloud about the nitrogen cap, which it was still equating with a ban on construction. Three industry groups — the Building Trades Employers Association of Westchester/Mid-Hudson Region, the Construction Industry Council of Westchester and Hudson Valley, and the Westchester County Building and Construction Trades Council — formed their own coalition, which issued a press release on the Thursday before the environmentalists' conference. It asserted that the nitrogen cap would kill two major development projects in Port Chester, urban redevelopment in New Rochelle, affordable housing projects in Mamaroneck, and several new developments in Kings Park. To emphasize the group's position, more than a thousand union construction workers would confront the environmentalists by holding a demonstration outside the Citizens Summit.

The press release went beyond the sky-is-falling pronouncements to propose the formation of a Long Island Sound Regional Management Authority, comprising the federal government, New York and Connecticut, and the counties in New York (Connecticut has no county government). The regional authority would use the Long Island Sound Study's findings to develop a cleanup plan. But before anything could be done to improve the Sound, the authority would have to quantify how it would affect the region's economy. The authority would look for ways to pay for the cleanup, through federal and state grants, user fees, bonds, or new taxes, and it would be bound to have money in place before it started any cleanup.

The regional authority had no more chance of being accepted than Audubon's Long Island Sound Coastal Area Commission. The Long Island Sound Study was well on its way to writing its own cleanup plan, and too much had been invested in it for a new management authority to take over. But the proposal indicated that the construction industry wanted a voice in the cleanup. And along with the proposal, the press release contained another assertion: "[I]ndustry officials noted that environmental groups, led by the National Audubon Society, have performed a valuable service to the region by leading the cry for scientific studies to quantify the actual harm Long Island Sound has endured." This statement effectively conceded that environmentalists were not necessarily the enemies of economic well-being after all.

On the evening of the day the construction industry coalition issued its press release, Robert Funicello spoke with David Miller on the phone. Funicello said that he had been told by Dolph Rotfeld, whose engineering firm handles many sewer construction and repair projects in Westchester County, of the Teamsters demonstration. Miller arranged to have breakfast with Rotfeld the next morning. You environmentalists are nice guys, Rotfeld told him, but you're going to put us out of work. When Miller responded that the sewage plant improvements would be large construction projects that would create jobs, the two realized they had a common interest. After the breakfast meeting, Rotfeld talked to Ross Pepe and George Drapeau, the leaders of the Construction Industry Council who had written the coalition's press release. Pepe and Drapeau told Rotfeld they agreed with Miller that the groups had a common interest and that they would be open to pursuing it in the future, but that the Teamsters demonstration would go on as scheduled.

That Saturday morning was cold and blustery, and about two thousand union workers gathered outside the front entrance of Stouffer's, along the strip of corporate parks that line Interstate 287 in Harrison and White Plains. Inside, Miller gave the opening speech of the Citizens Summit. His theme was that great accomplishments were possible if labor and environmentalists realized that their interests

The Soundkeeper
Terry Backer, a former fisherman, became Soundkeeper in 1987.
The Soundkeeper was affiliated with the successful Hudson Riverkeeper
program, and Backer became a forceful and passionate advocate for
cleaning up the Sound. Courtesy of Save the Sound.

were the same. Soundkeeper Terry Backer, whose collar was as blue as
the protesters', talked to the demonstrators outside. Our differences
are minor, he said. Environmentalists and workers both want the same
thing — money from Washington to rebuild the sewage plants, work
that would create jobs and clean up the Sound. Later, inside the hotel,
a New York assemblyman named George Pataki spoke to the environmentalists about the link between a strong economy and a clean environment.

Two weeks later, Pepe, Miller, Funicello, and Rotfeld met at an Italian restaurant across the road from the Westchester County Center in
White Plains. "Once we got the concept down that we'd agree to dis-
agree on some things but we'd seek our commonality, which was funds,
then it all came together very quickly," Miller said. The Clean Water–
Jobs Coalition, as it was called, ended the bickering over whether the
Sound should be cleaned up and instead focused attention on how to

pay for it. Coalition leaders agreed to direct a contingent of environmentalists and construction representatives to lobby for state support in Albany and then fly to Washington, D.C., to ask for federal money to upgrade the sewage plants.

Albany listened. Miller believes that the coalition's trip to the Capitol, and the involvement of George Pataki, led directly to priority status for the Sound five years later in New York State's Clean Air–Clean Water Bond Act, which Pataki — who became governor in 1995 — campaigned for heavily. The bond act eliminated a major headache for New York State officials, because no longer would they have to tell local governments that they had to invest perhaps hundreds of millions of dollars in their sewage plants and that they would have to pay for it themselves.

Washington, though, proved far more difficult. Although the coalition had no trouble persuading congressmen whose districts bordered the Sound — Christopher Shays, Nita Lowey, and Rosa DeLauro foremost among them — to sponsor bills that would fund sewage plant improvements, those bills did not come close to passing. The Reagan administration had made it clear during the 1980s that it would no longer fund sewage plant improvements, and the Bush administration concurred. It was true that in May 1988, President Ronald Reagan — through EPA Administrator Lee Thomas — had declared the Sound to be "an estuary of national significance." And it also was true that Washington had authorized and funded the Sound study. But resolutions and studies were relatively easy; Washington had little intention of giving away money to actually clean up the Sound. The yearly grants for sewage plant construction were replaced by a so-called revolving loan fund: federal money was funneled to the states, which could lend it to local communities at low interest rates. When a town paid back the money, it could then be loaned out again to another community. The major flaw in the program was that, even at low-interest rates, cities like Bridgeport and New Haven, which were often near bankruptcy, could not afford the loans.

In July 1988, a year after the first onslaught of hypoxia, New York's Senator Daniel Patrick Moynihan tried to amend the Clean Water Act, to restore money for sewage plant construction grants. New York State would have gotten more than $1 billion in extra funds over eight years if the Moynihan amendment had passed. But the Senate's budget amendment rules required that the money be siphoned out of the space program. In the United States Senate, cleaning up polluted water lost to exploring outer space by a two-to-one margin.[6]

The Sound's advocates, though, were nothing if not persistent. They went to Washington again during the nitrogen cap debate, when Westchester County needed $200,000 to pay for alterations at Rye's Blind Brook plant to cut the nitrogen discharge almost in half. Two hundred thousand dollars did not seem like serious money, but county politicians did not want residents of the Blind Brook sewer district to pay it through a tax increase. Instead, county and state officials, backed by U.S. Representative Nita Lowey, who represented Westchester County, solicited the federal government, through the Environmental Protection Agency. EPA officials in New York took the request to their superiors in Washington. All agreed that $200,000 was not much money. All agreed that it would be put to good use. Those in New York who were asking for the money saw it as a small request and as a symbolic one — if the federal government came through with $200,000, maybe it would be a signal that it would reconsider its policy. Washington, no doubt, had the same perception. The answer was no.

The refusal worried and angered people working on the Sound cleanup. Once nitrogen levels in wastewater were stabilized at eight to ten milligrams per liter, they probably would have to be cut in half again to truly restore the Sound. The technical ability to achieve those levels was not in question. Jeannette Semon had done it at Stamford. Malcolm Pirnie Inc., a consulting firm in Harrison, New York, had cut nitrogen to five milligrams per liter and then to three and a half milligrams per liter in a small experimental project at Norwalk's treatment plant. The drawback was the firm's estimate of how much these systems would cost if built on a scale that could handle Norwalk's daily flow of fifteen million gallons: $50 million to $66 million. Reducing nitrogen for $4.40 a gallon would cost more than $4 billion if every treatment plant had to reach that goal. Costs of that magnitude would strain municipal budgets in relatively wealthy communities like Westchester, Greenwich, or Roslyn, but they would probably prove impossible in poorer cities. Yet if Washington would not part with $200,000, how likely was it that $4 billion would be forthcoming?

And of course, as always, New York City was a dilemma unto it-self, if only because of its size. The city had its own budget to worry about. The cleanup of the Sound would have to compete for funding with other environmental projects, including some that would benefit the Sound itself. City officials, for example, were planning to install a forty-million-gallon concrete tank in Flushing that would store sewage underground during rainstorms, eliminating most of the combined sewage overflows that were polluting Flushing Bay. That tank alone was projected to cost $170 million.[7]

The city's treatment plants presented their own problems. The economies of scale so loved by accountants and engineers had channeled seven hundred million gallons of sewage a day into four enormous plants, which over time had become physically squeezed by the growing city. Those four facilities were processing almost 70 percent of all the Sound's sewage. Nitrogen removal would require either a drastic cut in water use, to give the plants room to lower nitrogen by employing Jeannette Semon's method, or major reconstruction and expansion. With their treatment plants already wedged into crowded neighborhoods, city officials said that expanding the facilities would require that they build out over the Sound itself. That scenario seemed unlikely at best, if only because the environmental review needed to win approval would be of nightmarish length and scope.

The estimate at the time was that it would cost the city as much as $3.5 billion for nitrogen removal. That prospect filled some of those who cared about the Sound with despair that the job would never get done. The officials guiding the Long Island Sound Study were aware of this fiscal reality. Their response was to form a Finance Steering Committee, consisting of business people, citizens, and government officials. The committee — with the help of a consultant — explored alternative ways to pay for the cleanup. All possibilities were open for discussion, with two exceptions. The first, obviously, was federal funding: the committee assumed that Washington would provide little or nothing. The second was property taxes. "I insisted that none of the options include increasing the real property tax," said Paul Noto, the mayor of Mamaroneck, who was co-chairman of the steering committee. "That's something the municipalities simply could not afford."

The committee recommended a series of fees and taxes on products and activities that affected the Sound. A water-use fee, for example, of one, five, or ten cents per thousand gallons would raise as much as $15 million a year in Connecticut and $150 million a year in New York. (It might also have the coincidental benefit of prodding people to use less water, which might free up the space in treatment plants needed for nitrogen removal.) Other suggestions included taxes on nitrogen fertilizers, toilet paper, plumbing fixtures, and gasoline used for boats; and increased fees for boat registrations and docking space. The fees and taxes would raise as much as $230 million a year — money, the committee insisted, which would be spent on nothing but the cleanup of the Sound.

Still, $230 million a year would hardly solve all the Sound's problems, assuming that the fees and taxes would be embraced. And there was no guarantee of that. The fees and taxes would have to be passed by the respective state legislatures and signed by the governors. Accomplishing that task would be hard enough in Connecticut, where the Sound is a major geographical feature and represents 100 percent of the state's coastline. New York presented a different problem altogether. In a state with waterfront on the Atlantic Ocean, New York Bay, Lake Champlain, and two Great Lakes, Long Island Sound makes up just a small part of the coastline. Its ecological significance might not mean much to upstate politicians who would have to approve, for example, a water-use fee to be charged to their constituents in Buffalo and Rochester. And there was a precedent for the quick demise of ideas about how to pay for the cleanup of the Sound. In the spring of 1988, U.S. Representative Joseph DioGuardi, the New Rochelle Republican who would go on to lose that year's election, had announced a proposal to raise money for the Sound by charging developers in the Sound region a fee equal to 1 percent of their development costs. Developers hated the idea, and even environmentalists, who considered development the evil that was killing the Sound, mustered little enthusiasm for it. The proposal disappeared like a lead sinker on a fishing line.

One of the most influential worriers about the cost of saving the Sound was New York City's DEP commissioner Albert Appleton. Appleton had the advantage of speaking from a position of respect in conservation circles as a committed naturalist and environmentalist. He had been president of the New York City chapter of the National

Audubon Society and had been influential in gaining protection for several islands and wetlands along Staten Island's northern and western shores, where herons and egrets lived in densities and diversities that were surprising given the area's heavy industrialization. When he began to speak publicly about the cost of cleaning up the Sound, he made sure he refocused people's attention on the Sound as an estuary, not merely as the receptacle for treated sewage. Appleton is a gentle, bearish man and a skilled debater and litigator who was trained at Yale Law School. Beginning in January 1991, he made a series of appearances and gave interviews in which he argued that it would be hard to implicate New York City's treatment plants in the Sound's hypoxia because their nitrogen output had not increased since the 1950s, and hypoxia, of course, had peaked in the late 1980s. (Only when asked did Appleton acknowledge that thirty years of nitrogen buildup might have pushed the Sound to the brink.) "The connection between nutrient removal in the East River [that is, the four plants between Throgs Neck and Hell Gate] and oxygen depletion has yet to be made," Appleton told me. "If nitrogen removal in the East River is irrelevant to Long Island Sound, let's spend that money doing something that helps the East River or Long Island Sound."

At the National Audubon Society's first Citizens Summit, in Stamford in January 1991, Appleton told a crowd that enthusiastically supported a quick cleanup: "It's easier to play 'let us bash New York City' than to put into place difficult land-use controls. We are not willing to pay the bill for the political weakness and political failures of others to deal with these problems." That point of view angered people concerned about the Sound, who saw it as Appleton's way of preparing to excuse New York City from taking part in the cleanup. "I think that's a cop-out," Soundkeeper Terry Backer told me on a mild June morning as we stood on the dock near the converted oyster house that serves as Soundkeeper's headquarters. "He's got to fix his sewage treatment plants no matter what Connecticut and New York State do. Let him worry about his problems. New York's not going to get stuck with the bill. That's what we're here for—to make sure everybody pays their share."

Appleton's point, though, was one with which Backer and many others agreed: engineering strategies by themselves would be inadequate to restore the Sound's ecological vitality. Pipes, bricks, concrete, nitrification, denitrification—they would do little if the Sound's true nature as an intricate mesh of plants, animals, and minerals was ignored. "There's no question that we are going to have to make an investment in Long Island Sound. But so's everyone else," Appleton told me. "The city's going to have to play its part in a significant way." But, he added, "We have to look at a whole ecological approach to the Sound." And the way to do that, he said, was to begin with one of the key components in defining an estuary—its wetlands.

Half the Sound's wetlands have been obliterated in recent centuries, a rate of destruction consistent throughout North America's coastal waters. Some biologists believe that estuaries would not be nearly so overloaded with nitrogen if tidal marshes were intact. Appleton and others proposed the creation of new marshes and the restoration of damaged ones—giving the estuary, in a sense, more of the estuarine characteristics that make it so ecologically productive and so valuable as an absorber of nitrogen. Their efficiency in using nitrogen can be so great, in fact, that when researchers studied various ways of cutting the nitrogen flow to Laholm Bay, near the southern tip of Sweden, by 50 percent, they found that improving farming practices, building sewage plants, and decreasing acid rain would be three times as expensive per unit of nitrogen removed as restoring marshes.[8]

But marsh construction and restoration was in its infancy in America and elsewhere. The use of nature to control pollution has hardly been the first solution for engineers whose careers are founded on attempts to control nature. Curtis C. Bohlen, a wetlands ecologist at the Chesapeake Bay Foundation in Annapolis, Maryland, estimates that creating a salt marsh costs about $20,000 an acre. More problematical than the money was a biological reality: plants in the northeast stop growing in winter and so have little need for a constant stream of food. Land is another problem: a marsh built to treat sewage must be far larger than the treatment plant it replaces. "The difficulty is not so much total acreage of salt marsh but having the salt marsh in the right places," Bohlen said. If the goal is easing hypoxia's grip on the western Sound, in other words, it would make sense to build marshes near the western Sound's nitrogen sources. "New York City is a problem because of its size," Bohlen said. "But there are smaller communities along the Sound and you could start hitting some of them with constructed wetlands."

The vegetation planted in man-made salt marshes will immediately start taking nitrogen out of the water and using it to grow, but a man-made marsh takes decades to match the biological complexity of a natural salt marsh. The complex web that encompasses bacteria, diatoms, amphipods, fiddler crabs, egrets, and striped bass simply cannot be manufactured to order. It takes at least a decade for a man-made marsh to start behaving like a natural one, Bohlen said. "You don't want to think of it as a substitute for a natural system," he said. He added, however, "Aesthetically it's more pleasing than another bunch of vats with pipes sticking out of them." Augmenting the vats and pipes with marshes was what Appleton was talking about when he argued for abandoning the traditional engineers' approach: "We're really talking about a holistic strategy versus an old-fashioned sewage-treatment strategy."

The holistic strategy, he said, must include controlling the pollution in storm water running off farmland and urban and suburban streets; improving septic systems to stop sewage from seeping into groundwater; and devising and carrying out plans for wise development in coastal areas. Undeveloped lands must be left alone to serve as buffers and filters for pollution; development must be concentrated in already built-up areas. Despite the intense development surrounding the western half of the Sound, there was still room for good planning, Appleton argued. And there was a political constituency for it, if not yet at all levels of government then at least in a vanguard of the electorate. "The problem is not a planning problem," Appleton said. "The problem is politics."

Not surprisingly, Appleton's ideas found supporters in the environmental community. What was new, however, was that some government officials also were starting to see that a strategy consisting only of upgrading sewage treatment plants might be too narrow to be effective. That it had taken them the better part of the century to reach that realization was less important, perhaps, than the fact that their minds were finally acknowledging the well-entrenched folly. As Robert Bendick, the New York State DEC's deputy commissioner, put it: "You shouldn't just continue to do what hasn't always worked in the past."

For the next year or more, the people working on the plan to clean up Long Island Sound retreated. There was not much to debate publicly. The cleanup strategy had to be written. The National Oceanic and Atmospheric Administration had to pull together the troublesome water circulation computer model. Ever since it had been decided that computer modeling would be the key diagnostic tool, it had been assumed the final plan would await the final model. But NOAA continued to be stymied by the East River and its contribution to the Sound. The tides in the East River, the Harlem River, and the Sound; the flow and the tides of the Hudson River; and the tides of New York Bay all carried water and pollutants into and out of the Sound in ways that defied easy understanding. In 1993 the Sound's management committee decided that unless it took some action, it risked losing public interest in and support of the cleanup. So the management committee chose to release the cleanup plan before the computer model was finished, and in 1994 EPA Administrator Carol Browner, Connecticut Lieutenant Governor Eunice Groark, and New York Governor Mario Cuomo held a formal signing ceremony making the Comprehensive Conservation and Management Plan the policy of the states and the federal government.

In many ways, the plan simply reiterated previously agreed-upon goals and decisions. It said, for example, that dissolved oxygen levels were to be increased, to eliminate the ecological damage humans were causing. It listed the no net-increase policy as one of the actions to be accomplished. It said New York State would make sure that all its sewage plants were treating wastewater at the secondary level — which is what the Clean Water Act, by then more than two decades old, also mandated. And it said the computer model would be finished, with the understanding that a completed model would be the foundation of the cleanup plan.

In the meantime, under the guidance of an independent group of scientists who were serving as peer reviewers of NOAA's work, the Sound study's management committee hired HydroQual — the company that assembled the water quality model — to put together a detailed water circulation model of the East River. The idea was to use HydroQual's work as a way to check the accuracy of NOAA's results. The two models meshed, and in July 1993, the management commit-

Cleanup Plan
In 1994 Governor Mario Cuomo of New York,
U.S. EPA Administrator Carol Browner,
and Lieutenant Governor Eunice Groark of
Connecticut held a formal signing ceremony to
make the Sound's cleanup plan the policy of
the states and the federal government.
Courtesy of Save the Sound.

tee approved NOAA's effort. It was then linked with the water quality model. Using data collected in 1988 and 1989, researchers succeeded in getting the model to reproduce the actual conditions on the Sound in those years. By November of 1994, the management committee approved the combined water quality–water circulation model — called LIS 3.0 — and began trying cleanup scenarios. Simultaneously, the committee made another important decision: rather than figure out different nitrogen-reduction goals for each community, the cleanup plan would set one goal for everybody. By doing so, the committee hoped it could eliminate complaints that one community was being held to a higher standard than another.

The basic cleanup scenario devised by LIS 3.0 was what the researchers called the limit of technology option — in other words, what would happen to the Sound if all the treatment plants used the best technology available to remove as much nitrogen as possible. The basis of comparison was the summer of 1988, when oxygen in two hundred and fifty square miles of the Sound fell below three milligrams per liter and remained at that level for seventy-three days. The researchers found that by removing nitrogen to the limit of technology, they could keep oxygen levels from dropping below 3.1 milligrams per liter anywhere in the Sound; that the area in which oxygen fell below 3.5 milligrams per liter could be reduced to fifty-five square miles; and that the drop below 3.5 milligrams would last just four days. The cost of that achievement would be $2.5 billion—considerably less than the earlier estimate of $6 billion, but still serious money. So the researchers pressed on with other scenarios.

The one they settled on as having the best cost-benefit ratio was an across-the-board nitrogen reduction of 58.5 percent over fifteen years. If treatment plants could do that, compared with 1988, oxygen would fall no lower than 3 milligrams per liter; the area in which oxygen dropped below 3.5 milligrams would be reduced to sixty square miles; and the drop below 3.5 milligrams would last three and a half days. If oxygen could be kept at those levels, hypoxia would have virtually no effect on the abundance of winter flounder or lobsters; its effect on the abundance of scup would be reduced by 61 percent; and its effect on fish abundance in general would be cut by 97 percent. The death rates of the larvae of animals sensitive to hypoxia would be reduced by 67 percent. The researchers estimated that those improvements would be about 80 percent of what could be achieved under the $2.5 billion limit of technology option. The cost would be $650 million—about one-quarter of the limit of technology.

That cost-benefit ratio was hard to argue with, and, although there were some quibbles over whether the $650 million estimate was legitimate, no one really challenged the theory that the 58.5 percent solution would work. There were skeptics, though, who believed that in practice compromises would doom the plan. Terry Backer, for example, thought that officials were using an artificially high nitrogen amount from which New York City would begin its cuts toward 58.5 percent. The result in fifteen years would be something less than a 58.5 percent reduction. "New York City wants to be able to dump more sewage than they are allowed by law," Backer said. "If this plan goes forward it will give them a free ride for years before they have to make any real reductions." While Backer argued his case, however, planning continued.

On February 5, 1998, the policy committee — Jeanne Fox and John DeVillars, the regional administrators of EPA, and John Cahill and Arthur Rocque Jr., the environmental commissioners of New York and Connecticut, respectively — approved the 58.5 percent goal at a meeting in Manhattan. Within fifteen years, starting from August 1999, the communities along the Sound would have to reduce the amount of nitrogen they put into the Sound each year from 39,000 tons to 16,185 tons. At the insistence of environmentalists, especially the National Audubon Society, the policy committee also promised that New York and Connecticut would restore at least two thousand acres and one hundred river miles of fish and wildlife habitat within ten years.

February 5, 1998, was a day of celebration for those who had made Long Island Sound the region's most important environmental issue. The squabbling was over. All that remained was to see if the solution would work.

TWELVE

The New Sound

Twice in late July 1987 I dropped down off a dock in Port Chester into an eighteen-foot Boston whaler, settled in as comfortably as possible — the boat had no seats — and eased out of the harbor with Joe Santoro, a local fisherman, for a night of bass fishing.

The first night we caught nothing. We watched as the sky darkened with clouds at sunset, and thunderheads gathered, and lightning flashed in the distance. After midnight we gunned the boat back to harbor in a downpour. The second night was clear and warm, and haze hung on the horizon. We chased bait fish in the coves between Port Chester Harbor and Greenwich Harbor. The bait pail full of mossbunkers, we settled near islands and reefs, casting and letting the bait set, feeling the running tide carry the mossbunker to where a cluster of rocks formed a sluice: a favorite place for bass to feed. We drank beer kept cold in ice that was supposed to be for the bass. Joe had caught two hundred bass already that season, twenty on one hot night. We hooked only two bluefish, which Joe eyed as if he had snagged a pair of old galoshes, and one bass, but it was too small to keep. Our last stop was off Rye, and at midnight, as we motored east toward Port Chester, a gargantuan moon the color of a cooked lobster slipped out of the water between New Haven and Shoreham.

Fishing is a chancy pastime. Nothing seemed unusual about coming home with no bass. But on those late July nights sea creatures of all kinds may have been feeling the clench of dropping oxygen levels. If we had been out in the glare of the afternoon we probably would have encountered the research boat on which Barbara Welsh was methodically watching hypoxia strangle the Sound. The still waters we had floated on so patiently were already virtually without oxygen. But who knew? The Sound on a calm July night was a beautiful place.

On one level it was a good thing that we could not see what was going on under the water. Seeing it would have been inexpressibly sad. And yet if we could have had some sense of it — not just Joe Santoro and me, but everyone who had been out on the water, the beaches, the marshes, and the seawalls during those weeks — if we could have heard the roar of the rivers of sewage, tasted the sour drops of acid rain, watched the uncountable discharges of storm sewers; if we could have seen the algae growing and dying, felt whatever the flounder and blackfish felt as oxygen disappeared; if we somehow could have seen into the future, seen that the Sound had become little more than a stagnant, weed-choked sink — perhaps then we would have been hit with a gut revulsion, a raw emotion to move us to act. Perhaps it would not have taken another four years merely to get a policy that mandated sewage plants to cap their nitrogen flow at 1990 levels and almost eleven years to get an agreement to begin reducing nitrogen.

The restoration of an ecosystem is a process rather than an achievement. Once we reach the point at which we can say confidently that Long Island Sound is healthy, that hypoxia is a problem of the past, that the mistakes we made for too many years are behind us, we must continue on, to make sure that we establish a way of life that treats the Sound as a part of ourselves rather than merely as a commodity for us to use. It is not inevitable that we will get there, or that we will get there on schedule. Chesapeake Bay is a cautionary example. For years, an EPA estuary study of the Chesapeake was considered a model for the Long Island Sound Study. But the cleanup plan that the Chesapeake officials devised fell far short of its 1987 goal of reducing nitrogen by 40 percent by the end of 2001: the actual nitrogen reduction was a mere 17 percent.[1] For encouragement we can remember that the destructive pollution of the lands and waters we depend on is relatively new. It does not have to be inevitable.

Saving the Sound will require two kinds of solutions. Because hypoxia has the potential to kill the Sound, it is imperative that hypoxia be brought under control. That work is under way, and the effort and commitment are sincere, but money remains a problem. When the Long Island Sound Study's policy committee agreed in 1998 to require a 58.5 percent reduction in nitrogen over fifteen years, its members gave themselves an escape clause: they would review the cleanup's progress at intervals during those years, and if it seemed as if the cost would be more than $650 million, the 58.5 percent goal could be lowered. The well-being of the Sound, in other words, might still be sacrificed for economic expediency.

There is, perhaps, a simple way to avoid that, a solution that a number of people concerned about the Sound have been calling for for years: the federal government must resume making money available for sewage plant upgrades, particularly in water bodies, like the Sound, that have cleanup plans founded on federal research and money.

At the 1991 meeting in South Norwalk at which the nitrogen cap was voted on, Robert Bendick of the New York State DEC decried the dissolution of the "partnership" of the past, which saw the federal government provide 75 percent of the money for sewage construction projects, with state and local governments splitting the remainder. "It is our position that that partnership ought to continue," Bendick said. "There is a continuing federal role in helping us."

Constantine Sidamon-Eristoff, the EPA regional administrator in New York, agreed, but said that merely wanting it to happen would not be enough. The federal government would need a demonstration of political will. "The partnership must be prepared to work on political levels as well," he responded to Bendick. "We're going to be able to get things done just as well as the political coalition we put together works."

People in government understand that government responds to groups: the more people who support a position, the more likely government is to do the things those people want. Government officials concerned about the Sound have been saying that for years. "Organize from the grass roots. If we want grass-roots government, let's make grass-roots government work," Lee Koppelman, director of the Long Island Regional Planning Board, told a conference held by the Long Island Sound Taskforce back in October 1987.

In early 1991, at an Audubon Society conference in Stamford, Leslie Carrothers, who was soon to step down as commissioner of the Connecticut DEP, told the audience: "I can't emphasize enough the importance of having private organizations form coalitions to advance their interests on the Sound." If that sort of democratic impetus succeeds in getting treatment plants fixed, it will bring us to the second kind of solution: maintaining the ecosystem. The foundation of the new attitude toward the Sound must be the realization that it is not the Sound's "function" to be the receptacle of our unlimited abuse. When that attitude is spread widely enough, the kind of behavior that imperils the Sound will be unacceptable. And although the new attitude must germinate and grow in individuals, the most enlightened environmental groups must help popularize it. It is here that environmental groups have a great responsibility.

Serious, well-organized, deeply felt environmental activism is relatively new to Long Island Sound. The well-being of the Hudson River, by contrast, has found tenacious constituents in the Hudson River Sloop Clearwater, Scenic Hudson, and the Hudson River Fishermen's Association/Riverkeeper, all of which formed in the mid-1960s when the threat to the river—intolerable levels of industrial waste and an unacceptable plan to build a power plant along one of its most beautiful reaches—grew critical. On the Sound, hypoxia did not become a palpable threat until the late 1980s. When it did, new, local organizations arose, and older groups grew and strengthened. And, also unlike the Hudson, the Sound has no coherent history to encompass its elements. Or rather, the Sound has had no historians to unify it in one compelling view—no one who has done for it what historian Carl Carmer and author-activist Robert H. Boyle have done for the Hudson. Long Island Sound, in other words, has rarely been considered as a *place*.

John Cronin, who for almost two decades worked as the Hudson Riverkeeper, and whose success in patrolling the river inspired followers on the Sound, Delaware Bay, Puget Sound, and two dozen other waterways in North America, has said that although no one wants pollution, neither does anyone believe his individual role in polluting is important: "Everybody wants to be an exception, and the government goes along. Big business thinks they're an exception because they employ a lot of people and are important to the economy. Small business thinks they are an exception because—hey, the point isn't to go after the little guy, is it? Municipalities insist that they have to be exempt because they represent the taxpayers who the laws are meant to protect. So the result is, nothing much ever gets done."[2]

Cronin also has expressed what amounts to the antidote to that condition: when an individual, or a company, or a government pollutes the Hudson, Cronin takes it personally. When we start to believe and to feel that the Sound is our place, we will take pollution personally. We would not allow someone to pollute our home or our yard. Nor will we allow anyone to pollute the Sound when we realize it is our home and our yard.

The environmental groups along the Sound can foster that sense of place. They can make sure the essential connections are recognized. They can help see to it that everyone realizes that the pollution of the Sound, its restoration, and its eventual ability to function as a healthy, unimpaired ecosystem are the responsibility of all. "Long Island Sound is not just the government's concern," Soundkeeper Terry Backer said. "It's too important to leave to the government. If we allow government to do this on their own, they're going to bog down in the bureaucracy and take too long to do it."

What may be most critical for the Sound is the stamina of the environmental groups. David Miller of the National Audubon Society believes that at some point attention must shift from sewage plants to changes in lifestyle that will likely prove far more difficult and take far longer. "If you don't," Miller said, "you'll put a cork in the dike and ten years later you'll spring a leak somewhere else."

Those changes will be a hard test. Any larger view of nature and human behavior is going to require a larger view of Long Island Sound—what it is, what it is best used for, what uses it can sustain, what will destroy it. The Sound must become something more than just the reason that waterfront property costs so much.

A change in behavior from one that exploits the Sound to one that nurtures it will have to be preceded by an increase in the number of people who use the Sound and an increase in the number of places where they can reach the Sound—in a word, public access. It is no simple matter now for residents of inland towns to get to the shore. Beaches and shoreline areas are often restricted to town residents. But the cleanup of the Sound will need a breadth of constituency that extends far beyond the coastal towns. In their book *Turning the Tide,* Tom Horton and William Eichbaum argue that increased public access would be critical in saving Chesapeake Bay. Their proposal for the Chesapeake should be adopted for the Sound: a wide range of water-related recreational opportunities for everyone who lives within a short drive of the watershed, and multiple-use public access to every significant tributary.[3]

The development boom of the 1980s and 1990s forced environmentalists to focus some attention on land preservation. The Long Island Sound Study's Comprehensive Conservation and Management

Plan called for the restoration of at least two thousand acres and one hundred river miles of fish and wildlife habitat within ten years. Environmental groups went farther in 2000, though, by making open space preservation the focus of a second round of Listen to the Sound meetings. The specific goal was to create a Long Island Sound Reserve of shorefront nature preserves, pocket waterfront parks, boat-launching and fishing areas, and underwater and intertidal lands for wildlife. The idea quickly won support of government officials in both New York and Connecticut.

Many of those who spoke at the ten Listen to the Sound meetings in 2000 connected water quality and open space preservation to the need for reforms in land use and development practices, just as those who spoke during the 1990 meetings drew that connection. Governmental oversight of the Sound is fractured, varied, and often in conflict; the governments and agencies that regulate the Sound view it as a domain for which they must compete among each other for control — the Coast Guard and the Army Corps of Engineers and the EPA and the DEP and the DEC, not to mention local boards, agencies, and coastal commissions. The Audubon Society's Citizens' Agenda recommended that a regional Long Island Sound Coastal Area Commission be established to guide development in ways and areas that would ensure the health of the Sound. I believe the power should be more decentralized. Instead of one commission, a number of commissions, corresponding to local watersheds, should guide development and land use. The members of each commission would live in that watershed, and one or several would sit on a body like the regional Long Island Sound Coastal Area Commission, the purpose of which would be to watch that the goals of protecting the Sound are followed. The Sound as an ecosystem would be treated as one political entity, whose well-being depended on the well-being of the ecosystem.

For those concerned with the link between development and pollution, the failure of the Davids Island project in New Rochelle was reason to open champagne. The damage caused by developments built in inappropriate places — sewage, storm water, visual pollution, loss of public access — must be made part of the accounting when building proposals are considered. Al Appleton's explanation is worth quoting again: "Pollution is free garbage disposal — it's using a public resource to subsidize a private activity. All we're really asking private activities to do is pay the true cost of doing business. We who are the public no longer want to use Long Island Sound to subsidize certain kinds of economic activities."

Restoring the Sound to health will restore confidence in it. Far too many people have abandoned the Sound as a place to swim or fish. They will return as the Sound grows cleaner. But once they do, the opportunity must be snatched to enlist them as stewards of the Sound. Perhaps nothing would foster this as well as a strong local economy built on the products the Sound can yield on a sustained basis. One of the sadder things to happen during the summer of 1988, when sewage and medical waste were washing up on beaches throughout metropolitan New York, was that proprietors of fish markets in towns near the Sound erected hand-lettered signs proclaiming that they did not sell local fish. A clean Sound would allow local fish to be sold locally, with pride. It would allow the oyster industry to expand back into the New York waters of the western Sound, which for decades have been closed to shellfishing. It would allow people to dig their own oysters from public oyster beds. Local oysters would be sold in towns near the Sound, and not just shipped away to San Francisco. Shad from the Connecticut River, mussels, clams, lobsters, bluefish — these and other foods would be harvested and used locally.

As a local, Sound-based economy develops, so perhaps would a way of life based on the Sound. But our knowledge of the Sound must grow. The Long Island Sound Study has provided a scientific foundation. Local organizations, led by Richard Harris, a biologist who lives in Westport, and Save the Sound (which is the new name of the Long Island Sound Taskforce) are measuring water quality on a regular basis in sub-estuaries like Southport Harbor, the Norwalk River, Cos Cob Harbor, Milton Harbor, and Echo Bay. Grade schools use the Sound for environmental studies. Yet a basic knowledge of the watershed, of the ecosystem, of how the Sound was nurtured and abused in the past, must extend beyond those limited forums. The Sound — and its ports and marshes and rivers in relation to the Sound — must become our place, the place to which we owe our allegiance and care.

It has the inherent power to be the one issue that connects all others. It has that power because the health of estuaries and coastal waters would no longer be the concern only of government or of environmentalists. The principle is the same, whether you live on Long Island Sound or the Hudson River or Chesapeake Bay or San Francisco Bay. Once accepted, it would bring with it, almost assuredly, an end to the abuse and exploitation that have dragged the Sound to the brink of death.

The ideal community does not exist, of course, but there is at least one region of the Sound that can serve as a model. Norwalk Harbor and vicinity have seen great improvements in water quality, the city and state have made a large investment in controlling pollution there, and the harbor is the center of the Sound's revived oyster industry. Norwalk has a busy recreational boating community. Guarding the harbor's mouth is Adriaen Block's Archipelagus — the Norwalk Islands: Chimon, Sheffield, Shea, Betts, Copps, Cockenoe — which contain one of the Sound's best bird rookeries, a concentration of herring gulls, great black-backed gulls, snowy egrets, great egrets, black-crowned night herons, and glossy ibises that is a reminder of what the abundance of wildlife must have been like when Block himself first sailed the Sound. With its long, narrow shape, its wide opening at one end and its narrow inflow at the other, Norwalk Harbor is a small estuary whose problems and solutions reflect those of the Sound at large.

Norwalk has gotten the attention it has because of its oystering heritage. After the disease outbreaks of the late nineteenth and early twentieth century, and in spite of storms that buried oyster beds, oystering lingered on the Sound in several ports. Weather-beaten wooden structures with signs bearing the old oystering names of Sealship, Rowe, McNeil, Wedmore, and Thomas lined the waterfronts of Bridgeport and New Haven, while Decker, Radel, Sterling, Lovejoy, and Ellsworth sat on the banks of Norwalk Harbor. Sloops continued to work Bridgeport natural bed, although by the 1930s the fleet was merely a remnant — where four hundred sailboats thrived in the 1870s, forty at most scraped out a living in the 1930s. Sloops raced each other in the morning on their way to the bed, then spent the day dredging what they could from the bottom.

"It was hard work, but there was — well, I won't say a thrill — there was something about sailboating that really got you," Clarence Chard, an oysterman from Greenwich, recalled at age seventy-four, in 1976.

"We liked that up there even though I say it was hard work." Chard remembered Norwalk as the center of the diminished industry: "In Norwalk, why, there were several oyster houses up there where they shucked them. One of them, the biggest one there, the Andrew Radel Oyster Company, had an immense building there. . . . I think they had around thirty openers working there at a time. And that's quite an experience to watch a group. A lot of them were colored, and they'd all work with a rhythm, and they'd get to singing, and it was worth seeing and hearing. They'd open the oysters, and they'd be put in cans, and then, of course, they'd be sent to the markets and hotels."[4]

But business through the 1930s and '40s, and into the '50s, was a matter of surviving, not prospering. Oyster companies and independent oystermen hung on, hoping to meet expenses until a good year or two could put them ahead. And then in 1958, a devastating wave of starfish swept over the beds, and even survival became impossible for almost everyone in the oyster business. Starfish had long been a kind of aquatic pestilence to the Sound's oystermen. In the 1880s, stars ate their way through $1.5 million worth of Connecticut oysters in three years. Starfish are fantastically efficient oyster predators. Creeping in across the beds, the stars latch onto the oysters and, with enormous strength, pry open the shells. The oysters don't yield easily. But the starfish can hang on for several hours, pulling the oyster apart with a pressure of nine pounds per square inch. When it has gained an opening of 1/250th of an inch, it slips in its reversible stomach and sucks out the oyster meat.[5] A one-year-old starfish can eat five juvenile oysters in a day. But starfish travel in hordes, not as individuals; on a research boat I once saw a twenty-minute trawl yield about three hundred juvenile starfish. "They can wipe out an oyster bed over the weekend," John Volk, Connecticut's director of aquaculture, told me.

Oystermen used to help the starfish unknowingly by dredging them off the beds, cutting them into pieces, and throwing the pieces back into the water — unaware that one cut-up starfish can regenerate into several new individuals. New York State also helped starfish when it closed virtually all of its oyster beds because of concern that they were contaminated with pathogens, in the western end of the Sound. With no oystermen controlling them, the starfish ate and reproduced freely. As the stars crept east into Connecticut, oystermen fought back with cotton mops tied to a frame, which they'd tow over starfish-encrusted oyster beds, entangling the stars and then killing them by dipping the mops into vats of hot water on deck.

"It was an uphill battle for my brother and myself to raise any oysters," Clarence Chard recalled. "See, we would go to Bridgeport and bring the seed home and plant it. But I can remember one year in particular, we 'starred' every day from the spring till cold weather set in, in the fall. We'd star all day long. And I'll tell you, it was pretty discouraging and expensive. Because they'll move in like a blanket sometimes, the stars will. Just cover the bottom. I've seen the time when we could throw a ten-bushel dredge overboard and bring it up solid-full of stars. So you can imagine what chance you've got if you have small oysters. Why, they clean it up in pretty quick order."[6]

In 1958, when the fading industry badly needed a strong year, the Sound's oysters produced one of the heaviest "sets" since the start of local oystering. But the tiny oysters were like so many unshelled peanuts for the starfish. Mature oysters were not much of a problem either: a large starfish can eat ten a day. The stars scoured the beds, causing ten to fifteen million dollars' worth of damage. Few oyster companies survived, and few independent oystermen continued to work. But among those that did was Tallmadge Brothers, an old company with an oyster house on the west bank of Norwalk Harbor, and as the decades passed and Tallmadge Brothers lasted and grew, the state of Connecticut began to work with the company on a plan to return oystering on Long Island Sound, at least partly, to the stature it once had.

In the late 1950s, two young twin brothers from Norwalk, Hillard and Norman Bloom, bought out the owners of Tallmadge Brothers. It was almost a family transaction—Hill Bloom's wife's grandmother was a Tallmadge. The Bloom brothers had started oystering in 1947, dredging seed oysters under sail on Bridgeport natural bed with, among others, Clarence Chard and his brother Bill. After the Blooms bought Tallmadge Brothers, seven or eight of the other Norwalk oyster companies became available—done in by the final blow of the 1958 starfish invasion—and the Blooms bought those as well.

In the late 1960s, a new generation of oysters set successfully across Bridgeport natural bed, luring a handful of independent seed men back to oystering by 1970.[7] Tallmadge Brothers, meanwhile, and several of their smaller competitors, were successfully cultivating their own seed. The aquaculture division of the Connecticut Department of Agriculture took notice, and thought that the state might be able to help build Bridgeport natural bed back up again. Imitating the cultivation practices of the private companies, the aquaculture men decided to produce more oysters by giving the oysters the hard bottom they needed to grow and develop — and the best way to do that was to dump shells in likely spawning locations.

Bridgeport natural bed was chosen as a field laboratory because of its history of phenomenal production, dating at least as far back as the first half of the nineteenth century. But the bed had very little shell left. Oystermen, working with no guidance or regulations, had scraped most of the bottom clean. The aquaculture division, however, had been monitoring the Sound's waters for oyster larvae for years. John Volk, aquaculture's director, believed that ample mature oysters remained — particularly in the Housatonic River, whose current swept the larvae around Stratford Point to the Bridgeport bed — to populate a resurgence if the hard bottom could be provided. But the division needed proof — and a lot of it — to persuade the state legislature to back a shell-planting program.

In 1977, Volk began sinking bags of shell at marked locations across the bed. He searched for oyster larvae in water samples. Once or twice a week he scooped up some of the shells to see if larvae had attached themselves. He knew of the bed's potential, but he also knew the odds against success were great because of the enormous peril that faces an oyster as it metamorphoses from egg and sperm, to larva, to mature bivalve.

A larval oyster will form only if a microscopic egg drifting through the water happens to connect with an even more microscopic sperm cell — an encounter of seemingly impossible randomness. Oysters compensate for the odds with enormous fecundity. They spawn in warm weather, when the Sound's water temperature has risen to 68 degrees, clicking on the biological thermostats of mature females grown plump with eggs. The waters of the Sound's north shore become vibrant with a tumult of microscopic activity: each female squirts out between twenty-three million and eighty-five million eggs several times during the June–September spawning season, while the males that surround her respond by broadcasting thick clouds of sperm. Soon the tides and currents are carrying millions of planktonic oyster larvae on a journey of two weeks' duration and tremendous danger. The incipient oysters are both morsels of food for a bewildering number of predators, and sitting ducks for parasites, diseases, oil spills, and fatal shocks of toxic wastes.

If the larvae dodge these threats, their survival odds improve again because of a dramatic change in behavior. Oysters being estuarine creatures, they have evolved the ability to withstand the great differences an estuary brings to the plants and animals that live there. They need salt water but they can tolerate as little as three parts of salt per thousand or as much as forty parts per thousand. Starfish are not as adaptable: they must have at least fifteen parts per thousand. So it is to the larval oysters' benefit to avoid the saltier end of their toleration range. Yet if the oyster larvae — spawned in the rich waters of harbors and river mouths — merely drifted with the tides and currents, they would be swept by river flow far out into the salty heart of starfish territory. To avoid that, the larvae migrate — not north-south like a bird, but up and down, timed to the ebb and flood of the tide. When the tide is dropping, so do the larvae, falling to the bottom to wait out the seaward pull. When the tide reverses, the larvae become buoyant, and the flood carries them into the upper estuary's fresher water, which lets at least some of the oysters evade the salty waters loved by starfish. The long, rich oyster beds of the Housatonic River are replenished in this way, which allows the river to produce enough larvae to be washed downstream and onto Bridgeport natural bed.

The larval oysters drift for two weeks before another change occurs: they sink for good. Now their survival requires that by chance, among thousands of acres of soft sandy and muddy bottoms, they find something hard to cement themselves onto. If they don't, they die. The perfect foundation is an old oyster shell — it is hard, it disintegrates after a year or two, and its calcium is taken up by the young oyster to build its own shell.[8]

Oystermen had known that for a long time. When John Volk started his experiment, oystermen had been planting shells on the bottom of the Sound for one hundred and fifty years. Until the 1820s, oyster shells had been sent to the limekiln or the village road-master for paving thoroughfares. But then a City Island oysterman named Fordham kept his shells and spread them across the bottom of East-chester Bay, becoming in all likelihood oystering's first shell-planter. It apparently was not a practice that gained immediate acceptance, be-cause as late as 1855 oystermen from Norwalk, Rowayton, and Bridge-port were hitting on the idea independently and claiming to have in-vented it. Connecticut's oyster companies have continued to plant shell throughout the twentieth century on the beds they lease for their private use.[9]

Volk pursued his experiment for a decade, building up the proof, larva by larva, and convincing the state legislature that enough oysters remained in the area to repopulate Bridgeport natural bed if only they had the shell—or the cultch, as oystermen call it—to grow on. It was time to expand. In 1986, the aquaculture division bought twenty thou-sand bushels of shell from the local oyster industry and persuaded the oyster companies to kick in another ten thousand bushels. The success of that year's set emboldened the state to enlarge the project, buying and planting about $1 million worth of shell a year starting in 1988.

In the past, oyster companies that needed shell had been able to buy it locally. "Shellermen" on the mouth of the Housatonic tonged fossil shell for cultch from the late nineteenth century until the 1950s, when oystering all but died on the Sound. The men worked in sharp-ies, in water as deep as sixteen feet, probing down through the bottom muck to reach the ancient shells. (When the Stratford breakwater was built, test borings found oyster shells buried eighty feet deep.) A good day's work yielded sixty bushels. The men lugged the shells to the river bank by balancing wheelbarrows across a thin plank that linked their vessels to the shore. There the shells dried in piles until spring and summer, when schooners arrived to buy them and transport them to oyster grounds elsewhere.[10] But shelling in the Housatonic was a dead industry in 1987, so Volk had to search south to Chesapeake Bay, and each spring from 1988 until 1996, ten to fifteen barges brought fos-silized shell from Maryland into the Sound. When the shell reached Bridgeport natural bed, Tallmadge Brothers supplied the boats and the crews—three hours a day for ten days throughout the spring, a service valued at about five hundred thousand dollars. The boats blasted the shells off the barges with high-powered hoses, washing them and spreading them—more than 6.2 million bushels—two or three feet deep across three thousand acres, about 2,000 bushels per acre.

Volk told me he could not be sure of the ultimate potential of Bridgeport natural bed—he did not know how far it could be expanded or at what point the cost of the shell-planting would not be matched by the return in oysters. But for now, acre by acre, year by year, a small piece of its old glory had been revived. A $6 million investment in shell generated $60 million worth of market oysters. "It's bringing life back to the entire bed," Volk said.

Independent oystermen harvest the seed from Bridgeport natural bed. As many as two hundred men work in small boats and haul bushel-and-a-half dredges by hand, which hinders the kind of excessive harvesting that in the past depleted the bed. "That type of equipment is not an efficient process, and that in itself is a management tool," Volk told me. A strong, efficient hand-dredger can take fifty to a hundred bushels in a day—tiny seed oysters, a year or two old, to be sold, transplanted, cultivated, and protected from predators until they reach market size in four or five years. "These are areas that have always been known to produce seed oysters, so that's the true value of these beds," Volk said. "There are not that many areas in the Sound that are chronically known for seed production."

An oysterman will fill a bushel with two thousand individual oysters, or spat, to be sold to an oyster company for about seven dollars a bushel. The bushel of spat will grow to become seven to ten bushels of market-size oysters, worth about sixty dollars a bushel. Throughout the 1990s, Bridgeport natural bed was yielding sixty thousand bushels of seed.

Most of the independent oystermen sell their spat to Tallmadge Brothers, the firm that Hill and Norman Bloom bought in the 1950s. The company supplies these modern natural growthers with parts and equipment, and it loans money if they need it. In return, the oystermen are happy to do business with Hillard Bloom, who took over when his brother died. "Bloom's check is always good," said Soundkeeper Terry Backer, who has worked Bridgeport natural bed.

Today there are thirty-four oyster companies in Connecticut, but Tallmadge Brothers dominates the Sound's oyster industry. The company controls twenty-one thousand acres of oyster beds — three thousand acres for growing seed, to complement the seed it buys from independent oystermen, and eighteen thousand acres, from Greenwich to New Haven, for growing market-size oysters. It employs forty-five workers in its biggest plant, in Norwalk, and operates smaller facilities in Bridgeport and New Haven (as well as in Port Norris, New Jersey, on Delaware Bay). Of its twenty-one vessels, fifteen are in Norwalk — harvesters, suction boats for taking up shells to be replanted, star boats for killing starfish. Its Norwalk plant, where workers box oysters in a large, spotless refrigerated room, is a renovation of the old Andrew Radel oyster house. Out back, visible from the Norwalk River, a massive pile of spent oyster shells rises in a chalky mound from the parking lot; Tallmadge Brothers plants a million bushels of shell on its own beds.

Some of Tallmadge Brothers' most productive territory can be found among the sand-and-gravel shallows around the Norwalk Islands, about a mile downriver from the company's oyster house. "Norwalk Islands is historically known for seed production," Volk told me. "But more so than seed, it's best known for its growing grounds, for fattening grounds for oysters."

Hill Bloom believes the islands are excellent growing grounds because they protect the oysters from storms that could smother them with sediment, and because they form, in effect, a baffle that sifts organic food out of the water that washes down the Norwalk River. Bare branches mark the Tallmadge oyster beds, a remnant of the practice in New Haven Harbor that had so startled a French visitor in the 1860s. When the tide exposes a finger of sand, flocks of American oystercatchers — pelican-sized birds, with chestnut backs, thick orange bills, and orange eyes in ebony heads — descend for a rest from the hard work of splitting bivalve shells. The company's boats circle endlessly, lifting dredge after mucky dredge to the deck, where the crew separates oysters from debris. The Norwalk Islands coddle more than two thousand acres of shellfish beds. They are the heart of a Sound-wide oyster industry that employs five hundred people, and yields more than five hundred thousand bushels of oysters a year, with a dockside value of $26 million. Twenty-five oyster companies lease sixty-five thousand acres of Connecticut-owned beds. Worked to their maximum, they produce three thousand bushels an acre — oysters that are worth more per bushel than the famous Chesapeake oysters, and which, as in the past, are packed and shipped throughout the United States.

"It is one of the finest quality oysters you'll find in the country," said Volk with unabashed enthusiasm. "They're in big demand around the country. Sometimes it's hard to find a Connecticut oyster in Connecticut. I tell people if you want a Connecticut oyster you should go to Fisherman's Wharf in San Francisco."

Yet as impressive as the reclamation of the Sound's oyster beds has been, the industry does not approach half its peak. And still, ninety years after the cases of typhoid and dysentery were traced to Connecticut and New York, the biggest deterrent to oystering on Long Island Sound is sewage. Connecticut maintains about eight hundred monitoring stations to test the water on the state's oyster beds. In many areas — off Norwalk, Darien, and Westport, for example — the bacteria in the water rise predictably after a heavy rain, forcing the state automatically to close those beds anytime an inch and a half or more falls within twenty-four hours. Seventy percent of Connecticut's oyster beds remain off-limits for oystering because the waters are unsafe; virtually all of New York's Sound waters are closed to shellfishing. (Like all coastal states, Connecticut participates in the United States Food and Drug Administration's National Shellfish Sanitation Program. State inspectors take approximately sixty-six hundred water samples a year from the Sound. All shellfish processing and handling facilities are inspected at least twice a year. Each bushel of oysters harvested for market is inspected and certified for compliance with FDA regulations.) The contamination of oyster beds is a problem that grieves many who care about Long Island Sound, who believe that the most compatible exploitation of an estuary is the prudent harvesting of naturally grown food.

"It's an appropriate use of the water," said Terry Backer. "It's an industry that's very sensitive to the environment, and has to be. It's what the Sound should be used for." In 1988, Backer gave up his occupation as a commercial fisherman — oysters and lobsters were his main quarry — to become the Soundkeeper. He works out of an old oyster house that sits on pilings on the east side of Norwalk Harbor —"Frederick F. Lovejoy — White Rock & Grassy Hammock Oysters," proclaimed a salvaged sign that was propped against a pillar in the low-ceilinged main floor the first time I visited there.

Backer was one of the founders of the Soundkeeper's parent organization, the Connecticut Coastal Fishermen's Association, a group established in September of 1986 to harass polluters — through the courts and public embarrassment — into obeying the laws that are supposed to protect the Sound. The fishermen's association had christened itself with an announcement timed for maximum publicity. On the eve of the annual Norwalk Oyster Festival, in September of 1986, it held a press conference at a restaurant overlooking the Norwalk River to say that it was suing Norwalk, Bridgeport, and Stratford in federal court for more than five thousand violations of the Clean Water Act at their sewage plants since 1980. Hudson Riverkeeper John Cronin, who is perhaps as savvy in public relations as anyone among local environmentalists, attended the press conference as a director of the new fishermen's association, and made sure everyone knew that a malfunction at Norwalk's sewage plant had forced the local oyster beds to close.

"The Oyster Festival is not going to be using Connecticut oysters," Cronin said that day. "They'll be using oysters from Rhode Island, from Long Island, from every place but Connecticut. And we're sitting in the center of oyster country here."

A year later, Backer wanted to show me that very little had changed. The Soundkeeper takes some good-natured needling from people who say he looks as if he's just reported from central casting. When I first met him, Backer was in his late thirties, and years of hauling lobster traps and oyster dredges had thickened his arms and chest with muscles that stretched the fibers of the T-shirts he favored in hot weather. He took his smokes out of a pack that he kept rolled up in his sleeve. A mat of red steel wool hair popped out from under his Greek fisherman's cap. His beard was red and long. In one ear he wore a gold earring shaped like an anchor. He drove a pickup truck that held a rusting

Sewage Treatment Success
The Norwalk sewage treatment plant was among the worst on the Sound in the
1980s. Every hour, 600,000 gallons of inadequately treated wastewater poured
into the Norwalk River. The plant has since undergone a $40 million upgrade
and is now one of the Sound's best. Courtesy of Save the Sound.

oyster dredge and chain. But while Terry Backer may have looked like
someone playing a role, he knew the Sound well and defended it with
an uncompromising passion from a blue-collar perspective.

We skimmed upriver in a skiff, passing under a railroad bridge and
a drawbridge and skirting a strip of salt marsh that somehow had remained undredged. The sewage treatment plant appeared on the east
shore, a complex of low, brick buildings. Backer maneuvered close to
the plant's outfall. Exposed mudflats nearby were black. He steadied
the bow of the skiff against the fast, silent stream of wastewater that
poured out of the plant. White particles flecked the water — cellulose,
Backer said, the remains of toilet paper. He said the river was two feet
deep. There was no way of telling because through the opaque effluent
the bottom was not visible. I reminded him of the fishermen's association's lawsuits, and asked him why this was allowed to continue.
"They can't fix it overnight," he said. "It's a monumental problem.
They never did any maintenance."

The Norwalk facility, built as a primary settling plant in 1931, was upgraded to a secondary plant in the mid-1970s. Operational problems caused it to malfunction constantly. Temporary closures of the shellfish beds became routine. The lawsuit filed by the Connecticut Coastal Fishermen's Association finally forced the city to follow the regulations that the state regulators were not enforcing. The city settled out of court with the fishermen's association for $175,000 — half going to the association and half to be used in various programs to benefit the harbor. The city also agreed to bring the treatment plant up to code. It hired Malcolm Pirnie Inc., an environmental engineering firm in Harrison, New York, which took over operation of the facility in 1989 and began requiring a higher level of professionalism among plant employees.

Like the Sound, Norwalk's river and harbor teem with marine life in the best of times — bergall, blackfish, flounder, sea robin, bluefish, mossbunker, and pipefish are common, and mud snails, mussels, crabs, and, of course, oysters live amid the bottom muck. With fresh water flowing downriver and salt water pushing up with the tide, Norwalk River divides into the two layers typical of an estuary; in warm weather it also stratifies by temperature, with warm water floating atop cooler bottom water. As in the Sound proper, the stratification is a key precondition for a drop in oxygen. But how far oxygen falls is determined by other factors.

Virtually all the river's marshes were dredged away, leaving a waterway that is essentially a narrow ditch with seawalls and bridge abutments that restrict tidal flow, so the rise and fall of the tide tends to slosh the water back and forth rather than flush and replenish the river. The minimally treated sewage the Norwalk plant was releasing added a 15 million gallon a day supplement to the river flow. Dense blooms of plankton turned the harbor brown. In short, it was a mixture of conditions guaranteed to damage the river. Hypoxia hit frequently and severely. On August 17, 1987, for example, a ferocious drop in oxygen killed about a million fish, according to Richard Harris, a Westport resident who has coordinated a highly praised water-quality monitoring project on the river since 1987. During another particularly bad period — September and October 1991 — oxygen plummeted repeatedly, doing too much damage to quantify. "God knows how many fish died," Harris told me one June day when I went with him and a couple of his assistants as they took measurements from South Norwalk upstream to where the river narrowed in downtown Norwalk.

The Malcolm Pirnie firm brought in a young engineer named Fred Treffeisen to run its Norwalk operation in 1990. Treffeisen found a plant that was a remnant of another era, with antiquated equipment that he was forced to use until replacements could be designed and installed. "We have some really old stuff here," he told me one morning, a decade after he started at the plant and just months before the improvements he instituted were to be finished. "We have some stuff that should go into a museum. Every time new stuff comes on line, we breathe a sigh of relief." Treffeisen and Pirnie began by arranging tanks and equipment to experiment with removing nitrogen, on a small scale, to four different levels. The point was to figure out what the Norwalk plant could achieve and how much money and effort it would take to achieve it. They learned that they could get quick, interim nitrogen reductions for about $1 million worth of improvements. For considerably more — about $40 million — they could increase the capacity of the plant from 15 million gallons a day to 20 million gallons; add a system that removes chlorine from the disinfected discharge, to limit the lethal effects of chlorine in the river; and also cut the nitrogen flow from 20 milligrams per liter to less than seven. That 66 percent reduction in nitrogen would be big enough to allow Norwalk to sell pollution rights, under a trading system adopted by the state, to other Connecticut plants that were having difficulty reaching the 58.5 percent goal that the states and federal governments had agreed on.

Treffeisen told me all this when I went to meet him one morning in his office at the plant, which was in the last stages of the $40 million upgrade. The office was strewn with reports and blueprints and thick manuals giving design specifications for the plant. Propped against one wall, one in front of the other, were half a dozen heavy metal plaques, each one noting some milestone in the annals of Norwalk civic engineering. Forged across the top of the biggest were the words, "Sewage Disposal Plant Erected 1931." It was one of Treffeisen's museum pieces, perhaps the only one that would not have done damage had it been left in place. We went outside for a look at the plant. It was

Oystering's Revival
Norwalk is the center of the Sound's oyster industry, which has recovered from
the setbacks of the late nineteenth and early twentieth centuries. Because
of the need to protect the oyster beds, Norwalk's sewage plant was
equipped with tanks, filter, and a chlorination system to treat
storm water, which can be heavily contaminated with
pathogenic bacteria. Courtesy of Save the Sound.

a cold morning in early December, the sky pale blue, the wind sharp.
Patches of thin ice dotted the parking lot. Brown, brittle weeds bent in
the wind. Fred wore a bluish-green doeskin shirt, unbuttoned, over a
white polo shirt, a green hardhat, olive green pants. His walkie-talkie
was clipped to his belt.

We stopped briefly in the room in which the amount of chlorine
being fed into the wastewater was measured automatically, and then,

outside again, at the chlorination tanks themselves — concrete vats shaped into a simple maze to slow the flow of the wastewater, so it stays in contact with the chlorine long enough to be disinfected. The water was dark but clear. The treatment plant, and his management of it, are under constant scrutiny because of the shellfish beds, he said. "If there's a mishap I have to notify state aquaculture and they shut them down immediately. Any little mishap and I'm on the phone in thirty seconds."

At the dechlorination tanks, further south on the site, the water poured over a concrete embankment and through a pipe that discharged it about two hundred feet away at the bank of the Norwalk river, where Terry Backer and I had watched the opaque wastewater pour out in 1987. "We like to say it's safer to swim in our effluent than at the beach," Fred said. The water was foamy as it flowed from the pipe, the result of mixing and aerating as it poured over the waterfall. A couple dozen gulls were gathered near the outfall.

We climbed about five feet to the top of an embankment that followed the east shore of the river. It had been built to protect the plant from flooding. Mud flats stretched from the levy to the water. Malcolm Pirnie would soon be planting marsh grasses on the flats, Fred said. We looked at a series of empty concrete tanks. When the plant was upgraded and expanded, they were added to hold storm water that pours through the plant when it rains. If the rain stops before a million gallons reaches the plant, the water is treated with the regular flow of wastewater. If the storm water exceeds a million gallons, it spills over a weir and flows through a series of rotating drums outfitted with fabric filters, after which it is chlorinated. Norwalk is also planning to separate its combined sewers, to keep contaminated storm water out of the river and the Sound (Bridgeport, meanwhile, is spending $27 million to eliminate forty combined sewer overflows that discharge into Black Rock and Bridgeport harbors, and will use a remote telemetering system to monitor its remaining nineteen CSOs; New Haven is spending $225 million to separate its combined sewers).[11] Treating the storm water might allow Connecticut to keep shellfish beds open after it rains.

With the wind gusting, we walked out onto a steel catwalk that spanned the tanks in which nitrogen removal takes place. Five long, narrow tanks ran parallel. Four were in use. The fifth was empty and we could see a grid of circular aerators, connected by PVC pipes, on the bottom. Plant operators use those to control the amount of oxygen pumped into the wastewater, and therefore to control the organisms that consume organic material and nitrogen. It is the same system that Jeannette Semon pioneered at Stamford, but Pirnie's engineers figured out how to recirculate the wastewater and use one tank for all the biological treatment processes. That was economically efficient — they avoided having to build extra tanks. But they did not have to compromise their nitrogen goal. One thousand four hundred seventy pounds of nitrogen flow into the plant each day; five hundred pounds are discharged — a 66 percent reduction.

Malcolm Pirnie is also designing ways to squeeze even more nitrogen out of the wastewater. By adding a battery of aeration tanks that would double the size of the plant (without changing the number of gallons the plant can treat), plant operators would be able to cut nitrogen to less than four milligrams per liter, or 294 pounds — an 80 percent reduction. By adding sand filters (which would require a doubling of the operations staff), the plant could get down to two milligrams per liter, or a 90 percent reduction. The cost of those two additions would be $15 million. "It looks simplistic and it sounds simplistic, but on the real level it's very sophisticated biology," Fred Treffeisen told me. The day was too cold for much outdoor reflection, but as I drove away, I couldn't help recalling what Joseph Lauria, one of Fred's colleagues at Malcolm Pirnie, had said several years earlier: "The days of somebody's pal getting a job in the sewage treatment plant are going to be in the past."

I drove across the drawbridge that links East Norwalk to South Norwalk. The river sparkled in the bright sun and I glanced quickly south for a glimpse of the Norwalk Islands and, beyond, Long Island. I was reminded of the day, thirteen years earlier, when I had gone with two ornithologists from the Connecticut Audubon Society — Milan Bull and Arturo Izurieta — to Chimon Island. We had met at a public boat ramp near the drawbridge and, with Arturo at the controls of the outboard, had motored down between the bulkheaded shores, the restaurants and marinas and remnant strips of cordgrass. Milan and Arturo were heading to Chimon to hack away the wild grape, creeper, brambles, cat briar, bittersweet, and poison ivy that were choking the island's paths. They had taken me along so I could see the nesting birds Chimon is noted for — the thousand pairs of herring gulls and fifty pairs of great black-backed gulls, and the hundreds of great egrets, snowy egrets, yellow-crowned night herons, black-crowned night herons, little blue herons, green-backed herons, and glossy ibises. The birds were not at all happy to see intruders during nesting season and tried so hard to harass us with their noise that when we left, after three or four hours, I was harried and bewildered — but also exhilarated that such wildness existed on the Sound. Milan Bull is an accomplished naturalist and committed environmentalist, but we did not exchange one word about the condition of Long Island Sound that day. There was no need to. We (or I) had almost no awareness that there was anything serious to discuss.

I thought of that day as I left my interview with Fred Treffeisen, and I thought of how innocent and ignorant I had been, and of how I had been far from alone in that naivete. And I thought how far the Long Island Sound region had come, how it had taken four hundred years of continual exploitation to push the Sound to the point where knowledgeable people believed that it might die. And of how it had taken just over a decade to reach the point where saving the Sound now seemed like it might actually become a reality.

Dead Oysters, Dead Lobsters

Long Island Sound is nothing if not complex, and an understanding of hypoxia is not tantamount to an understanding of the Sound's ecosystem. That truism was underscored in the late 1990s, when first oysters and then lobsters suffered broad die-offs. Although the causes are not yet clear, researchers suspect they might be linked to a slight increase in the Sound's water temperature, which in turn might be linked to global warming. And they provide a good lesson about the ways that progressive, scientifically based, and broadly supported environmental restoration projects are susceptible to larger forces.

The oyster mortality was caused by two parasites, MSX and dermo, that had been seen in the Sound before but which are more commonly associated with southern estuaries such as Chesapeake Bay. MSX was particularly devastating. John Volk, the head of Connecticut's Aquaculture Department, told me that it hit hard in the summer of 1997, in the shallow oyster beds of Clinton and Madison, and inside the Norwalk Islands. The damage was extensive, Volk said, because those waters are thick with oysters. The beds were just starting to recover in early 2000. "It's going to take a few years to rebuild the stocks and get back to record levels," Volk said.

Water temperatures in the Sound were unusually high from 1996 through 1999. In the winter of 1998–99, for example, the temperature in the western Sound never dropped below three degrees centigrade, according to Matthew Gates of the Connecticut Department of Environmental Protection. Most years it drops to one degree centigrade and on occasion falls below zero. Biologists believe the higher temperatures allowed the parasites to thrive. Despite the damage, Connecticut's thirty-four oyster companies all managed to stay in business, partly because they shifted their attention to harvesting clams. Oystering and clamming also began to attract a new wave of independent harvesters. Unfortunately, they got into the business not because shellfish were so abundant, or because shellfishing was so lucrative, but because their usual catch — lobsters — had been even more devastated than oysters.

The crisis first attracted attention in the fall of 1998, when lobstermen near City Island began pulling up traps with dead or dying lobsters. The 1999 season started off well but by late summer the phenomenon repeated itself, and began to spread east. In October I went to the Byram River in Port Chester one morning and found several lobstermen who had not quite given up for the season. Among them were Pedro Alexandre and his mate, Pedro Vicente. Alexandre had been fishing out of Port Chester for nine years since emigrating from Portugal. He turned out to be a cousin of John Fernandes, the lobsterman who had been devastated by the severe hypoxia of 1987, and in fact was in the same house in Rye that Fernandes had lived in before moving to Florida. As we talked, Vicente baited sixteen traps, slipping a dead fish into a plastic mesh bag and tying it to the inside of each trap so it hung suspended. Each trap was weighted with a barnacle-encrusted brick or concrete disc. Vicente slid the traps down a ramp to Alexandre, who hoisted each and arranged it on the deck of his boat, the *Seahawk.* Normally the two Pedros fish 1,600 traps, pulling each every four days. But since the die-off hit, Alexandre had cut back to only several dozen, and even those had been catching nothing. On this morning he was making a modest effort, more out of habit and hope than from any realistic expectation of catching lobsters.

"Now is empty 100 percent," he said. "No small ones, no shorts, no nothing."

He and his mate were thinking of looking for construction work, he said. He lit a Marlboro Light and started the *Seahawk,* filling the dockside water with bluish diesel fumes. He shrugged. "Today maybe I check a few traps more, but I think it's over. I put them back in because you never know." He piloted the boat down the river and through Port Chester Harbor, picking up speed as it passed the Byram breakwater. We sped south. The blue sky gave way to a bank of clouds, and the water was lead-gray. I was apprehensive, thinking back to the day I had spent on the Sound in October 1988 — a cool day that was wet and windy, and which turned out to be one of the most miserable experiences of my life. But the water was relatively calm today and I concentrated on watching the two lobstermen let out the traps they had just baited and then haul in sixteen traps that had been out for several days. The catch: one legal-size lobster, three short lobsters, and a dozen crabs, several of which were dead. In a normal year, those traps would have been filled with lobsters and crabs of all sizes.

Other lobstermen had similar experiences and reported odd phenomena that they linked to the die-off. John Makowsky, a fourth-generation fisherman from Norwalk, said he had always been able to find short lobsters and egg-carrying females in deep refuges, even when oxygen levels were low. "Those areas are all empty of lobsters now. Never have I seen those areas completely depleted," he said. Vegetation that usually clings to the traps and ropes died. The water was unusually clear—visibility was ten, twelve, or fourteen feet deep in areas where fishermen usually were not able to see their hand below the surface. Some traps brought up a rotten-egg smell—hydrogen sulfide, which Barbara Welsh had reported smelling in 1987. Bait remained uneaten in traps for two weeks. Barnacles encrusted lobster shells. Lobstermen who catch their own bait in gill nets reported hauling up fish they had never seen and could not identify. Joe Finke, a Long Islander who has fished for lobsters for twenty years from Lloyd Neck to Prospect Point, said he hauled in 244 pounds on September 14 and 198 pounds the next day. He did not fish at all on September 16 and 17 because of Hurricane Floyd. The next three times out—September 20 and 21 and October 8—he caught 45 pounds, 41 pounds, and 44 pounds, respectively. Divers who descended near Huckleberry Island off New Rochelle found lobsters dead in their burrows. Wholesalers began reporting that lobsters that had been alive at the dock were reaching warehouses dead on arrival; those that were alive on arrival died after two days.

The die-off was not as bad in the eastern end of the Sound. Some lobstermen reported a mortality rate of 10 to 15 percent. But lobstermen there had different troubles. Mike Theiler, who fishes in the New London area, said that up to half of his fall catch consisted of lobsters moving east through the Race. That migration never took place in 1999, perhaps because the lobsters that would have moved through were killed farther west. And many lobsters—up to 70 percent, by some accounts—suffered from a shell-rot, the cause of which remains a mystery to scientists. The shell-rot did not kill the lobsters, but it made them unsightly and therefore hard to sell. It also made them vulnerable to predators like starfish. "You get a big ball of starfish as big as a basketball," Theiler said, "and in the middle is one shell-rot lobster. They're pulling it apart."

The result has been a crash in the sale of Long Island Sound lobsters. "I have specific customers that will not buy Long Island Sound lobsters at any price," said Steve Burt, a distributor who works out of East Norwalk. "They do not want them at all."

Through the fall, government officials and biologists were stumped. But in November they announced that scientists at the University of Connecticut had found a culprit for the die-off (the cause of the shell-rot remained unknown). A microscopic parasite called paramoeba was eating away at the crustaceans' nervous systems, tissues, brains, and other organs. Like MSX and dermo, paramoeba had been a small, benign presence in the Sound until recent years. What triggered it remains a mystery, although biologists suspect several causes or combinations of causes. Warm water is one. Perhaps the parasite increased in abundance as the Sound's temperatures rose, or perhaps the warmer waters lowered the resistance of the lobsters — cold water animals that are at the southern limit of their inshore range — and made them vulnerable to a parasite. David Simpson of the Connecticut DEP said that lobsters prefer to live in water with a temperature range of five to twenty degrees centigrade. In the summer of 1999, he said, the temperature of the western Sound was above twenty degrees for fifty days, more than double what it had been in any of the previous four years.

The lobster die-off occurred in late summer, after dissolved oxygen levels in the Sound rebounded from their summertime lows, but the annual stress of hypoxia might have made the lobsters vulnerable. Lobsters had been incredibly abundant in the Sound in the 1990s, perhaps because they had been so well-fed: the lobstermen engage in a form of aquaculture, baiting their traps, catching and feeding numerous young lobsters, and freeing them until they grow to legal size. But even when they are abundant, lobsters become scarce when dissolved oxygen levels reach 2.2 milligrams per liter or less. Almost all of the Sound between the Bronx, Westchester, Queens, and Nassau experienced oxygen concentrations of below two milligrams in 1999, and large areas fell below one milligram, Simpson said. Waters with less than one milligram contained no lobsters. What happened to them? Several lobstermen said that when the western Sound is hit with severe hypoxia, lobstermen farther east report catching more lobsters than usual — the herding phenomenon that scientists had said in the 1980s was a likely result of hypoxia. Both the herding and the unusually high population perhaps stressed the lobsters, making them more vulnerable to an opportunistic infection or infestation.

Ernie Beckwith, Connecticut's marine fisheries director, told me, "If you step back from this thing and take sort of a philosophical view of it, we've been looking at increased lobster abundance year after year for a decade. And that just isn't normal. In a normal population there's peaks and valleys. So you step back and say this is just mother nature doing the kinds of checks and balances that she does." That "philosophical" point of view, of course, is easy to take when the indirect causes of the die-off are unknown, because it absolves us of any blame. The opposite extreme, perhaps, is one that seems equally plausible — that the die-off of oysters and lobsters was linked to increased water temperatures, which were linked to global warming. If that turns out to be the case, the prospect is even gloomier than that of oystermen and lobstermen losing their means of making a living.

"Think globally, act locally," has long been the environmentalists' maxim, and the Long Island Sound Study is a rare example of a region working together to do that. And yet in the case of lobsters, at least, that local work has been undermined, and the cause might be environmental degradation from far beyond the Sound region's borders — and beyond its control.

NOTES

INTRODUCTION

The Sound

1. Blanchard, *Long Island Sound*, 6; Whitman, *Complete Poetry and Collected Prose*, Library of America, 1982, p. 696; interview with Rhoda Kornreich, president Jay Heritage Center, Rye, N.Y.; Day, "The Devil's Belt," 79; Dwight, *Travels*, 368; Fitzgerald, *Gatsby*, 19–20, 152.
2. Ingersoll, "Oyster Industry," 89.
3. U.S. Environmental Protection Agency, Long Island Sound Study fact sheet, Long Island Sound Study office, Stamford, Conn.
4. U.S. Environmental Protection Agency Web site, www.epa.gov/region01/eco/lis/drainmap.html.
5. Blanchard, 8.
6. National Oceanic and Atmospheric Administration, 20; US EPA, Long Island Sound Study fact sheet.
7. Connecticut Department of Environmental Protection, *Principal Fisheries*.
8. U.S. Environmental Protection Agency, *Economic Importance*.
9. Leopold, *River of the Mother of God*, 254.

CHAPTER I

The Birth of the Sound

1. National Oceanic and Atmospheric Administration, *Long Island Sound*, 15; Needell et al., *The Quaternary Geology of East-Central Long Island Sound*, 3; Lewis and Needell, "Maps Showing the Stratigraphic Framework and Quaternary Geologic History of Eastern Long Island Sound," 6; Jorgensen, *A Guide to New England's Landscape*, 79–82; Lewis, ms. in press, 24.
2. Bell, *The Face of Connecticut*, 79; Lewis, ms. in press, 22–23.
3. Bell, 82; Platt, *American Forest*, 54; Lewis, ms. in press, 22–23.
4. Sutton, *Audubon Society Field Guide*, 3–4; Bell, 79; Lewis, ms. in press, 23.
5. Sutton, 135; Bell 87; Lewis, ms. in press, 23.

6. Bell, 79; Lewis, Ralph, on Connecticut College Web site, http://camel2.conncoll.edu/ccrec/greennet/arbo/publications/34/CHP1.HTM; Lewis, unpublished ms., 23.

7. Lewis, 1; Lewis Web site; Platt, 53; Jorgensen, *Sierra Club Naturalist's Guide,* 60; Lewis, ms. in press, 23–24.

8. Lewis, ms. in press, 25.

9. Bell, 79; Lewis interview.

10. Bell, 87; Lewis interview.

11. Interview with Barbara Davis, local historian in New Rochelle.

12. Lewis, Web site.

13. Danckaerts, *Journal,* 77.

CHAPTER 2

Early Residents

1. Sauer, *Sixteenth Century,* 64–66; Jennings, *Invasion of America,* 199; Boorstin, *Discoverers,* 264. Sauer says that Gomez sailed north along the coast; Stokes (*Iconography,* v. 2, 20) thinks Gomez sailed south directly from Cape Cod to Florida, or perhaps back to Europe, and never approached New York or the Sound.

2. Jameson, *Narratives,* 39–44; Ceci, "The Effect of European Contact," 178.

3. Jennings, 29; Cronon, *Changes in the Land,* 42; Ceci, 307.

4. Jameson, 68.

5. Sturtevant, *Handbook,* 163.

6. Ibid., 162.

7. Sturtevant, 162; Bennett, "Food Economy," 385.

8. Ceci, throughout.

9. Handbook, 163; Jennings, 91; Cronon, 44; Bennett, 385.

10. Cronon, 162.

11. Cronon, 22.

12. Jennings, 199; *Sturtevant,* 160.

13. Wilson, *The Earth Shall Weep,* 47.

14. Jennings, 29; Cronon, 42; Ceci, 307.

15. Ceci, 53–54; Sauer, 59–60.

16. Jameson, 48.

17. Cronon, 30; Kochiss, *Oystering from New York to Boston,* 81.

18. Jennings, 92–93; Cronon, 95–97; Ceci, 24.

19. Jameson, 68–71.

20. Ibid, 68.

21. Ceci, 64.

22. Cronon, 49; *Handbook,* 161.

23. Jameson, 71.

24. Jameson, 220.

25. Ceci, 36.

26. Jameson, 68–74.

CHAPTER 3

Adriaen Block and the First Explorers

1. Sauer, *Sixteenth Century North America,* 54–60; Stokes, *Iconography,* v. 2, 13.
2. Hart, *Prehistory,* 17.
3. Ibid., 48–51.
4. Ibid., 20–21.
5. Hart, 19, 51.
6. Hart, 20, 50.
7. Stokes, v. 2, 69; almost everything written about the early history of the Sound credits Block with the "discovery" of the Sound but puts the first voyage in 1614 on a vessel called the *Onrust.*
8. Jameson, *Original Narratives,* 39–43. My identification of "the river of Siccanamos" as the Mystic comes from *History of New London Connecticut from the First Survey of the Coast in 1612, to 1852,* published in 1852 by Frances Manwaring Caulkins. In Jameson's edition of deLaet's *New World,* published in 1909, he identifies the river as the Thames. But Caulkins convincingly argues that "the river here described was probably the Mystic. The variation of the soundings, the sand points, shoals and creeks, all apply to that neighborhood." She then, in a footnote, quotes a manuscript by one Asa Fish, Esq., describing the river's shoals and channels and sandbars. Caulkins goes on to say, "The Mystic, also, was peculiarly the river of the Pequots, although the name *Pequot River* was afterward given to the Thames, that being the largest river of the Pequot territory and the one principally visited by the English and Dutch traders. The tribe, however, was most numerous in the vicinity of the Mystic and their fortresses commanded its whole extent."

    She adds, "In some particulars the account is not precisely accurate; nor could we reasonably expect that the first rude survey of a coast embarrassed as this is, with creeks, coves and islands, should exactly correspond with charts made two or three centuries later. In a part of the description, it is evident that the Mystic is confounded with the river next surveyed. When it is said, 'navigation extends fifteen or eighteen miles,' we can not doubt but that the geographer has misplaced a fact which, in the original surveys, referred to the Thames."

9. Jameson's version of deLaet refers to this "small stream" as the Frisian River, which Jameson identifies as "Four Mile River." I have been unable to find "Four Mile River" on modern charts. Perhaps it was once a name for the Niantic, although Caulkins, writing fifty years before Jameson, refers to the "Niantick," and makes no reference to "Four Mile River." E. B. O'Callaghan's version of de-Laet refers not to the "Frisian River" but to the "Little Fresh River." As Caulkins notes, "The adjunct *Little* was necessary to distinguish it from the Connecticut, which had been previously named by the Dutch, Fresh River." DeLaet wrote at least two versions of *New World,* one in Dutch, the other in Latin. Caulkins apparently read O'Callaghan's translation as well as the Latin version, which was

written later than the Dutch version, and noted that it "does not name the Little Fresh River, but notices what is evidently the same stream, under another name"—the "Frisius."

10. Jameson, 43–44; Stokes (v. 2, 71) believes that Block's goal in surveying the coast was to find the river the Hudson had sailed into, and that he entered the Connecticut thinking that it was the Hudson.

11. Where this fire took place is a matter of some dispute. Stokes (*Iconography*) believes it was near Albany, where the natives were thought to be friendlier and more disposed to trading. Hart (*Prehistory*) suspects it was near Manhattan, where the *Tijger*, the *Fortuyn*, and the *Nachtegael* were said to be moored three abeam. For evidence, he points to the excavation, in 1916, by workers digging a new subway extension at lower Manhattan's Greenwich Street and Dey Street, of the charred prow, keel, and frame of a ship, which, tests indicate, were burned around 1614. Although no proof exists that the timbers were those of the *Tijger*, archaeologists believe, at least, that they are the remains of a Dutch ship dating from the early seventeenth century (telephone interview with Museum of the City of New York).

12. American authors, under the impression that they are discussing the first ship to sail the length of the Sound, translate *Onrust* as "unrest" or "restless," but Hart rejects that translation and Stokes presents an explanation for the name not based on any translation. Hart believes *Onrust* may better be interpreted as "trouble," in reference to the fire that destroyed the *Tijger* and to Block's difficulties with his competitors. Stokes suggests that the name has nothing to do with any restlessness associated with a life spent on the high seas or trouble encountered on the Hudson. Rather, he says, the yacht may have been named after "the small island of Onrust, between the north point of the province of North Holland and the island of Texel, the last bit of land which ships pass in leaving Holland on sailing from Texel." Stokes's reasoning for looking beyond the restless/unrest interpretation is fraught with ethnic bias: "the Dutch are not an imaginative people," he writes. And yet, despite his faulty reasoning, he may have been correct: early Dutch explorers, after all, called Martha's Vineyard "Texel," which is the name of one of the West Frisian Islands, along Holland's north coast, and the Thames River, in Connecticut, was called the "Frisian River."

13. Hart, 22–33.

14. Ibid., 48–52.

15. Ceci, "The Effect of European Contact," 20.

16. Cronon, *Changes in the Land*, 95–97; Jennings, *Invasion of America*, 92–93.

17. Cronon, 99.

18. Moloney, *The Fur Trade*, 46; Cronon, 99.

19. Moloney, 50–62; Cronon, 106.

20. Cronon, 95–97; Jennings, 155, 190.

21. Ceci, 78, 88, 190.

22. Ibid., throughout.
23. Cronon, 100–101.
24. Sale, *The Conquest of Paradise*, 313–314.
25. Moloney, 58.
26. Murphy, *Fish-Shape Paumanok*, 40; Ceci, 59.
27. Dobyns, *Their Number Become Thinned*, 8–35.
28. Jennings, 26.
29. Sale, 304–305.
30. Jennings, 15.
31. Matthiessen, *Wildlife in America*, 70–71.

CHAPTER 4

The American Mediterranean

1. Kochiss, *Oystering*, 52; Ingersoll, "Oyster Industry," 61, 80.
2. Dwight, *Travels*, vol. 3, 369.
3. Stokes, *Iconography*, v. 2, 94.
4. Danckaerts, *Journal*, 256.
5. Dwight, *Travels*, vol. 3, 368–369.
6. Ibid., 198, 212–213.
7. Albion, *New England*, 47.
8. Morgan, *Connecticut as Colony and State*, 139–141.
9. Cronon, *Changes in the Land*, 148–149.
10. Morgan, 139–141.
11. Morgan, 139–141; Morris, *Encyclopedia*, 136–137.
12. Morgan, 139–141.
13. Bailey, *Village*, 131.
14. Weigold, *American Mediterranean*, 69.
15. Morgan, 139–141.
16. Schmitt, *Mark Well*, 6–25, 119–125.

CHAPTER 5

The Industrial Age

1. Chandler, "Industrial History," 3, 9, 10, 22, 23, 57, 58; Brecher, *Brass Valley*, 3.
2. Day, *The Rise of Manufacturing*, 4–6.
3. Chandler, 58–59; Brecher et al., eds., *Brass Valley*, 1–2.
4. Chandler, 21, 25–26; Brecher et al., 3, 5.
5. Chandler, 27, 29–30; Morris, 730.
6. Bingham, *History of Connecticut*, vol. 2, 668.
7. Day, 24.
8. Chandler, 61–79, 442.

9. *The New Encyclopaedia Britannica,* vol. 26, 433; Connecticut Board of Health, *Second Annual Report,* 140.

10. Connecticut Board of Health, *Second Annual Report,* 13–14.

11. Mitchell, James, ed., *The Random House Encyclopedia.* New York: Random House, 1977, 1768–1769.

12. Burrows, *Gotham,* 184–185, 588–591, 787–788.

13. Bingham, 722–724; Connecticut Board of Health, *Second Annual Report,* 11–15.

14 Connecticut Board of Health, *First Annual Report,* 103, 108–111.

15. Connecticut Board of Health, *Second Annual Report,* 140; Bingham, 722–724.

16. Bingham, 719, 722–724.

17. Connecticut Board of Health, *Fourth Annual Report,* 44.

18. Interstate Sanitation Commission, *Annual Report 1937,* 6–7.

19. Suhr, "Comments on Sewage Disposal," 1.

CHAPTER 6

Oystering

1. Ingersoll, 61, 63–64, 78, 88.

2. Rowe, "The Oyster Industry," 430–431; Ingersoll, 62.

3. Ingersoll, 62, 80, 84–85.

4. Rowe, 421; Ingersoll, 61, 85.

5. Kochiss, 156–157; Oral History Project, *Oystering: Oral History Interview with Clarence Chard.*

6. Rowe, 430–435.

7. Raymond, *Rowayton,* 79–81.

8. Ingersoll, 78–80.

9. Kochiss, 154.

10. Ingersoll, 86.

11. Kochiss, 156–157, 164, 166.

12. Ingersoll, 58–60, 77–78, 86–94.

13. Kochiss, 177.

14. Interview with John Volk, Connecticut Aquaculture Dept.

15. Ingersoll, 89, 58; Albion, 196.

16. Connecticut Board of Health, *Seventeenth Annual Report,* 243–264.

17. Shute, "Were the Shellfish Safe?" 188.

18. Chandler, 79.

19. Rowe, 421–422.

CHAPTER 7

Sprawling Suburbs

1. Weigold, 56; Jackson, *Crabgrass Frontier,* 81.

2. Jackson, 160–176.

3. Patton, *Open Road,* 69–70; Jackson 175.

4. Weigold, 86–89, 107.

5. Jackson, 176; Patton, 70.

6. Jackson, 234–236.

7. Patton, 77–78.

8. Jackson, 249–250, 162–163.

9. Miller and Moffat, *Listen to the Sound*, 19.

10. Commoner, *Closing Circle*, 20–21.

11. Horton and Eichbaum, *Turning the Tide*, 58–59.

12. Groffman, "Is Rainfall Polluting Our Waters," 30–32; Horton and Eichbaum, 58–59.

13. Population-Environment Balance, *The Cost of Population Growth*, 13; Natural Resources Defense Council, *Ebb Tide for Pollution*, 15.

14. Horton and Eichbaum, 73; Population-Environment Balance, 2.

15. Horton and Eichbaum, 62.

16. Commoner, *Making Peace*, 49; *Closing Circle*, 140–141; Jaworski, 30.

17. Groffman, 29–30.

18. Fisher, *Polluted Coastal Waters*, 15; Commoner, *Making Peace*, 39.

19. Commoner, *Making Peace*, 39.

20. Jason Grumet, New York State Environmental Conservation Department, interview.

21. Fisher, throughout.

22. Groffman, 29–31.

23. Barbara Dexter, SUNY Purchase, personal communication.

24. Jaworski, 30–32.

25. National Oceanic and Atmospheric Administration, *Long Island Sound*, 27.

CHAPTER 8

Strangling the Sound

1. Odum, *Fundamentals of Ecology*, 51.

2. *New York Times*, "Growing Harm Seen to Key Fish Source," 1, August 17, 1987.

3. Horton and Eichbaum, 9.

4. U.S. Environmental Protection Agency, *Water Quality Modeling Analysis of Hypoxia*, section 1, p. 2.

5. Odum, 268.

6. Commoner, *Closing Circle*, 23.

7. Interview with Gerard M. Capriulo, SUNY Purchase biologist; Connecticut Department of Environmental Protection, *Long Island Sound Atlas*, 35.

8. Dexter, "Plankton of Long Island Sound," 6–7; Connecticut DEP, 35; Perry, *A Sierra Club Naturalist's Guide*, 16.

9. U.S. Environmental Protection Agency, *Long Island Sound Study Status Report*, 18.

10. Parker and O'Reilly, "Oxygen Depletion in Long Island Sound," 15, 19, 58–60.

CHAPTER 9

The Brink of Disaster

1. Briggs, "Notes on the American Lobster," 1; Lund and Stewart, "Abundance and Distribution of Larval Lobsters," 48.
2. Lund and Stewart, 48.
3. Stewart interview; Briggs, "American Lobster Fisheries," 2.
4. Briggs, "Notes on the American Lobster," 4–5.
5. Briggs, "Movements of American Lobsters," 24; Briggs, "Notes," 3; Briggs and Mushacke, "The American Lobster in Western Long Island Sound: Movement," 23.
6. Briggs, "Notes," 6; Briggs interview.
7. Briggs interview.
8. In the late 1980s, the tiny marina in which Abel Miguel kept his boat was sold to a developer and turned into waterfront houses. Miguel moved his operation to Long Island's north shore. He and his nephew, Luis Mendez, were pulling traps off Sands Point in April 1993, when a speedboat approached their vessel. The three men in the speedboat were wearing masks and were armed with guns. They opened fire, hitting Miguel three times in the abdomen and groin. Mendez escaped injury when he jumped overboard. Police believe that Miguel was the victim of a territorial dispute. The men who shot him were found guilty, but the convictions were overturned because of a judicial error; a second trial ended in a hung jury; at a third trial they were acquitted. Miguel recovered and has returned to lobster fishing on the Sound.
9. Welsh and Eller, "Mechanisms Controlling Summertime Oxygen Depletion," 276.
10. Welsh interview; Welsh and Eller, 276.
11. Welsh and Eller, 266.
12. Ibid., 268.
13. Ibid., 268.
14. Welsh interview.
15. Welsh and Eller, 276–277.
16. U.S. Environmental Protection Agency, *Long Island Sound Study Status Report and Interim Actions*, 22–23.
17. U.S. Environmental Protection Agency, *Long Island Sound Study Annual Report 1989–1990*, 11.

CHAPTER 10

Sewage

1. Suhr, "Comments on Sewage Disposal," 2–3.
2. Interstate Sanitation Commission, *Annual Report for the Year 1937*, 18, 24, 25.
3. Ibid., 18, 24.

CHAPTER 11

The Cleanup

1. U.S. Environmental Protection Agency, *Water Quality Modeling Analysis of Hypoxia,* section 2, p. 1.
2. Interview with Mark Tedesco, EPA's Long Island Sound office.
3. Miller and Moffet, *Listen,* 18–19.
4. Ibid., 24–25.
5. Tedesco interview.
6. May, Clifford D. "Solution to Ocean Waste is Baffling Lawmakers," *New York Times,* July 19, 1988, 23.
7. Fried, Joseph P. "City Plan for a Huge Sewage Tank in a Park Divides Queens Group," *New York Times,* June 17, 1990, 20.
8. Groffman and Jaworski, "Is Rainfall," 33.

CHAPTER 12

The New Sound

1. Clines, Francis X. "Progress in Cleaning Chesapeake Bay, but Far to Go," *New York Times,* July 22, 2001, 16.
2. *New York Times,* July 19, 1988, 23.
3. Horton and Eichbaum, *Turning the Tide,* 285.
4. Oral History Project, *Oystering: Oral History Interview with Clarence Chard.*
5. Perry, *A Sierra Club Naturalist's Guide,* 237.
6. Oral History Project.
7. Kochiss, *Oystering,* 156–157.
8. Perry, 224–225.
9. Ingersoll, "The Oyster Industry," 17.
10. Kochiss, 171–172.
11. Interstate Sanitation Commission, *1999 Annual Report,* 9–10, 12.

BIBLIOGRAPHY

Albion, Robert G., William A. Baker, and Benjamin W. Labaree, *New England and the Sea*. Middletown, Conn.: Wesleyan University Press, 1972.

Bailey, Anthony. *In the Village*. New York: Knopf, 1971.

Bell, Michael, *The Face of Connecticut: People, Geology and the Land*. Hartford: Connecticut Department of Environmental Protection, 1985.

Bennett, M. K., "The Food Economy of the New England Indians, 1605–75," *The Journal of Political Economy* 63, no. 5 (February–December 1955) 369–97.

Bingham, Harold J. *History of Connecticut*, vol. 2. New York: Lewis Historical Publishing Co., 1962.

Blanchard, Fessenden S., *Long Island Sound*. Princeton: D. Van Nostrand Company, 1958.

Boorstin, Daniel J., *The Discoverers*. New York: Random House, 1983.

Brecher, Jeremy, Jerry Lombardi, and Jan Stackhouse, eds. *Brass Valley: The Story of Working People's Lives and Struggles in an American Industrial Region*. The Brass Workers History Project. Philadelphia: Temple University Press, 1982.

Briggs, Philip T. "Movements of American Lobsters Tagged off the South Shore of Long Island, New York," *New York Fish and Game Journal* 32, no. 1 (January 1985), 20–25.

———. "American Lobster Fisheries in New York Waters with Emphasis on Long Island Sound." Unpublished. New York State Department of Environmental Conservation, May 1, 1989.

———. "Investigations of the American Lobster in Eastern Long Island Sound." Unpublished. New York State Department of Environmental Conservation, Commercial Fisheries Research and Development Act Completion Report, April 12, 1984.

———. "Notes on the American Lobster (*Homarus Americanus*) Fisheries in New York." Unpublished. New York State Department of Environmental Conservation, March 31, 1989.

Briggs, Philip T. and Frederick M. Mushacke. "The American Lobster in Western Long Island Sound," *New York Fish and Game Journal* 26, no. 1 (January 1979), 59–86.

———. "The American Lobster and the Pot Fishery in the Inshore Waters off the South Shore of Long Island, New York," *New York Fish and Game Journal* 27, no. 2 (July 1980), 115–68.

———. "The American Lobster in Western Long Island Sound: Movement, Growth and Mortality," *New York Fish and Game Journal* 31, no. 1 (January 1984), 21–37.

Buckles, Mary Parker. *Margins: A Naturalist Meets Long Island Sound.* New York: North Point Press, 1997.

Burrows, Edwin G. and Mike Wallace. *Gotham: A History of New York City to 1898.* New York: Oxford University Press, 1999.

Capriulo, Gerard M. "Sea Microbes — the Yin and the Yang," *Long Island Sound Report* vol. 4, no. 3, Long Island Sound Taskforce.

———. "Planktonic Food Webs," *Long Island Sound Report* vol. 2, no. 2 (Fall 1985), Long Island Sound Taskforce.

Carson, Rachel. *The Edge of the Sea.* Boston: Houghton Mifflin, 1955.

———. *The Sea Around Us.* New York: Oxford University Press, 1951.

Caulkins, Frances Manwaring. *History of New London Connecticut from the First Survey of the Coast in 1612, to 1852.* New London: New London County Historical Society, 1985.

Ceci, Lynn. "The Effect of European Contact and Trade on the Settlement Pattern of Indians in Coastal New York, 1524–1665," Ph.D. diss., CUNY, 1977.

Chandler, George B. "Industrial History." In *History of Connecticut in Monograph Form,* vol. 4, Norris Galpin Osborn, ed. New York: The States History Company, 1925.

Commoner, Barry. *Making Peace with the Planet.* New York: Pantheon Books, 1990.

———. *The Closing Circle.* New York: Knopf, 1971.

Connecticut Department of Environmental Protection, *Long Island Sound: An Atlas of Natural Resources.* Hartford: State of Connecticut, 1977.

———. *Principal Fisheries of Long Island Sound 1961–1985.* Hartford: State of Connecticut, 1989.

Connecticut Board of Health, *First Annual Report of the State Board of Health of the State of Connecticut, for the Fiscal Year Ending November 31, 1878.* Hartford, 1879.

———. *Second Annual Report of the State Board of Health of the State of Connecticut, for the Fiscal Year Ending November 30, 1879.* Hartford, 1879.

———. *Fourth Annual Report of the State Board of Health of the State of Connecticut, for the Fiscal Year Ending November 31, 1881.* Hartford, 1882.

———. *Seventeenth Annual Report of the State Board of Health of the State of Connecticut.* New Haven, 1895.

Cronon, William. *Changes in the Land: Indians, Colonists, and the Ecology of New England.* New York: Hill and Wang, 1983.

Danckaerts, Jasper. *Journal of Jasper Danckaerts, 1679–1680,* Bartlett, Burleigh James, and J. Franklin Jameson, eds. New York: Charles Scribner's Sons, 1913.

Day, Clive. *The Rise of Manufacturing in Connecticut, 1820–1850.* Tercentenary Commission of the State of Connecticut, Committee on Historical Publications, XLIV. New Haven: Yale University Press, 1935.

Day, Thomas Fleming. "The Devil's Belt: History in Long Island Sound." In *The Rudder Treasury,* Tom Davin, ed. New York: Sheridan House, 1953.

Delaney, Edmund. *The Connecticut River, New England's Historic Waterway.* Chester, Conn.: Globe Pequot, 1983.

Dexter, Barbara, "The Plankton of Long Island Sound: The Biology and Ecology of Marine Copepods," *Long Island Sound Report* vol. 3, no. 1 (Spring 1986), Long Island Sound Taskforce.

Dobyns, Henry. *Their Number Become Thinned.* Knoxville: University of Tennessee Press, 1983.

Dwight, Timothy. *Travels in New England and New York,* 4 vols., Barbara Miller Solomon, ed. Cambridge, Mass.: Harvard University Press, 1969.

Fitzgerald, F. Scott. *The Great Gatsby.* New York: Scribners, 1996.

Fisher, Diane et al. *Polluted Coastal Waters: The Role of Acid Rain.* Environmental Defense Fund, 1988.

Groffman, Peter and Carole Jaworski. "Is Rainfall Polluting Our Waters," *Nor'-easter* vol. 2, no. 2 (Fall 1991).

Ferguson, Henry L. *Fishers Island, N.Y., 1614–1925.* Mamaroneck: Harbor Hill, 1974.

Hart, Simon. *The Prehistory of the New Netherland Company.* Amsterdam: City of Amsterdam Press, 1959.

Horton, Tom and William H. Eichbaum. *Turning the Tide.* Washington, D.C.: Island Press, 1991.

Horton, Tom. *Bay Country.* Baltimore: Johns Hopkins University Press, 1987.

Hunt, Morton M. *The Inland Sea.* New York: Doubleday, 1965.

Ingersoll, Ernest. "The Oyster Industry," *The History and Present Condition of the Fishery Industries.* Tenth Census of the United States. Washington, D.C.: Department of the Interior, 1881.

Interstate Sanitation Commission. *Annual Report for the Year 1937.* New York: ISC, 1938.

——. *Annual Report for the Year 1938.* New York: ISC, 1939.

——. *1999 Annual Report.* New York: ISC, 2000.

Jackson, Kenneth T. *Crabgrass Frontier: The Suburbanization of the United States.* New York: Oxford University Press, 1985.

Jameson, J. Franklin, ed. *Original Narratives of Early American History, Narratives of New Netherland 1609–1664.* New York: Charles Scribner's Sons, 1909.

Jennings, Francis. *The Invasion of America:* New York: Norton, 1976.

Jorgensen, Neil. *A Guide to New England's Landscape.* Chester, Conn.: Globe Pequot Press, 1977.

——. *A Sierra Club Naturalist's Guide to Southern New England.* San Francisco: Sierra Club Books, 1978.

Kochiss, John M. *Oystering from New York to Boston.* Middletown: Wesleyan University Press, 1974.

Leopold, Aldo. *The River of the Mother of God.* Madison: University of Wisconsin Press, 1991.

Lewis, Ralph S. and Sally W. Needell. "Maps Showing the Stratigraphic Framework and Quaternary Geologic History of Eastern Long Island Sound." U.S. Geological Survey, 1987.

Long Island Soundkeeper Fund, *The Soundbook.* Norwalk, Conn.: Long Island Soundkeeper Fund, 1992.

Lund, William A. Jr. and Lance L. Stewart. "Abundance and Distribution of Larval Lobsters, *Homarus Americanus,* off the Coast of Southern New England." *Proceedings of the National Shellfisheries Association,* vol. 60 (June 1970), 40–49.

Matthiessen, Peter. *Wildlife in America.* New York: Viking Press, 1959.

Miller, David J. and Jane-Kerin Moffat. *Listen to the Sound: A Citizens' Agenda.* Albany: National Audubon Society, 1991.

Moloney, Francis X. *The Fur Trade in New England.* Hamden, Conn.: Archon Books, 1967.

Morgan, Forrest, ed. *Connecticut as a Colony and as a State.* Hartford: The Publishing Society of Connecticut, 1904.

Morris, Richard B., ed. *Encyclopedia of American History.* New York: Harper & Brothers, 1953.

Murphy, Robert Cushman. *Fish-Shape Paumanok.* Philadelphia: The American Philosophical Society, 1964.

National Oceanic and Atmospheric Administration. *Long Island Sound: Issues, Resources, Status and Management Seminar Proceedings.* NOAA Estuary-of-the-Month Seminar Series No. 3. Washington, D.C.: NOAA, January 1987.

Natural Resources Defense Council. *Ebb Tide for Pollution: Actions for Cleaning up Coastal Waters.* Washington, D.C.: NRDC, 1987.

Needell, Sally W., Ralph S. Lewis, and Steven M. Colman. *Maps Showing the Quaternary Geology of East-Central Long Island Sound.* U.S. Geological Survey, 1987.

Odum, Eugene P. *Fundamentals of Ecology.* Philadelphia: W.B. Saunders Co., 1971.

Oral History Project: Friends of the Greenwich Library. *Oystering: Oral History Interview with Clarence Chard,* by Suzanne Kowalski. Greenwich, Conn.: Greenwich Library, 1976.

Parker, Charles A., John E. O'Reilly, and Robert B. Gerzoff. *Oxygen Depletion in Long Island Sound.* EPA technical report. Washington, D.C.: U.S. Environmental Protection Agency, 1986.

Parker, Charles A., and John E. O'Reilly. "Oxygen Depletion in Long Island Sound: A Historical Perspective," *Estuaries* vol. 14, no. 3 (1991), 248–64.

Patton, Phil. *Open Road.* New York: Simon & Schuster, 1986.

Perry, Bill. *A Sierra Club Naturalist's Guide: The Middle Atlantic Coast.* San Francisco: Sierra Club Books, 1985.

Perry, Charles E., ed. *Founders and Leaders of Connecticut, 1633–1783.* Boston: D.C. Heath & Co., 1934.

Population-Environment Balance. *The Cost of Population Growth in the Patuxent River Basin.* Washington, D.C.: Population-Environment Balance, 1987.

Platt, Rutherford. *The Great American Forest.* Englewood Cliffs, N.J.: Prentice Hall, 1965.

Raymond, Frank E. *Rowayton on the Half Shell: The History of a Connecticut Coastal Village.* Rowayton: The Rowayton Historical Society, 1990.

Rowe, Henry C. "The Oyster Industry." In *History of Connecticut in Monograph Form,* vol 4., Norris Galpin Osborn, ed. New York: The States History Company, 1925.

Sale, Kirkpatrick. *The Conquest of Paradise.* New York: Knopf, 1990.

Sauer, C. O. *Sixteenth Century North America: The Land and the People as Seen by the Europeans.* Berkeley: University of California Press, 1971.

Schmitt, Frederick K. *Mark Well the Whale.* Port Washington, N.Y.: Kennikat Press, 1971.

Shute, Malcolm. *Were the Shellfish You Just Ate Safe?* Hartford: Connecticut Health Bulletin, vol. 96, no. 4 (1982).

Stokes, I. N. Phelps. *The Iconography of Manhattan Island.* New York: R.H. Dodd, 1916.

Sturtevant, William C., general ed. *Handbook of North American Indians,* vol. 15. Washington, D.C.: Smithsonian Institution, 1978.

Suhr, Carl J. "Comments on Sewage Disposal in Westchester County." Unpublished. White Plains: Westchester County Department of Environmental Facilities, 1971.

Sutton, Caroline, ed. *The Audubon Society Field Guide to the Natural Places of the Northeast: Coastal.* New York: The Hilltown Press, 1984.

Teal, John and Mildred Teal. *Life and Death of the Salt Marsh.* New York: Random House, 1969.

U.S. Environmental Protection Agency. *Long Island Sound Study Annual Report 1989–1990.* Stamford, Conn.

——. *Long Island Sound Study Preliminary Management Plan for Hypoxia.* Stamford, Conn., 1989.

——. *Long Island Sound Study Status Report and Interim Actions for Hypoxia Management.* Stamford, Conn., 1990.

——. *Economic Importance of Long Island Sound's Water-Quality-Dependent Activities.* Marilyn Altobello for the Long Island Sound Study. Stamford, Conn., 1992.

——. *Water Quality Modeling Analysis of Hypoxia in Long Island Sound Using LIS 3.0.* Stamford, Conn., 1996.

Warner, Frederic W. "The Foods of the Connecticut Indians," *Bulletin of the Archaeological Society of Connecticut,* 37 (1972), 27–47.

Weigold, Marilyn E. *The American Mediterranean: An Environmental, Economic &* *Social History of Long Island Sound.* Port Washington, N.Y.: Kennikat Press. 1974.

Welsh, Barbara L. and F. Craig Eller. "Mechanisms Controlling Summertime Oxygen Depletion in Western Long Island Sound," *Estuaries* 14, no. 3 (Summer 1991), 265–78.

Wilkinson, Alec. "Riverkeeper," *The New Yorker,* May 11, 1987.

Wilson, James. *The Earth Shall Weep: A History of Native America.* New York: Atlantic Monthly Press, 1999.

World Resources Institute. *World Resources 1990–1991.* New York: Oxford University Press, 1990.

INDEX